MASS KILLERS:

How You Can Identify, Workplace, School, or Public Killers Before They Strike

MIKE ROCHE

Other Books by Mike Roche

The Blue Monster

Coins of Death

Karma!

Face 2 Face:
Observation, Interviewing and Rapport Building Skills:
an Ex-Secret Service Agent's Guide

About MIKE ROCHE

Mike Roche has over three decades of law enforcement experience. He began his career with the Little Rock Police Department, and spent twenty-two years with the U.S. Secret Service. The last fifteen years of his career were focused on conducting behavioral threat assessments of those threatening to engage in targeted violence. Mike was also assigned as the Intelligence Liaison to the FBI and CIA headquarters as well as being assigned to the Joint Terrorism Task Force (JTTF). He is the author of three novels and a nonfiction work on rapport building. Retired, Mike is currently a security consultant at Protective Threat LLC. and an adjunct instructor at Saint Leo University. He resides in Florida with his family.

Contents

I would like to dedicate this book to the loving memory of Barry Glover, friend, mentor and colleague. Barry retired as a captain from the Clearwater Police Department and moved on to faculty positions with USF and Saint Leo University. Upon my retirement from the Secret Service, Barry asked me if I would be interested in developing the class that this book is based upon. Barry exuded passion to educate the law enforcement community. His smile and drive are missed by all those who were honored to have known him, as well as his middle of the night emails. I miss those.

Despite the uncomfortable subject matter of this book, I hope that sharing my knowledge will assist in preventing a future tragic event and saving victims and survivors from enduring the suffering from the trauma of a mass killing.

MASS KILLERS

Introduction

On July 26, 2012, 6'7" Neil Prescott answered his front door wearing a t-shirt that said, "Guns don't kill people, I do." The visitor at the door was a police officer investigating threats of workplace violence. In law enforcement, you would call the t-shirt "a clue." The next day, detectives from the Prince George's County Police Department returned with a search warrant to search Prescott's residence for weapons.

The reason for the visit with a search warrant was that Prescott had made threats to his employer, Pitney Bowes over the telephone. According to the search warrant, the detective was informed by an employee that Prescott said, "I am a joker. I am going to load my guns and blow everybody up." He reiterated the threats in subsequent telephone calls. He also stated he would like to see the supervisors brain matter splattered all over the sidewalk. Prescott had recently been terminated from his employment at Pitney Bowes as a subcontractor. The subject, who was a gun enthusiast, legally possessed twenty guns and ammunition.

Prescott uttered these threats six days after the Aurora, Colorado, shooting by James Holmes during the movie, *The Dark Knight Rises*. The vigilant employee listening to the threats alerted the police to mitigate any possible violence stemming from these threats. Those who knew Prescott came to his defense saying that he was the type of person who made provocative statements and wore shirts with outrageous slogans, but that violence would have been out of character for him. In today's culture, irresponsible comments concerning threats of violence cannot be tolerated. The graphic threats coming from a subject who had recently been terminated from his employment and displayed a high interest in collecting firearms, were cause for alarm. The police acted appropriately to diffuse the situation.

Prescott was taken to the Anne Arundel Medical Center for a psychiatric evaluation. He was charged with misuse of a telephone, but the case was dismissed by a judge who found the charge vague. After several weeks of mental health counseling, he was released to his parents' custody. Prescott was ordered to continue taking prescribed medication and attend counseling. Had the police not been called, would he have engaged in a workplace shooting? No one will ever know. The quick response averted any possibility of violence. The psychiatric therapy that Prescott received may have diffused and stabilized Prescott, thus interrupting the road to violence.

Texas State University studied 84 active shooter incidents in the U.S. that occurred in the first decade of 2000. These shootings are not common occurrences, thus they garner national headlines and riveting news coverage. Despite the rarity of these murderous rampages, there is no way to measure how many of these potential shootings were mitigated and properly managed by the vigilance of the community.

The common definition of mass murder involves the killing of four or more individuals in a single location. Spree killers are multiple homicides committed in multiple locations. As this book explores the mindset of mass killers, I have chosen not to confine my overview to the defined typology of mass murders and spree killers. The two types often share similar characteristics. Although political assassinations may specifically target a single individual, quite often they are not concerned about bystander casualties, such as the attempt on President Ronald Reagan.

Celebrity killers will also often share related traits. This book will explore the thought process of those who intend to kill indiscriminate targets without regard to the result. Although some killers may have failed in their attempts, their thought process is still worth examining for investigators.

There is always a concern that a book such as this one could be read by someone considering targeted violence. Mass murders have occurred prior to this book and will continue well after. Most of the information contained in these pages can be accessed through public source gathering and materials. These killers target innocent subjects in shopping malls, movie theaters, the workplace, in schools, or at public events where people in a free society are the most vulnerable. Carnage is often launched in an effort to leverage the killers' public platform so that they can exit life in a grandiose manner.

This pattern has become increasingly disturbing to me as I witnessed many of the shootings unfold on television and the subsequent absence of accurate information being disseminated to the public. I am writing this book in hopes that the information here will shed some light on the mindset of the shooters. I hope to raise the awareness of some of the triggers and to arm law enforcement, school administrators, security professionals and human resource professionals with investigative techniques in identifying and conducting threat assessments of these individuals. Perhaps we can mitigate their conduct before we read about them in the newspaper.

Many, but not all, of these tragic shootings are preventable. Hindsight is always 20/20. The challenge is to identify patterns of conduct and behaviors that will allow for the intervention and mitigation of a possible shooter. When the 911 calls are made or shots are being fired, it is too late.

With current budget restrictions and increased caseloads, many police agencies are faced with insurmountable obstacles in identifying and prosecuting many of these mass killers. Their hands are often tied due to legal restrictions. It is tough for a detective to explain to her captain that she is investigating a subject who may become the next lone shooter when the captain is issuing orders to conduct a follow-up investigation on the theft of the mayor's golf clubs. The captain explains that the potential shooter has not violated the law. The same holds true when a campus police officer is told to suspend an investigation because someone is illegally parked in the president's reserved parking space.

In the school or workplace environment, administrators constantly tiptoe on a high wire. They must weigh the concerns of the safety of their community against the rights of the individual who has come under suspicion. The administrators know that whatever action they take, they will be closely scrutinized and face possible civil litigation.

By the end of this book, I hope to make you pseudo-psycho sleuths. This is a term that you will not be able to repeat three times in succession without stumbling. Perhaps the challenge in front of us is to conduct these investigations without stumbling. If the knowledge that I can impart through this book provides a window of opportunity to interdict a potential mass killer, then I have tremendous satisfaction.

Chapter 1
The Beginning

My view of conducting threat assessments was significantly altered in 1998. In my earlier career as a police officer, I disliked receiving calls to attempted suicides or to intervene on emotionally disturbed people (EDPs). I recall the book and the movie by Joseph Wambaugh, *The Choirboys*, in which the fictional police officer Roscoe Rules, challenges a suicidal subject. Rules tells the suicidal man that he lacks the fortitude to jump off the roof and that the world would be a better place if the suffering man did jump. The subject finally succumbs to the challenge and ends his life. I was never as cynical or unsympathetic as Roscoe Rules, but I never looked forward to answering EDP type calls.

I always took pride in my interviewing abilities as a police officer and then as a detective. As I was going through the new agent training for the Secret Service, we interacted with role players, who were employees from St. Elizabeth's Hospital in Washington, D.C. The role players simulated the type of individuals that we would interview concerning investigations of threats against the president. I learned that I was proficient at interviewing emotionally unstable subjects and I received encouragement from my classmates.

In 1998, I was assigned to conduct a protective threat assessment advance in Eugene, Oregon. I knew this would not be an ordinary advance, when I checked into my room at the River Valley Inn as my message light was already blinking. Assuming that the operator was checking to see if I needed turndown service or if my pillows were fluffy enough, I was disappointed when I checked the message to find out that the call was from the local FBI office. They had been alerted to a possible verbal threat made on the life of the president, which was overheard by a deputy sheriff on a CB radio.

Criminal investigations are typically conducted in a methodical, well thought-out procedure. With the president arriving in town in less than seventy-two hours, I did not enjoy that luxury. You as an investigator will have to make the assessment as to whether you have the time to approach the investigation with a more methodical and deliberate approach or if there are more urgent conditions. Monday morning quarterbacks will have little regard for your reasoning.

Armed with the data that had been developed by the Secret Service's Exceptional Case Study Program, I asked the FBI agent to accompany me to the residence of the subject who had allegedly made the threatening statement. My motivation was not only to speak directly to the subject, but also to determine the stability of his social setting and environment. I wanted to observe his family situation, living conditions, see what books he was reading, what sort of videos he was watching, what type of posters or art adorned the walls, what kind of mail was scattered on his table, and what sort of information his family could provide concerning his thoughts and stability.

There I was at 2 o'clock in the morning in a very rural environment in a secluded home with the FBI. We interviewed the subject and learned that he was primarily an innocent blowhard who made some wildly inappropriate remarks without engaging his brain before his mouth. Those statements would be subsequently followed up later in a case presented to the United States

Attorney's Office. I was able to walk away comfortably knowing the subject did not pose a serious threat to the safety and security of the president.

A subsequent case that came to my attention within the next 24 hours was much more significant. A subject began calling law enforcement agencies saying, "The bombs have been dispersed," prior to the president's arrival in Eugene. I requested that the explosives ordnance division (EOD) examine an area near the airport where the caller had stated that a bomb had been placed. The EOD team discovered an explosive device in close proximity to where the motorcade would exit the airport. This alarming development increased my heightened attention and the security for the protection of the president. A subsequent manhunt by the FBI was successful in ultimately identifying the subject and bringing him to justice.

The president's primary purpose for coming to Eugene, Oregon was to visit the site of a school shooting at Thurston High School in Springfield, Oregon. The shooting had occurred just weeks prior to President Clinton's visit. The shooter Kip Kinkel, killed his mother and father, then came to the school and killed two additional students while wounding twenty-four more in the cafeteria.

I stood there looking through the classrooms and the cafeteria and I could not understand how the sanctity of the school could be so violated. As I stood at the rear of the school and looked out across the majestic mountains of Oregon, admiring the beauty, I wondered what would possess a youthful individual to perpetrate such a heinous act and intentionally attack with the intent to kill fellow students at such a peaceful and serene environment.

Chapter 2
Experts

"When facts are few, experts are many"
—Donald R. Gannon

After the attack on America on September 11, 2001, I was on a break while working at an FBI command post. We were monitoring all the TV channels. Most channels were filled with the doom and gloom from various talking heads. I paused to listen to Colonel Oliver North, who was providing his knowledge and experience on the subject. He told the story of being stranded in Little Rock, Arkansas, in a hotel room on that fateful day. He was disgruntled at having to watch various talking heads espouse the theory that additional attacks were forthcoming. North made the assertion that many of these experts gleaned most of their knowledge from reading other people's books, and possessed very little reality-based knowledge. Oliver North asserted that Al Qaeda and the terrorists had utilized and expended all of their resources on this attack, and that it would take months, if not years, to launch a subsequent attack. He claimed that there would be no follow-up attack. As it turned out, Colonel North's assessment was correct.

I do not consider myself an expert on conducting threat assessments of mass murderers. I do however, consider myself extremely knowledgeable in the subject. Yes, I have read many books and studies while conducting hundreds of interviews and threat assessments of subjects who potentially posed a threat to others. I consider myself a student of life. The day I stop learning is the day I stop living. I have benefitted from the laborious research and experience of many others. I believe we throw the term "expert" around a little too loosely in our society, when many experts are seldom called to substantiate their viewpoints and there are no measures to gain or to gauge their self-ascribed expertise. I have listened to many of these talking heads proffer unsubstantiated claims and judgments while others lack substantive resumes to make the judgments that they are professing.

When I provide this eight-hour class, I tell my students to raise the "not true" flag if they do not agree with me. I am typically surrounded by a great deal of experience and knowledge. I have been challenged a few times and we discuss our disagreements. I appreciate the interaction. You may not agree with everything I say in this book and hit me up on Twitter, email, or my website and we can discuss our disagreements.

Chapter 3
Not a New Phenomenon

Although we have become focused on current trends of the types of targeted violence, this type of violence is not a new phenomenon. In August, 1966, at the University of Texas, a 25-year-old former Marine and current student at the school, ascended the 27 floors to the observation deck of the University of Texas clock tower and began firing. At the end of his massacre, 16 people died and 32 were wounded.

The gunman, Charles Whitman grew up in Florida. He had an abusive father who allegedly abused him both emotionally and physically. Charles possessed a genius level IQ of 172. As an altar server at church and accomplished pianist, he was also an Eagle Scout. No one understood the darkness that prevailed behind the façade of the all-American family or Whitman.

In an effort to escape his father's torment, he enlisted in the United States Marine Corps. He kept this a secret from his father, who was furious when he found out that his talented son had enlisted in the military. While in the Marines, Charles entered into the Platoon Leadership Corp. This program promoted education among the enlisted marines. As a member of this program, a Marine's enlistment was held in abeyance while he attended college. Upon successful completion of college, he would be commissioned as an officer in the Marine Corps.

Whitman enrolled at the University of Texas in Austin, as an engineering student. During his early days of enrollment, he made general statements concerning the strategic location of the clock tower and how a sniper could hold off an army from this high vantage point. Were these statements the observations of a tactically trained Marine or thoughts of a darker intent? In 1966, this type of remark would not have caused alarm. While a student, he married. His grades were not up to the standards of what the Marine Corps, expected and he was called back to active duty and had to withdraw from the University of Texas.

He subsequently ran into disciplinary problems in the Marines, and he was court-martialed for gambling. Whitman eventually completed his enlistment obligation with the Marines and returned to the University of Texas, where he majored in architecture. His mother finally escaped the shackles of her abusive husband and moved to Austin to be close to her son and his young bride. According to his journal and the recollection of two friends, Whitman struck his wife from which he felt a tremendous burden of guilt for his physical assault. He was concerned of following in his father's footsteps.

Whitman began seeing a psychiatrist over concerns of violent impulses that he was experiencing. He confided in a psychiatrist that he had thoughts of climbing the clock tower with a rifle and killing people. He also complained of debilitating migraines. There was no documented follow-up by the psychiatrist, nor were there any notifications made to authorities.

The day before his rampage, Charles Whitman started at home by drafting a suicide note. He was interrupted by some friends, who detected nothing unusual. His friends said Whitman seemed at ease and stress-free. After they departed, Whitman continued typing his letter. He complained of irrational thoughts and migraines. He professed his love for his wife. Later that evening, he executed both his mother and his wife. His motive appears to have been related to saving them the hardship of enduring what was about to happen.

The next morning, he drove to the clock tower where he carried in his cache of weapons and premade sandwiches that would provide him sustenance during his onslaught. With a genius IQ, his planning was thorough. He rented a mover's dolly to help with his load of supplies. He brought toilet paper, water, deodorant and other supplies. Upon his arrival at the top floor, he killed a receptionist who challenged his presence.

Whitman began firing indiscriminately at the innocent targets below. Police response was slowed when a local radio station called for a civilian response to the sniper. Numerous well-intentioned Texans with long rifles responded in an effort to help stop the massacre. The police were eventually able to gain entry to Whitman's sniper position and killed him.

Whitman asked that an autopsy be performed to learn what caused his violent thoughts and to donate funds from his estate to mental health causes. A subsequent autopsy revealed that Whitman was suffering from a brain tumor, which provided a possible explanation into his lack of impulse control and migraines. His brain had a small tumor about the size of a nickel. The tumor was located in the thalamus region and the growth was applying pressure on the hypothalamus and the amygdala, which is the emotional regulator of the brain. It is also possible that due to the violent nature of his upbringing, he learned to accept violence as part of the normal course of life and an acceptable way to end his own life.

He had made remarks concerning his visualization of utilizing the clock tower as a sniper position. In the 1960's, this kind of rhetoric would have been easily discounted. Whitman shared his homicidal thoughts with a psychiatrist. As horrible as this tragedy was during a simpler time in America, Whitman's story and images were splashed across the cover of all of the major publications of the day, including Time and Life magazines. The nation was fascinated by the seemingly all-American boy who had become such a killer devoid of compassion, slaughtering innocent people, including those who were rendering aid to the wounded.

In 1984, in a suburb of San Diego, California, James Oliver Huberty entered a McDonald's in San Ysidro and during a seventy-seven minute rampage, discharged two hundred and fifty rounds killing 21 and wounding 19 others. A sniper from the San Diego Police Department was able to neutralize Huberty, but only after a massive body count.

James Huberty, like Whitman, had a dysfunctional upbringing. He walked with a limp because of childhood polio. His marriage was filled with domestic violence. He worked in Ohio as a welder. Because of a motorcycle accident, he suffered from a disability, which caused his arm to twitch uncontrollably. This trait is not conducive to stabile employment as a welder and he lost his job.

Huberty was described as an angry loner and had difficulty getting along with others. He often spoke of killing others and confided in one person that if losing his job was the end of making a living for his family, he was planning to take everyone with him. He initially moved to Mexico to seek employment. Later, he moved back across the border to San Ysidro, where he had obtained employment as a security guard.

Huberty suffered from various paranoia beliefs that centered on a survivalist mentality. He feared the manipulation of the currency by the Federal Reserve Bank and feared Soviet Cold War aggression against the United States. He was a believer in a nuclear Armageddon and stockpiled food and weapons in anticipation of the final assault of evil against good.

He was fired from his position as a security guard two weeks before the killing. Huberty may have recognized that he was suffering from anxiety, as he placed a call to a mental health care provider the day before the killing. There is no evidence that he spoke with a clinician. His message was not returned as there was no indication that his call was an emergency.

The Hubertys ate lunch at another McDonald's. They returned to their home and while he was gathering his weapons, his wife inquired as to what his plans were the rest of the day. He told her he planned to "hunt humans." The statement apparently brought no alarm to his bride. Nor did his previous threats of violence.

We can identify a number of factors of concern in the Huberty case. He suffered from extreme paranoia. His career had been altered due to a disability. He relocated away from possible social and family support systems. All relocations are stressful. I have found that relocations, even the ones you look forward to, are stressful and disruptive. From my own experience, it normally takes a year to adjust. Add to this his termination as a security guard and his acceptance of violence at home. He was obviously making inappropriate statements. Could you predict that he would enter a McDonalds and begin shooting? No. You could identify that he was deeply disturbed and suffered from unbearable stressors that could likely lead him down the path to violence.

At the Luby's Cafeteria in Killeen, Texas, 1991, diners were enjoying companionship and good food. George Hennard drove his pickup truck through the front of the restaurant coming to a crashing halt inside. Many diners were in shock by the impact of the vehicle, and initially responded to the car in an effort to render aid and assistance. Hennard began firing at the diners killing twenty-four and wounding an additional twenty before taking his own life. He had been previously employed as a Merchant Marine, but he had been suspended due to illegal use of marijuana.

Hennard was raised in an upper middle-class environment. His father was a surgeon and, his mother was known to be very domineering. As a result, he had a strong dislike of females. He may have obtained some inspiration from the movie *The Fisher King*. The movie starring Robin Williams, depicted a shock disc jockey who offends a critical fan. The fan enters a bar and engages in a killing spree. A ticket stub from *The Fisher King* was found in the killer's pocket. Did the movie provide inspiration or affirmation of Hennards beliefs?

As history dictates, these mass shootings are not new. Many more predated these cases. All three of these cases amassed a significant body count and an additional psychological toll on the survivors. What is concerning, are the efforts of the modern killers to eclipse the casualty count of previous incidents. Their plans have become more devious.

Chapter 4
No Snap and Checklists

The approach of this book is to provide a road map to utilize an overall assessment approach of the individual. I utilize a holistic behavioral approach. Like an archaeologist who uncovers our history, we are sifting through the layers of a person's life. My goal is to remove the sediment in an attempt to reveal the inner self. By looking at all facets of the individual's past and current experiences, I hope to develop a clearer picture. That means talking to neighbors, former co-workers, former schoolmates, teachers, supervisors, relatives and examining academic, military, employment and police records.

So often, it is easy to dismiss aberrant behavior with phrases like "he snapped," or "he was a nice boy next door," or "he was the brilliant student," or "he was the former war hero." These people do not just hit the snooze alarm in the morning and decide to become mass killers. There has been a gradual buildup to the cataclysmic event, and the evidence traces left behind are abundant. In many instances, individuals planning an attack do not go to bed the night before, instead choosing to stay up in preparation for the final assault. The alarm clock is a reminder to engage in the attack.

I have often been asked about using computers or checklists. I am not in favor of either approach. I believe computer models can be utilized to "thin the herd" and help to identify a smaller pool of possible suspects, but I still believe in good old-fashioned Sherlock Holmes deductive reasoning and investigative work.

In 2004, while I was living in Florida, all the hurricane forecast models projected the path of Hurricane Charlie to have a direct impact on the Tampa Bay region. The computers forgot to tell Charlie where Charlie was supposed to go. The hurricane made an abrupt right-hand turn, came ashore, and slammed into Punta Gorda, Florida, cutting a swath through Central Florida. So, despite the voluminous data that had been inputted into the computers, the models were wrong. Computers might be useful for writing a book, organizing your checkbook, having a good go of it in a game of chess, but when lives are at risk, I don't like to delegate that authority to a computer that has no emotional stake.

The use of checklists can provide a myopic view of analysis. I would much rather someone who has an overall sense or a holistic viewpoint of behavioral threat assessment. Checklists can be helpful reminders to stay focused and on track but often they become a crutch and those utilizing the checklists can develop a myopic viewpoint towards conducting threat assessments.

After 9/11, one war hero and Medal of Honor winner, retired General Joe Foss was detained by TSA while transitioning at the Phoenix airport, when his Medal of Honor triggered the metal detector. Instead of making a quick determination as to why the metal detector had been set off, the screeners operating off the checklist deferred the war hero to secondary inspection, so that he could be scrutinized. Now keep in mind, General Foss was 86 years old and posed little threat to anyone. He and his medal were enroute to West Point for a speech. The inspector's judgment was blinded by the micromanaging checklist.

We want to take a holistic approach and look at the situation from a macro viewpoint. In the past, we would focus solely on verbal statements, which encompass only one part of the totality of the picture. Deception is most easily manipulated through our verbal language. My book *Face 2 Face* examines deception and interviewing in more detail.

The FBI does a wonderful job of building profiles of serial killers, which can be used as an investigative tool by police departments in identifying and locating serial murderers. The method that we will use in this book is to take an individual who has been identified as displaying unusual patterns of behavior and to assess that behavior in order to determine whether that individual presents a potential threat to public safety. Threat assessments are not to be confused with criminal profiling utilized by the highly trained FBI's Behavioral Analysis Unit (BAU). I do not pretend to be a profiler.

Of the subjects that were studied in the Secret Service study, the profile reflected that their ages ranged from 16 years of age to 73 years old (although an 88 year old has since attempted a mass murder) and the overwhelming majority of the attackers were white males who had at least a high school education. As you can see, this profile has limited value to security guards at your local school or shopping mall. Essentially, you are looking for angry white males who had a high school education.

Chapter 5
Barking Dogs

I have a philosophy called the Barking Dog Theory. Anyone who has ever approached a home with a barking dog is well aware of the intentions of the dog; to guard the master's residence. When we served arrest warrants or search warrants, the barking dog was a known hazard. The real problem was when you entered the residence and heard the scratching of toenails on the linoleum floor and a low growl. You knew you were fixing to have an awful day as the dog was charging at you. While one dog is merely announcing its protection of its territory, the other one is in attack mode. Which is more dangerous?

While all threats must be investigated and taken seriously, the Secret Service study found only one tenth of those planning to attack, known as near attackers, made any direct threats to their intended targets or law enforcement. In this study, none of the 43 assassins made any direct threats. Why is this?

Those who are committed to violence typically do not want to show their cards and tip their hand. Their objective is success, and investigators should never underestimate their resolve or intelligence.

In his research of threatening letters to members of congress, Park Dietz the noted forensic psychologist, found little association between those writing threats and those that made inappropriate personal contact. He found that subjects who mailed threatening communications were significantly less likely to pursue a personal interaction with the intended target. Dietz also found similar conduct in those who sent inappropriate writings to members of congress and Hollywood celebrities. It is also not unusual for a letter writer to mention multiple targets. I often found letters, which mentioned numerous individuals.

Despite the Barking Dog Theory, law enforcement does not have the luxury of discounting such threats. They must all be investigated to determine the veracity and if the person communicating the threat has the means, capacity or motivation to carry out an attack. All inappropriate communications should be examined despite the lack of criminal wrongdoing. In this current culture, the media and public will question why law enforcement failed to follow up or warn the target.

Communications are not confined to letters. They also include phone calls, Internet postings and emails. All incidents must be preserved. Letters, emails, and postings should be printed and placed in a common file. If one communicator begins to send additional communiqués, this offender should have his or her own file. Original letters should be preserved with the original envelope in a plastic sleeve for later retrieval of fingerprints and DNA. The more persistent the communications, the more devoted and more likely the subject will attempt to make contact. The communications should be scanned and converted to digital files so that key word phrases can be easily searched. Writers tend to reuse the same phrases.

There are folks out there that author "poison pen" letters. These letters are an attempt to paint someone with a toxic brush to get them in trouble. In one of the most bizarre cases I worked, we received a late night call concerning the threatening behavior of a subject in a bar in New Orleans. He described plans to kill a U.S. senator and launch an attack on the White House. The details of the plan were concerning. Through interviews of the patrons of this bar in the French Quarter, we were able to determine that the suspect had initiated the call reporting his own behavior. We were compelled to conduct an investigation and serve search warrants throughout the night and the next day.

Some communicators become quite prolific. They will send numerous letters directed to many different agencies or individuals. Never assume that a person on the distribution list was notified of the letter. One person I investigated had been a prolific letter writer to many different organizations and officials. We went to his reclusive home to speak with him. He refused to answer his door. I knew I was at the correct house when I noticed the empty ink jet cartridges in his trash. He never threatened anyone, but his letters contained inappropriate content and warranted a follow-up.

In today's world of the Internet, there is irresponsible behavior. Many will post on social media platforms without engaging their brain and considering the consequences of their actions. There are always citizens willing to report inappropriate comments. Many others feel insulated by the anonymity of the Internet. The digital world is never private. I have lost count of the number of individuals who were shocked when I knocked on their door and asked about a threatening post.

There was a fellow driving down the road and his right front wheel came completely off the car. He skidded to a stop. He exited his car, retrieved his errant wheel and rolled it back to the car. He looked behind him and realized that his mishap occurred in front of the mental health hospital surrounded by a moat of a 12-foot chain-link fence with razor wire. As he sat there trying to decide how to proceed, one of the patients walked up behind him and said, "You know if you take one lug nut off of each of the other three wheels, you can hold the fourth wheel on the car until you arrive at a service station." The driver said, "That is an excellent idea. Hey, you seem normal, why are you on the inside of the mental health hospital?" The patient said, "I might be crazy, but I am not stupid."

The preceding story is a good illustration that you do not want to underestimate the intellect of those suffering from mental illness. Keep in mind that one out of every seventeen Americans suffers from some form of mental illness. Charles Whitman, the University of Texas school shooter, had an IQ of 172. Of those I personally interviewed, I found myself often enamored with their degree of intelligence and the tales they would weave. A former supervisor dismissed the individuals I dealt with as "just being crazy." This is a shallow and dangerous viewpoint.

Despite the fact that many of the shooters will not share their intentions with their target, many will leak their intentions to friends, family, and associates. In approximately two thirds of all cases, there was some sort of pre-incident leakage to people the attacker knew. Francisco Duran who fired an assault weapon at the front of the White House, provided an example of this indicator. In the weeks prior to his assault, Duran provided a business card to a coworker, on the back of which he had written, "Death to government officials" and signed his name. He told the coworker that the business card might be worth some money in the future.

In many of the post-attack examinations, it becomes obvious that the attacker had shared some potential insights to those around him. Often those who were included in the loop dismissed the disturbing comments as just crazy talk or thought he was joking. This sharing behavior was displayed frequently by those who engaged in school shootings.

In August 2013, Rockne Newell entered Ross Township municipal meeting, where he shot and killed three individuals because of an ongoing feud with the town over his junk-strewn property. His bathroom was a bucket outside and his home was essentially a storage shed. Ross officials had good reason for code enforcement. There were warning signs that Rockne was considering violence.

Rockne Newell told his father, Pete Newell and others that he planned to kill officials claiming he had nothing left to lose. He was desperate because he had been evicted from his land. Pete Newell shared conversations he had with his son "He said, 'My life's over Dad. I just got to stop them from doing it to anyone else, and I'm going to take care of it so they're not around to do it to anybody else." His father attempted to reason with him. His son replied, "I've got to do what I've got to do."

Deputies served Rockne Newell with papers notifying him that his property would be sold at a sheriff's sale. His father, Pete Newell, warned the deputies that his son had made threats, saying, "I'm telling you one thing, people are going to die over this." Sheriff Todd Martin said his deputies misunderstood the threat to be against the sheriff's department, not against others. A threat is a threat, regardless of whom it is targeting. In hindsight, I am sure those deputies would have handled this reported threat in a different manner. The sheriff admitted that his office had a long volatile history of threatening behavior with Rockne Newell. I am sure they viewed calls concerning the killer as a nuisance. They may have said, "Oh, it's just that crazy Rockne again." He had not acted upon his threats in the past. But in today's culture, you cannot discount this type of speech. Direct threats are against the law.

The best way to find evidence of this behavior is to interview those in the inner circle of the subject. This is quite often a small circle, as many are social isolates. They typically would not be announcing this behavior on blog postings. They may share their homicidal thoughts with those they are most intimate with or those who have gained their trust.

In the days before computers, written journals and diaries provided an insight into the thoughts of the writer. We know that Arthur Bremer, the shooter of presidential candidate George Wallace, maintained a diary. John Hinckley the shooter of President Reagan also maintained a journal that went undiscovered during an arrest at an airport in Nashville, Tennessee. In today's digital world, journals and diaries are commonly maintained on computers or tablets. If you can examine email traffic, Facebook postings, Twitter and Word documents, you may be offered an opportunity to open a digital window to the soul of the attacker.

Chapter 6
Motives

After every one of these mass shootings, we often want to understand the why. That is the most commonly asked question after a tragedy. We all want to know how the boy in homeroom, the former altar server, the neighbor down the street, or a former coworker could engage in such violence. Although many of the shooters have multiple motivations, we typically see that they come from a list of four individual motivations. The four motives are: achieving fame, suicide, revenge, and bringing attention to a perceived grievance.

The first of four motivations is, very simply fame. Many of the shooters want to attach some significance to what they perceive as a meaningless life. If you look into many of these cases, you will see that they failed to live up to their own potential and were failures in life. Initial reporting of the Aurora, Colorado shooter wondered how someone who had achieved such academic excellence would resort to such a heinous act. As more information became available, the psychological autopsy disclosed that the shooter had in fact failed in his academic endeavors, and was asked to leave the University of Colorado. You can just imagine the disappointment and rejection that he must have felt. Like many students, attackers attach their identity to their goals and objectives as the endgame of their academic pursuits. For the Aurora shooter, his identity as a neuroscientist was ripped away from him. He was now going to have to return to his parents' home in San Diego and face the scrutinizing and humiliating gaze of his neighbors and others.

As disturbed as this mindset sounds, many of the shooters were looking to put an exclamation mark on their lives. The attackers wanted to go out in a grandiose manner, where everyone would remember who he or she were. They would have their own dedicated page on Wikipedia, the story of their death would be above the fold on the Washington Post and the lead story on every newscast across the country. TMZ, Facebook and Twitter would be ignited by the story of their life. The Columbine shooters debated which directors would direct the movie about them after the shooting. This conversation occurred when they considered a potential body count of two hundred and fifty students.

Dr. Katherine Ramsland the noted forensic psychologist wrote in *Inside the Minds of Mass Murders: Why They Kill,* that many killers would factor in these "Rehearsal Fantasies." This term describes how killers view the world. Just as many authors, fantasize about being interviewed on Oprah Winfrey; many killers picture the news accounts of their attack and demise.

Arthur Bremer, the shooter of presidential candidate and Alabama governor George Wallace, provided insight into this thought pattern in his diary. He had initially begun surveillance and targeting of President Richard Nixon. He had followed Nixon to a summit in Toronto, Canada, but due to robust security, he concluded that his attempt would be another failure in his life. He then lowered his objective and began targeting Wallace. He lamented in his diary his concerns that no one would really care that Wallace was shot. His concerns were that he would be relegated to some back pages of the newspaper especially, if there was a more significant international event such as a storm.

I believe very strongly that fame is the number one motivation of these individuals. They are using the 24/7 news cycle's insatiable need for stimulation as a leverage to raise their own platform of fame. We can look back in history and review the case of Charles Whitman, the University of Texas tower shooter. His face was plastered all over the front page of Time and Life magazines. In today's society, there is a cascading avalanche of news reporting which becomes almost white noise. For the victims, it is a tragedy that the world has become so busy that it will not slow down to acknowledge the significance of an innocent person's death. Many of the shooters realize they must accomplish a spectacular act that is shocking to the conscience in order to capture the headlines and attention of the country and world. In journalism, this is referred to as, "If it bleeds, it leads."

I use a term called the *negative emotional vortex* to describe the attacker's mindset. If you were to stand in the shooter's flip-flops, you would be able to see how the world is collapsing around them. It all comes down to frame of reference. For a high school student, devastation translates into doing poorly on the SAT exam, failing algebra, or breaking up with a girlfriend of two days. For a middle-aged adult, the frame of reference is exponentially increased so that the negative emotional vortex could result from a painful divorce, his gold fish died, the bank foreclosing on his home, and being fired from his job of twenty years. Regardless if the shooter is a teenager or an adult, this vortex is his reality.

Not everyone who endures personal tragedies and adversity is going to turn into a mass killer or even contemplate this path to violence. For many who lack coping skills, these unbearable stressors begin to exert pressure and turn the individual into a boiling cauldron of emotions. For those who lack coping mechanisms, the cauldron can eventually boil over and lead to unwarranted consequences.

The second motivation often dovetails into the first motivation. The second motivation is the permeation of suicidal thoughts. Simply put suicide by cop. Many of the shooters have a history of failed suicide attempts. For some who are not very adept at killing themselves, what better way is there to ensure your own death than by presenting yourself with a firearm pointed at a well-armed and highly trained police force. Although many of the attackers will commit the ultimate act of taking their own life, many have professed their willingness to be eliminated in their attempt at executing their mission.

John Hinkley had visions of the Secret Service splattering his blood, and we have seen this in multiple situations including Arthur Bremer, who felt that merely the attempt of an assassination would result in his infamous death and bring fame to his insignificant, meaningless life. In examining the lives of the shooters, the Secret Service found that approximately two thirds exhibited a history of at least one previous suicide attempt, and many made multiple attempts.

It appears that most of these individuals had no expectation to live beyond their brutality. Aaron Alexis, the Navy Yard killer knew that his life would end in his assault. In many instances, the killer ended the shooting spree by taking his own life. Suicide could have been precipitated by the arrival of first responders, but it was the attackers plan to place an exclamation mark after his name, so they could demonstrate to everyone that his life was not meaningless and that everyone will remember him in death.

Kip Kinkel, the Thurston High School shooter, taped two bullets to his chest and a knife to his leg to ensure his death at the end of his rampage. Kinkel was concerned that during his murderous rampage, he would run out of bullets, and he would not be able to end his own life, so he had one bullet for each gun taped to his chest. However, he was tackled before he could finish his killing spree. While in custody, he pleaded with the detective to kill him. The Boston Bomber, Tamerlan Tsarnaev, was killed while making a final brazen armed assault against police officers in Watertown, Massachusetts. Wade Michael Page, the shooter at the Sikh Temple in Wisconsin, took his own life after firing upon the first officer to arrive. Seung-Hui Cho took his own life at Virginia Tech, as police officers gained entry into Norris Hall.

It appears that the fortunate jamming of ammunition in the drum-fed magazine, caused James Holmes, the Aurora shooter, to stop shooting, and he was taken into custody alive. Weapons malfunctions have ended a number of shootings prematurely.

Police officers endure countless training scenarios to compensate for gun jams, but video games do not address this variable.

Two other philosophies have been discussed concerning the commitment of suicide at the end of a killing spree. One is that the killer has become so overwhelmed by grief over his actions that he chooses to end his life. Another is that he has been hardened through the operant conditioning of video games to essentially feel and embrace the mindset of *game over.*

I ascribe to the belief that these individuals planned to commit suicide from the beginning. The majority of these killers believed that essentially their lives were over. They were consumed with the darkness of mental illness such as depression. The acceptance of violence within our society has cemented the belief that violence has become a suitable means of placing an exclamation mark on their life. One individual told me that he was not afraid to die, but he could not continue to face the pain of living. He said he was exhausted with living.

Some individuals, were solely committed to ending their own lives and decided that it would be more effective to have a highly trained police officers do the job. There have been a number of individuals, who lay in wait for the president, in hopes that the Secret Service or police officers would kill them.

Not only has violence become integrated into our society, but there has been a decline in spiritual mediation in resolving inner conflict. There are those who handpick religious teachings to substantiate or affirm their beliefs. Others feel betrayed or abandoned by organized religion. Of all the school shootings perpetrated by students over the last two decades, only one has occurred at a faith-based institution. In April 2001, Elizabeth Bush was a recent transfer from public school to Bishop Neumann High School in Williamsport, Pennsylvania. Despite her embracing a pacifist ideology and desire to become a nun, she was overwhelmed by rejection and subsequent despair. She fired one shot, wounding another student in the cafeteria.

I do not want to stand on a soapbox discussing the spiritual degradation of American society, but this topic does require some examination. The lack of spirituality could be one underlying element that would need further exploration and study. None of the individuals I interviewed professed regular attendance at church or prayerful meditation. One potential school shooter embraced an agnostic viewpoint. However, John List, murdered his family, while espousing his commitment to being a devout Christian.

Gallup and Pew surveys indicate that weekly church attendance is around thirty-six percent. The accuracy of the respondent's response must be viewed with skepticism. Many people will not be forthcoming with their lack of church attendance.

David Olson of the Evangelical Covenant Church, author of *The American Church in Crisis,* estimates church attendance to be approximately 17.5%. In another study published in 2005, in The Journal for the Scientific Study of Religion, C. Kirk Hadaway and Penny Long Marler estimated church attendance was 17.7%. The actual number of heads in pews is difficult to determine with certainty.

It has been speculated that the foundation of faith is one of the reasons that African Americans are less likely to engage in targeted violence. Suicide rate of blacks is about half that of whites. Those who study and analyze this data, and possess more expertise on the subject than I do, often cite the embracing of a religious foundation by the black community as a causal factor in the disparity.

I am making an unsubstantiated observation that those who find peaceful meditation through a higher authority have stronger emotional coping skills to deal with adversity in their lives. Atheists will strongly disagree with this position. Those who are comfortable with their religious position or absolute non-believers will have less inner conflict. Some who have a rigid interpretation of religious beliefs could also suffer from considerable internal strife.

The third motive is an age-old motive that can probably be traced back to the beginning of time. That motivation is revenge. In the distorted prism through which these killers view life, they often look at seeking revenge against those who rejected them. One of the most basic motivations in life is of acceptance. Most of us want to be included. Imagine how you feel when you are left off the guest list for a party. Regardless of whether you wanted to attend, you are hurt that you were not included.

We heard in the words of Seung-Hui Cho, the Virginia Tech murderer, who claimed he was seeking revenge against all those who made his life miserable. At a recent a school shooting at Taft High School in Kern, California, the shooter was attempting to exact revenge on the individuals who bullied him. Many of the shooters appear to be making a statement of fame, but also to demonstrate a mistake society or a particular organization has made. By organization, I mean school, work or other social system in which the offender feels rejection.

Certainly, in workplace shootings and domestic targeted violence, revenge is a strong motivation. A rejected spouse, who allowed hatred to take hold, could view eliminating the source of that hatred as a viable option. Domestic revenge creeps over into the stalker mentality, that "if I can't have you, then no one will have you." O.J. Simpson fit this profile as well as Richard Farley, whose obsession with Laura Black, another employee ended in his being fired and engaging in a rampage at his former workplace. Jason Rodriguez in Orlando, Florida, stated that the engineering firm he was fired from, "left me to rot." He entered the business and killed one, injuring six others.

The fourth motive, which we do not witness as often, is to bring attention to a perceived wrong. These would be individuals who are trying to raise the relevance and significance of a platform that is often driven by political or religious beliefs. One must view life from the same lens these individuals see life. It is perhaps a distorted view, but it is their perception of reality.

The shooting in Wisconsin at the Sikh Temple, was carried out by Michael Wade Page a devout believer in the white supremacist movement. James von Braun, the 88-year-old shooter at the Holocaust Museum lived the majority of his life consumed with anti-Semitic beliefs. A shooting was averted at the Family Research Council in Washington, D.C., after Floyd Lee Corkins, who volunteered at a gay advocacy center, launched an unsuccessful attempt at a mass shooting. He wanted to make a statement against those that opposed same-sex marriage. The Boston Bombers may have utilized this motivation, as their platform to seek justice against America because of a perceived injustice to Muslims. Analyzing their behavior suggest that this conduct was a veiled excuse, and the real motive was to exact revenge out of frustration at not being able to attain their dreams of success. Christopher Dorner, the former LAPD officer stated in his manifesto that he wanted to bring attention to his perceived injustice and discrimination by the police department.

Motivation is the reason we get out of bed in the morning. It is inspiration that drives us to seek accomplishment. This same concept is the reason mass killers engage in acts of targeted violence against innocent citizens.

Chapter 7
Target Selection

The selection of a target can be a fluid decision by the attacker. The selected target is based upon the attacker's motivational platform. As we have already seen and as we move forward, we will see a number of instances where the individual attackers change their targets and in some cases, multiple times. Arthur Bremer initially focused on President Nixon, but because of stringent security and more accessibility to presidential candidate George Wallace, he changed his target. John Hinckley had initially focused on President Jimmy Carter, but then changed to President Ronald Reagan and perhaps even considered killing Jodie Foster. John David Chapman, who assassinated John Lennon, had initially considered several other celebrities, but chose Lennon because of his accessibility.

With mass public killings, the target selection is once again based upon motivational factors. We can look at the horrible shooting at Sandy Hook Elementary School. The target selection was based upon Adam Lanza's familiarity with the school, the knowledge that he was unlikely to encounter an armed protector, as well as confined areas that limited escape paths. This theory is speculative and the reasons for target selection would only be proved upon forensic examination of computer hard drives or writings by Adam Lanza.

Floyd Lee Corkins, who attempted to conduct a mass killing at the Family Research Center, considered a list of four conservative groups. An unarmed security guard was able to subdue Corkins after being wounded. The shooter had desired to smear Chick-fil-A sandwiches in the faces of his victims, thus making a statement about both the conservative advocacy group and the restaurant.

With the recent Aurora, Colorado shooting at the movie theater, we can only speculate that perhaps the Batman movie *Dark Knight Rises* could have been an inspiration, but this information may not become public until judicial proceedings are complete. What we do know is in the two aforementioned examples as well as in Columbine and other previous shootings, one would assume that the attackers had considered the fact that their targets were physically confined to a space that would reduce the opportunity for escape and increase their killers success in their killing fields. The likelihood of not being confronted by armed individuals could have played a part in the site selection. The shock value of the target selection should not be ignored.

Symbolism can also factor into the selection process. The workplace or the school can convey the loss of innocence or the perceived hatred by the organization towards the killer. Symbols of power can also be the target, such as a corporate headquarters or government building. For others, mental illness is a factor in choosing a target. Russell Weston, who killed two Capitol Police Officers, believed he needed to locate the "Ruby Satellite" sealed in the Capitol vault to eradicate an imaginary deadly illness.

Society has become desensitized to violence. Whether it is the body count in Afghanistan or an episode of workplace violence in which "only" two people die, the assertion can be made that these killers are looking for shock value. Previous mass killings become the standard to surpass. Columbine and Virginia Tech have often been cited by potential school shooters as body counts to strive for and eclipse. The Norwegian shooting of seventy-two children has also been cited by several shooters as an inspiring event.

In most instances, some manner of physical surveillance was conducted. It is during this preoperational surveillance that the attacker's signature and exposure becomes greater and more likely to be detected. One would assume that the Aurora shooter had attended movies at the location and was very familiar with the layout. I would be shocked if he had not tested the rear exit door to check for an alarm. If in fact, there was a buzzer or an alarm and he was detected, I am sure he had already prepared a response that he merely needed to step out to answer his cell phone to avoid disrupting moviegoers. There is some evidence that Seung Cho at Virginia Tech had practiced chaining the doors on the academic building that he chose as his killing field. There were also anonymous bomb threat calls prior to the shooting. It is unclear if these were related or whether again this was Cho gauging the response of campus first responders to a potential emergency.

I am not suggesting that because James Holmes could have been identified as a potential attacker simply because he attended movies at the theater. Known and familiar targets are often selected because of the comfort level. With workplace shooters, if a former disgruntled employee begins surveillance of the employer, this should be an indication to call law enforcement. In the instance of school shooters, they are members of the student community, and unless they are scribbling surveillance notes, as in the case of the Columbine shooters, the likelihood of being discovered is limited.

Chapter 8
Attack Related Behaviors

Every one of the studied attackers by the Secret Service displayed at least one attack related behaviors. The first one to examine is an interest in or obsession with assassinations. Like any good student, attackers will attempt to gather research and available information. They will study previous attacks to identify strengths and weaknesses of previous mass killers. Evidence was developed that the Tucson shooter of Congresswomen Gabby Giffords had conducted computer searches on mass shootings. We know the Virginia Tech shooter had idolized the Columbine shooting and demonstrated this by writing a term paper about it in high school. This correctly brought the attention of not only the English teacher, but also his parents and they were able to obtain appropriate mental health assistance. Adam Lanza studied other mass murders and the Norwegian shooting in particular. Arthur Bremer claimed in his diary to have been reading a book on Sirhan Sirhan, the killer of Robert Kennedy.

Stephen Kazmierczak, the shooter at Northern Illinois University studied Ted Bundy, Jeffrey Dahmer, Hitler and read *Hunting Humans: The Rise of Multiple Murderers* by Elliot

Leyton. He confided to a close friend that he was enthralled from how the serial killers planned and how they avoided detection.

If you were to ask a suspect, whether or not he was interested in or obsessed with previous assassinations or shootings, he would probably deny interest. Instead, you can approach this topic by asking what he is reading. What are his favorite books and why? Is there a particular character he likes and why? You may have an opportunity to explore their bookshelf if you are conducting an interview in his residence. In one person's apartment I entered, there were several copies of Janet Evanovich's books. That revelation provided little insight, other than he was enamored with a fictional smart-alecky, bounty hunter named Stephanie Plum.

Another question to ask the suspect is where he obtains his news and what he has recently researched or looked up on the Internet. This inquiry must be conducted delicately. If the subject has paranoid tendencies, you risk him becoming Concerned about spy satellites and black helicopters. Most employers provide no personal protection of employee privacy on network computers and thus, computer history can be checked easily.

Inquire as to what genre of movies the suspect prefers and explore his favorite flicks. Ask them what was it they enjoyed most about the movie and which characters they identified with or liked the most. If you are familiar with the movie, it provides an opportunity to share and explore, while also developing rapport. If he mentions a movie I had not viewed, I will research the movie and rent the video. The key is to view the movie from his perspective, not yours. You should also determine whether the suspect has developed an obsession with a particular movie. Watching the movie can provide insight into his viewpoint.

Ask what kind of music the suspect listens to and find out if there are particular songs or groups that he likes. Later, you can pull up the lyrics of those songs so that you can try to gather what the lyrics may suggest.

It is best to frame these questions in casual terms, so it does not sound like you are focusing in so much on the responses. Your goal is to demonstrate genuine interest in an attempt to establish a rapport with them. You may find it more useful to use the strategy of spacing out the questions and sprinkling them in between other questions, so that the subject of your interview does not recognize the pattern that you are exploring.

When we are preparing for a road trip, we may consult a map, preprogram the GPS unit, or conduct some research on our destination such as the hotel. This is the same technique demonstrated by someone preparing to engage in an act of targeted violence. They will utilize some planning measures. The Columbine attackers demonstrated the greatest planning acumen to date. Their planning and preparation began a year in advance. They made meticulous notes, conducted surveillance, acquired weapons, manufactured explosives, and developed cover stories. They practiced exploding their bombs and honing their skills. They spent hours target practicing with their newly acquired weapons. They fashioned utility belts and even match strikers, so they could ignite their incendiary devices.

In some instances, the individual will conduct minimal surveillance because he is very familiar with the setting. The Sandy Hook shooter had attended the school. This would also be the case in workplace violence, where an employee is intimately familiar with the surroundings. The attacker may display some stalking tendencies as he is trying to develop the courage to execute the attack, or to monitor the arrival and departure of specific individuals. In 2012, Jeffrey Johnson was seen lurking in front of the entrance to the fashion company that fired him from two years earlier. He lay in wait for the arrival of Stephen Ercolino, who was shot multiple times as he arrived at the entrance. The two had a long-standing feud that simmered for several years.

An attack-related behavior displayed more frequently among shooters of individual targets such as a celebrity or political figure is that the attacker will attempt to penetrate or breach security at various locations. Many times these individuals will either blend in with a group or use social engineering techniques to manipulate security personnel. They will often use the ruse of, "I am an old friend" or "I am an aid," or "I am carrying information of paramount importance." They will often use name dropping techniques and we-teaming efforts. This was the philosophy developed by Gavin DeBecker and described in his book, *The Gift of Fear*. In we-teaming, attackers will start utilizing "we" to get this information to the politician or celebrity. "We" are allies and share a common goal. It is essential these techniques be discussed with security personnel, who should be instructed to summon someone or to defer them to the check-in table. If possible, the intruder's story should be verified and vetted. This is not always plausible during a major event. The suspects can be creative and employ the old default excuse that they were looking for the bathroom or the coatroom.

These killers want to succeed. There will be times that they will utilize disguises or blending techniques to infiltrate a crowd. As we know with the Aurora shooter, he posed as just another moviegoer. Ramzi Yousef, who was arrested in the bombing of the World Trade Center in 1993, acquired clerical garb and planned to disguise himself as a priest carrying a Catholic Bible at the Pope's visit to Manila. His plans were thwarted by unanticipated fire at his bomb-making factory. Others have worn trench coats and acquired haircuts to make themselves resemble law enforcement officers. In his diary, Arthur Bremer wrote that he attempted to blend with the crowd by being one of the most enthusiastic hand clappers.

Some have demonstrated a proclivity to previous assaultive behavior. This demonstrates the inability to control emotions. Most of these killers had minimal criminal history, but I have encountered a few who had arrests for assault. These would be in the minority. The Navy Yard shooter, Aaron Alexis, displayed a history of assaultive behavior.

The one common thread that is woven through the fabric of all of these killers and attackers is that they were suffering from personal turmoil. Perception is reality. One's personal turmoil could be insignificant to another. Quite often, their inability to manage comes down to coping skills and social support. John Huberty, the McDonald's shooter in San Diego, had moved from Ohio and lacked the social support of his extended family and friends. Would this have made a difference? We can only speculate he may not have felt as isolated if he had a social support network to rely upon. The Virginia Tech shooter suffered from a self-imposed isolation and was socially inept. He would have benefited from a nurturing, supportive environment and in closer proximity to his parents. He responded positively in high school to therapy and the loving support of his family.

During the study conducted by the Secret Service, only about one third of the attackers sought mental health treatment in the year prior to their shootings. I believe the majority of these attackers suffered from some form of mental defect. The fact that many of them had not sought treatment in the year prior is not in itself evidence that they did not suffer from a mental illness. People who are fully adjusted in life do not commit suicide or go on a murderous rampage. Half of those in the study suffered from delusional thoughts. The question is the depth of those delusional thoughts and how consuming were they. If that person lacks the proper coping mechanisms, these deficiencies can be a roadmap to tragedy.

Despite the fact that most of these individuals suffered from some degree of mental health illness, the most important aspect is how these individuals could maintain their focus of thought. One individual I interviewed, could not scheme his way out of the urine-soaked recliner. I encountered others that had a high degree of intellect and one who had a Ph.D.; but both were defective in their mental thought process.

One individual, had an extremely high intellect, and despite being in the depths of schizophrenia, he was able to maintain his focus long enough to complete assignments. One of his former friends hired this individual to pressure wash his business. The subject diligently pressure washed the business for eight hours only pausing to add gas. The employer marveled at the determination and focus of the subject. The one question that you must ask is, despite some obvious mental health issues, the real concern is whether they can maintain focus, formulate a plan, adhere to it and execute the plot. Is he organized enough in his thoughts to carry out a plan? Never underestimate the determination and intellect of these people.

It is too easy to dismiss somebody as being crazy. Charles Whitman, the University of Texas shooter, had an IQ of 172. Another individual was a former military officer and graduate student before his life became consumed with paranoid thoughts. Stephen Kazmierczak, the Northern Illinois University killer, despite suffering from a long history of mental health issues, intentionally refrained from mental health treatment for five years, so that he could qualify under Illinois state law to legally possess and acquire firearms. He also was a highly functioning graduate student in psychology and had been awarded recognition by the dean of the college. Remember the humorous tale of the mental health patient instructing the gentleman to attach the tire to his car; he said, "I may be crazy but I'm not stupid."

As law enforcement professionals, we often discount those who have not demonstrated a previous criminal record as being a serious threat. Research indicates that most of these individuals had an insignificant criminal history and perhaps they had not come to the attention of law enforcement in the past. What we must examine is what stressors are occurring in their personal lives and what social support systems are in place to help them through these unbearable stressors. You must stand in their flip-flops and determine how they view their life. If they feel trapped in this negative emotional vortex, from which they see no way out, they may become desperate. There may be evidence of an escalation of concerning behavior demonstrated to those who personally know the subject. This knowledge becomes of paramount importance as to whether or not the individual has become a concern to others that know the subject.

I was alerted by another law enforcement agency of an individual of concern. As I began to look into the case, I discovered that the subject's financial situation was deteriorating, and he was being ousted from his domicile. He had entered into a business in which he was known, and made inappropriate statements that he planned to travel to Washington, D.C., and that no one would stop him from seeing the president.

As he exited the business, he looked back at the owner, and bid the shopkeeper farewell by saying, "It's been nice knowing you, I don't expect to see you again." It also turned out that the subject was wanted on a sexual assault in another state. Unable to locate him at his residence, I called the subject and spoke to him for several minutes before he terminated the call. He denied having intentions to harm the president, but I was not convinced of his truthfulness. He refused to provide his exact location, but I determined that our phone conversation occurred while he was driving in close proximity to the Washington metropolitan area. He was subsequently located in Pennsylvania, where he had run out of gasoline and money. A loaded shotgun was found in the car, and he was placed under arrest for the outstanding warrant. Did my phone call influence his decision not to act upon his statements? We will never know. He again reiterated the fact that he harbored no ill intentions toward the president. I have heard this repeatedly. The individual denies any animosity, but behavior or statements to others contradict the denials.

We have seen this repeatedly, especially in assassins and presidential attackers. They are attacking the position, and it has nothing to do with politics. The one exception that comes to mind is the John Wilkes Booth killing of Abraham Lincoln. Booth was consumed with his hatred of the politics and policies of Abraham Lincoln. John Hinckley was not acting upon a political platform when he stalked two presidents, one republican and one democrat. Despite his mental illness, he had a high enough intellect and functioning ability that he was able to develop, execute and carry out his plan. He was motivated by his desire to acquire the affection of an actress.

Shawn Achor, the author of The *Happiness Advantage,* conducted a survey of the happiest ten percent of individuals. He found the most important factor in being one of the happiest people is meaningful social connections. If you have no one to share your turmoil with, the irritants can weigh upon your conscience and become detrimental to your stability mentally, physically and socially. We have all been around an individual that has endured the personal wounding of a divorce. Many times, the psychological scars from the divorce will carry on for years. Two law professors from Ohio engaged in a bitter and contemptuous divorce lasting seventeen years. It is hard to imagine two attorneys not coming to an agreement, but this is a great demonstration of how deep the acrimony in a divorce can be and how long it can last.

Are the people closest to the individual concerned about the subject's behavior? Has there been an escalation in concern over the subject's increasingly alarming behavior? Most will discount the initial behavior as an acceptable response to stress. If this conduct does not abate over time and increases in intensity, there is legitimate cause for concern.

Chapter 9
Mental Health

Four events had an influence on the mental health care system transforming care from an institutionalized based system to an outpatient community based system. These influences have also increased the threshold for commitment of those in need of mental health treatment. If we look at history, we can see the deplorable conditions and the denigrating of human beings who were subjected to hospitalizations in the mental health system. These institutions were commonly understaffed, overpopulated with patients and utilized lobotomies and shock therapy as normal course of treatments.

Growing up on Long Island, I frequently drove past Pilgrim State Hospital. The hospital was a massive, foreboding structure that looked like it belonged on the set of some horror picture or the latest Harry Potter movie. I was always intimidated by the fear of breaking down on the highway alongside the fence in the darkness of night. That facility which is now closed, housed thirteen and half thousand patients. That is equivalent to the size of a small town with a fence around it, institutionalizing all the citizens. There were many facilities like Pilgrim's State not only in New York, but across the country. Estimates of institutionalized patients in mental health hospitals or asylums as they were called were believed to be around 400,000 people. Compare that with approximately 40,000 persons today.

Certainly new drug treatments and therapy treatments have significantly decreased the need for such facilities. The pendulum of mandatory care has swung far to the opposite direction. Quite often, those people who are in dire need of treatment are unable to obtain the necessary treatment from their current state. Between 2009 and 2011, states across the United States in efforts to reduce their budgets, slashed 1.8 billion dollars from mental health funding resources. As in the highly institutionalized settings, the current state of many mental health facilities is one in which resources are stretched thin and employees are poorly compensated resulting in an extremely high burnout rate.

In 1972, a young investigative reporter for ABC News New York, named Geraldo Rivera, explored and exposed the inhumane treatment of patients at the Willowbrook State School in New York. This facility housed approximately six thousand children suffering from various mental disabilities. Rivera, with the assistance of a recently terminated physician was able to obtain access to the gruesome patient areas. As a teenager, those vivid images were so disturbing that I can still recall them today. I can tell you that if animals at a zoo were treated in any such manner as these patients there would be outrage. Rivera's report raised the conscious awareness of these conditions and initiated a much-needed national debate over the treatment of mental health patients and those who were institutionalized.

In 1973, Dr. David Rosenhan, conducted an experiment to test the validity of patient diagnosis in the field of psychiatry. He along with three women and five men presented themselves as pseudo-patients at twelve different hospitals in five states. The pseudo-patients were to present symptoms of people suffering from various mental illnesses. In all cases, these pseudo-patients were admitted to hospitals. Many times, they were forced to follow drug therapy, and the average stay of these patients was nineteen days before being released. Could you image being one of these pseudo-patients forced to remain institutionalized and monitored for compliance to drug therapy? "Hey, I was just joking, I'm not really crazy." The clinician responds, "Sure you are, just take these pretty pink and blue pills and everything will be all right."

After Dr. Rosenhan disclosed his findings, one hospital essentially dared Rosenhan to dispatch pseudo-patients to their hospital. The hospital subsequently reported that out of 193 patients presenting themselves at the facility, 41 were identified as being pseudo-patients. Unfortunately, Rosenhan had not dispatched any pseudo-patients to the target hospital. This study created quite a stir in the mental health community, and emphasized that the diagnosis and treatment of patients is much more subjective than rigidly structured in science.

The last event that had significant influence on mental health treatment was the 1975 U.S. Supreme Court case, O'Connor versus Donaldson. Kenneth Donaldson had visited his father in Florida. He complained to his father that someone was attempting to poison his food. His father, concerned about his mental state committed him to the Chattahoochee State Hospital in Tallahassee. For the next 15 years of his life, Mr. Donaldson was institutionalized in Chattahoochee. This hospital was small by many standards, but still housed thousands of patients. The lone attending physician was an OB/GYN doctor.

The essence of the Supreme Court decision created the threshold that no person should be institutionalized who is not a danger to themselves or to others. In other words, are they homicidal or suicidal? This remains the current standard for most mental health commitments throughout the United States.

In the state of Florida, under the Baker Act, an individual may be involuntarily committed for 72 hours after a law enforcement officer becomes concerned that an individual is displaying symptoms of being a danger to himself or to others. This does not mean that the individual must remain for 72 hours in a treatment facility. It merely means that he must be seen within the 72 hours by a clinician. If he is seen by a mental health clinician within the first few hours of his admission and deemed to be stable enough that he is no longer a threat to themselves or to others, he is quite often released with a referral to an outpatient facility and perhaps a prescription for a handful of psychotropic drugs.

In order for someone to be detained past the 72 hours, the patient must be afforded the opportunity to a commitment hearing in front of a judge. That judge will listen to the evidence and render a decision as to whether further treatment is necessary or whether the subject could benefit from treatment on an outpatient basis. Most states have similar commitment laws. There are variances, and I would suggest that you consult with the legal authorities within your own state.

As demonstrated by the Donaldson case, decades ago it was easier for families to obtain help for their loved ones who were exhibiting signs of mental illness. There were abuses in which families dropped off a family member and never returned. Many families become frustrated in trying to obtain help for their loved ones. If a family member is not willing to obtain treatment voluntarily, the family must rely upon legal intervention. They can summon the police or go through the courts for an ex-parte order mandating treatment. Long-term treatment is reserved for those who are the most dysfunctional.

Because of these previous incidents, a debate and dialogue began concerning the institutionalization of the mentally ill. This stimulated movement in congress and as a result, they passed the 1980 Civil Rights Act for Institutionalized Persons. This provided the Department of Justice the ability to enforce civil rights for those institutionalized not just in mental health facilities, but also in prison facilities. Civil litigators are also willing to enforce unsatisfactory conditions in civil court.

Chapter 10
Pharmacology Cycle

With budgets being adversely impacted inpatient beds are at a premium as is adequate staffing. In the law enforcement community, I often witnessed what I refer to as the pharmacology cycle. That is when an individual is admitted on an inpatient basis. After an assessment, he receives treatment, prescribed medication, and is subsequently released back to the community.

Quite often, the patients cease the medication treatment. This occurs for a number of different reasons. It may be because they cannot afford the cost of the drug treatment, or they do not like the side effects. Side effects are quite common for these types of drugs, and can include loss of libido, brain fog, impaired judgment, mood alteration, and weight gain, among many others. Some proponents advocate that the drugs themselves are the causal factor for homicidal impulses. Another factor of noncompliance is the patient feels he is stabilized and no longer needs to take the medication.

Many of these drugs require a gradual withdrawal for proper termination. When the patients suddenly halt the drug treatment, they are once again confronted with a crisis. Law enforcement is summoned to quell the emergency and the cycle starts all over again. I lost count of the number of individuals who wore the hinges out on the "swinging door" of a mental health facility. Many of them had multiple volumes in their records.

My greatest sympathy was for the families of these individuals. They often struggled for years to obtain treatment that would restore their loved ones back to their former selves. I always admired the willpower of these families who stood by their loved ones during protracted treatment of mental illness. I remember the sister of one patient telling me that the movie *A Beautiful Mind* accurately portrayed the schizophrenia experienced by her brother and the struggles that the family endured. The family eventually becomes frustrated and has difficulty remaining engaged.

In August 2013, nineteen-year-old Michael Hill, entered the Ronald E. McNair Discovery Learning Academy in Decatur, Georgia, armed with an assault rifle and five hundred rounds of ammunition. After a brief exchange of gunfire with police, Hill was convinced by the school bookkeeper to put down his weapon and not injure any of the staff or students. Michael Hill's, brother, Tim Hill, told Piers Morgan on CNN that Michael had been hospitalized for mental illness ten times and there had been an ongoing struggle to regulate his medications. Michael Hill's family had become frustrated as he tried to burn the home down with the family inside, threatened his mother with a butcher knife, and threatened to shoot his brother, Tim.

A significant number of individuals who advocate for patients to choose their own treatment plan. Some adhere to holistic, nutritional or alternative remedies. In addition, some find that mediation, yoga and diet can assist in controlling mental illness. The National Association for Rights Privacy and Advocacy (NARPA) is a group that lobbies for independent choice. John Nash, a Princeton mathematician and the winner of the Nobel Prize in Economic Sciences is also an advocate of treatment choice. He was the focus of the movie *A Beautiful Mind,* which starred Russell Crowe. Although he battled schizophrenia, he has refused medications and has been able to manage his illness. This debate is above my pay grade and knowledge.

Chapter 11
Psych 101

This book and certainly this chapter are not meant to replace Elementary Psychology 101. It is merely meant to provide a very brief overview of some of the more prominent mental health illnesses that you will see in individuals who engage in or plan to conduct acts of targeted violence. When you hear mental health providers discussing various illnesses, you will have a general understanding of what they are discussing. It will assist you in avoiding the deer in the headlights look.

When we discuss mental health illness and motivations, it is helpful to consult a study that was completed by Ohio State University psychology professor Stephen Reiss. Most everyone remembers Maslow's Hierarchy of Needs. That is the triangle with the five basic motivational factors in everyone's lives. Dr. Reiss's research has put Maslow's Hierarchy of Needs on steroids and identified sixteen relevant basic motivational desires. The sixteen desires include the following: acceptance, curiosity, eating, family, honor, social justice, order or structure, exercise, power, romance, saving, social contact, status, tranquility, and vengeance.

We all possess a number of these basic desires. Notice number one on that list was acceptance. Most everyone has the desire for acceptance. We look for acceptance from our spouses, children, coworkers, supervisors and neighbors. How many friends or likes do you have on Facebook? How many Twitter followers do you have? How many connections on LinkedIn? We all strive for acceptance. When you are not accepted you begin to view yourself as an outcast, rejected by society and by your friends. This can be a harrowing experience. Think about this concept. How would you feel if everyone who truly mattered in your life rejected you? What would be the effects if you were not accepted by anyone who really mattered? The result could lead to devastation and total despair.

Another important desire in that group of sixteen traits is social justice. We are all looking for fairness in life. Rarely is that ever achieved. The level of injustice will dictate how embattled and bitter we become. Acceptance and social justice go hand-in-hand, and most of us seek social contact of some varying degree. Yes, some people are satisfied being alone, but are they truly alone or are they connected on the Internet and social networks and receiving stimulation through television or books?

Most of us crave physical contact and social contact with others. We discussed Shawn Achor's work in the study of happiness. His studies of the top ten percent of the happiest individuals all share the common denominator of meaningful social contacts or relationships. Social relationships are vitally important in allowing us to share our ideas, to gauge our actions, or to act as a barometer for emotions. Most of us desire to laugh, listen and to share experiences with others. It leads us to a status of tranquility and is important to most people.

Vengeance is a strong motivating factor. Many who were trying to reach up and achieve a higher status in life, but were denied that status can be embroiled in turmoil and vengeance. How many violent crimes occurred because of revenge? When somebody does us wrong, it is difficult to just forgive and forget. You can understand the frustration of those who were bullied, humiliated, castigated, ignored, or ostracized. They reach a point where they want to strike back and seek revenge against those who willfully disregarded of their personal feelings. We all have definitions of honor and varying levels of pride. Some nations have gone to war over hurt feelings and pride. Think of how common road rage has become.

When we are denied access to these basic desires, it can have dire consequences. These motivational factors are not only the reason we get out of bed in the morning and go to work, but also the reason some commit acts of violence.

Chapter 12
Mental Health Typology

Psychopaths and Sociopaths

Many people get wrapped around the axle concerning the definition of psychopaths and sociopaths. The best way that you can differentiate between the two is a description I heard in the play *Wicked*. One of the lines concerning the witch provides a good difference of the two pathologies. "Was her wickedness cast upon her (by social forces) or was she born with wickedness?" That is essentially the difference between sociopaths and psychopaths.

Psychopaths and sociopaths share many of the same traits and are both highly manipulative and very calculating. They are devoid of a conscience. Despite these ominous traits, many of them are capable of operating in the mainstream as your neighbor down the street or the boardroom executive. The nuance between whether they are socio or psychopaths is only useful for the causality of their illness. It has no effect on their actions, which are symptomatic of a shared psychosis.

Psychopath is one that is born with wickedness. From the research that I have read on Eric Harris, the Columbine shooter, he appears to fit the mode of the psychopath. He was highly calculating and manipulative of his parents, the criminal justice system, school authorities and friends. It is obvious that he was devoid of any conscience, as he was heard on the video laughing with glee during his murderous rampage. He enjoyed the act of killing. It appears that he grew up in a stable, middle class environment with two parents.

An example of a sociopath could be Stephen Kazmierczak, the shooter at Northern Illinois University. He grew up in a dysfunctional family in which his alcoholic mother would have him lay in bed with her viewing horror movies that were much too traumatic for a young child to see. He was tormented by his peers in school. This deeply disturbed individual was also impaired by other mental health illnesses, but society's failures had an adverse impact on his development. Stephen fanaticized of eating human flesh with glee.

Dr Robert Hare, who is one of the foremost authorities on psychopaths, estimates that somewhere around one percent of the population are psychopaths. Yes, good portions of those are probably incarcerated but not all. Some walk among our boardrooms, universities, and neighborhoods.

Depression

Depression is probably the number one malady many of the killers suffer from. Many individuals across America struggle with bouts of periodic or even sustained stages of depression. Statistics show that approximately 6.7% of the population suffers from depression. Many of us have experienced depression after the death of a loved one, divorce, becoming unemployed, poor health or struggling with a personal failure. The majority of the population endures these challenges and eventually sheds the cloak of depression. For those who become consumed with the depths of depression, they eventually claw their own way out, or through counseling and or medication, are able to stabilize their lives.

Those who are not able to stabilize their depressive symptoms can be overcome by the burden of the darkness within their lives, and often become victims of suicide. Many who are contemplating suicide feel there is no way out, and that this is their last remaining option to terminate their pain and alleviate the darkness.

They are sucked into the negative emotional vortex and they rarely consider the thoughts of others, including loved ones. This is evidenced by those who take their own lives in their homes, with full knowledge that their family will discover the body and the sanctity of the home will be forever tarnished by the scar of that memory. Sometimes, the victim intends that his or her loved one find the body so that person will live with the guilt. I have been at crime scenes when fathers and husbands took their lives in their own homes knowing that their children or their wives would be the ones to discover the body. This just demonstrates the depth of the darkness that they obviously endured.

The average age of the onset of depression is thirty-two years old. Why is thirty-two the average age of onset? It is a time in our lives where we are approaching middle-age when one would think we would be enjoying the happiest times of our lives, but quite often our lives become consumed with dreams unfulfilled. It is around that age that many marriages begin deteriorating, we perhaps experience impaired health, or we have reached stagnation is the ascent up the career ladder and become disgruntled at work. As a gerbil stuck on the wheel, we get caught running in place and not being able to see any improvement.

Although more women than men are diagnosed with depression this could be because men are less willing to receive treatment. Depression is probably the easiest mental health illness to conceal. Often times those who knew the victim of a suicide were shocked and surprised. They thought that this act was out of character for the deceased. Those who are closest to someone suffering from depression can perhaps pick up on subtle mood changes. Depression is an illness that can consume the individual inwardly, while externally they present an alternate image of happiness. Richard Jeni, the famed comedian, committed suicide despite his hilarious exterior. Lee Thompson Young, the always smiling and gentle-souled actor from *Rizzoli and Isles,* shocked his co-stars by committing suicide.

Men are much more likely than women to commit suicide in an approximately 3 to 1 ratio. The significant gender gap is based upon the culture that the two genders are nurtured. For men, violence is a much more accepted means to accomplish an end. Females are more willing to share their feelings with others and are more likely to seek treatment and counseling, which can certainly moderate the depth of the illness.

Those who are consumed in an intractable depression are swallowed by despair. Desperate people who have lost faith and hope are often motivated to perform desperate acts to end their suffering. The trail of despair does not happen overnight, but is a longer journey of tragedy.

Schizophrenia

Schizophrenia is a fractured thought pattern. The name stems from the Greek "splitting the mind." The disorder affects slightly over 1% of the population. The onset is typically in the late teens to early 20s. Schizophrenics often suffer from auditory hallucinations of hearing voices. The real concern arises when they listen to those voices and act upon the commands of those voices. One individual, was convinced that aliens were trying to poison his food, became consumed with the voices and told him the only way to stop the poisoning would be to kill the president or innocent children. He expressed no personal desire to kill the president and harbored no ill will toward the president. He was merely acting upon the voices commanding him to assassinate the president.

The Navy Yard killer, Aaron Alexis, appeared to have been suffering from paranoid schizophrenia. He was concerned that after an unprovoked altercation in the Norfolk airport with an elderly trio, they had dispatched three people to follow him. He believed these people were sending vibrations into his body via a microwave. He could hear voices coming through the walls, floor and ceiling. Were these voices commanding him to take action or merely tormenting him?

One person I spoke with told me that he could hear 100,000 voices, but only two spoke for the collective group. These two voices would at times argue with each other. I empathized with him that the noise level in his head must equate to an NFL stadium on Sunday afternoon. He agreed with the comparison. This man, who held a Ph.D., had become totally disabled by the ongoing war of voices in his head.

Schizophrenics are often consumed with delusional thoughts. I interviewed one subject who was convinced he was God. That was an interesting conversation. I interviewed another individual who was convinced that he was running the White House from his small home in a rural community. You must understand that as bizarre as this behavior sounds, this is the reality in their minds.

Many of these individuals who suffer from paranoid beliefs are truly convinced that black helicopters or satellites are hovering above them or tracking chips have been imbedded in the brain. With the recent revelations concerning NSA activities, I can only imagine that this news will exacerbate these ongoing paranoid beliefs. This thought behavior coincides with conspiratorial thoughts of the government tracking people or manipulating society in one manner or another. Common conspiracy theories are that the government was involved in the 9/11 attack, that the landing on the moon was staged, and any other wide-ranging conspiracies that have gained traction in the media.

Julia Roberts and Mel Gibson starred in the movie *Conspiracy Theory*. I play this in my classes to demonstrate a paranoid schizophrenic. Mel Gibson nails the portrayal of someone suffering from this disorder, as he preaches wide-ranging conspiracy theories to the occupants of his taxicab in New York. One of his theories is the polymer strip in U.S. currency as a tracking device used by the government.

One individual I investigated, who has been deceased for a number of years, was often consumed with thoughts of being tracked by satellites. One night, he filled my voicemail box with schizophrenic tangents and conspiracy theories. Because of his high intellect, he could initially present himself as being a functioning individual. However, this mask of sanity could only hold up for a short time and the façade would collapse quickly. In one instance, he was able to engage in a conversation with a fellow customer standing in line at a Wal-Mart store. He learned the customer was a rocket scientist for a major defense contractor.

The subject then suggested that they exchange business cards, which they did. The subject's business card provided the name inspired by the Brad Pitt movie *Meet Joe Black*. Under the name, Joe Black was inscribed, "Hired assassin for Condoleezza Rice and Colin Powell." The rocket scientist became aware of the mental instability of the subject and they parted ways. That was until he checked his voicemail, which was now filled with the ranting of a paranoid schizophrenic who was directing the rocket scientist to redirect the rockets toward specific targets and individuals in Washington.

While on surveillance with the FBI on an unrelated matter, I was parked in a parking lot where this Joe Black's girlfriend maintained a business. I sat and observed him from a distance as he engaged with his girlfriend and assisted in setting up displays. To the casual observer, he appeared normal. I looked at him with sadness, understanding that this man, who was now in his mid-50s, had been consumed by these personal demons from his late teens and it had led to his personal and permanent disability. I could only imagine what he would have accomplished in life if not for the impairment of a debilitating mental illness.

He and I developed a relationship, as I did with many of those suffering from mental health illnesses. Perhaps it was because I was one of the few people who would listen to them and provide an empathetic ear. I would hear from him and several of the others on a routine basis. When I stopped receiving phone calls, it usually meant that they either were in a treatment facility or had been arrested again. Unlike the flu, which goes away in a week, a person who suffers from mental illness is in for a long-term struggle to manage the symptoms. I was saddened when I had not heard from this one subject for a considerable time. I finally learned that he died several years ago. I do not know under what circumstances.

In 1998, Russell Weston entered the U.S. Capitol and killed two police officers that he believed were cannibals. Two years earlier, he had been interviewed by the Secret Service and the CIA, as his life was consumed with paranoid schizophrenia. He believed that President Clinton was a Russian clone and that Weston too was a clone. He travelled to the capitol in his belief that time was running out to avoid the "Black Heve," an imaginary deadly disease spread by cannibals. Only the "Ruby Satellite" kept in the U.S. Capitol vault could stop the disease. He had been interviewed by a number of law enforcement agencies, including the Secret Service. Weston had been in and out of psychiatric facilities for most of his adult life. He was also habitually noncompliant with medication and until that tragic day in 1998, no one thought he was a danger to act upon his delusions and hallucinations.

Estimates are that 50% of those suffering from schizophrenia are substance abusers. This is no doubt in response to dulling the demons or attempts at self-medicating. A good portion of the homeless population in America suffers from schizophrenia. This afflicted group could benefit from treatment, but is often disregarded and overlooked by society. There have been assertions that the Aurora, Colorado shooter suffered from schizophrenia. Although this may be possible, it is speculative to label anyone who has not been adequately assessed. I am sure that those clinicians who examined him have been able to determine a proper diagnosis.

Bi-Polar

Another illness that you will often see is bipolar disorder. The simple explanation is someone who has polar mood swings from a manic state to a depressed state. While in the manic state, they can be extremely focused extreme, and very productive to an exhausting extent. Anyone who watches the show *Homeland* on Showtime could witness the behavior of Carrie, the CIA analyst, who enters into a manic state near the conclusion of season one. Those affected by the manic state will engage in this hyper and manic activity for a period of days with little or no sleep, consumed with anxiety and urgency to complete various projects. Coming off of the manic high, they will fall into a deep depression, with long periods of slumber.

One individual left twenty-six voicemail messages at a Marine Corps recruiting station and mentioned a number of political figures. The initial voicemail messages were very hyper and interspersed with schizophrenic tangents spoken in a manic state. Toward the conclusion of the voicemails, the tone dramatically changed. The subject became depressed and his thought pattern turned desperate for attention as he was brought to tears.

It is when they are in this depressed state that they are the most vulnerable, when they are overcome by despair and desperate to end their darkness. Approximately 2.6% of the population suffers from bipolar disorder, and there have been good results with various prescribed medications to temper the mood swings. The average age of onset of bipolar disorder is approximately 25 years old.

Bi-polar is often confused by some as having multiple personality disorder. Dissociative identity disorder is completely different. Those who suffer from this ailment have at least two distinct enduring personalities. Although I have heard some interesting tales from those in the mental health field concerning those suffering from multiple personalities, I have not encountered someone who has experienced this disorder. I am not familiar with this ailment being associated with mass killers.

Some individuals will display symptoms of more than one illness. Often, while reviewing mental health records, I read different diagnoses for the same patient by different doctors. I do not become too concerned about the diagnosis. I want to be familiar with the symptoms that are being displayed and to understand to the best of my ability what the patient's reality is and how organized are his or her thoughts.

Chapter 13
The Great Narcissists

Narcissistic personality disorder (NPD) is an epidemic in America. Dr. Jeanne Twenge, who is one of the foremost authorities on narcissism, estimates that one out of sixteen individuals across the country is suffering from this disorder. It is not a disorder in the true sense of mental illness, as the newest DSM has removed the diagnosis. NPD is more in line with a need for behavioral modification. Drugs will not successfully alter the state.

Narcissism is an outcropping of societal and cultural influences. Those afflicted with narcissism have a very high self worth and elitist viewpoint. They believe in their superiority over others. They also have a strong sense of entitlement. They believe that they are entitled or owed their station in life or the trophies they have acquired. They also have a lack of empathy for others. They may project a superficial interest or concern, but deep down they are only concerned when it impacts their situation. As an example, the narcissist may ask you how your weekend was in general terms. You could wrongly assess that question as being out of genuine interest. But a narcissist is merely projecting a false façade and if you notice, most times he will not really ask any additional follow-up questions, unless there is a subject of concern or interest to them.

Professor Wayne Hochwarter, the Jim Moran professor of management at the Florida State University College of Business, asked more than 1,200 employees to provide opinions regarding the narcissistic tendencies of their immediate supervisors. The results indicate that approximately one in four supervisors display narcissistic traits. This can have corrosive results in the workplace. When I share this statistic in classes, it often elicits some under-the-breath chuckling. Most of us have been victims of narcissistic bosses.

Narcissists enjoy adoration and they will generally attract those who have a proclivity for sucking up to the boss. They love to display their trophies and accomplishments. When I worked at the Secret Service, we commonly referred to the office decorations as, "I love me walls." For some, you could hardly view the paint due to all of the certificates of appreciation, school certificates, and action photos. I have witnessed this in some business offices as well.

Professor Jeanne Twenge of San Diego State University has conducted considerable research in the field of narcissism and she has authored several good resources on the disorder. In her book *Me Generation*, she examines the self-esteem movement as empowering narcissism. When you are told that you can accomplish whatever you want and any criticisms are discouraged, the students of the self-esteem movement have difficulty adjusting to and handling adversity. It is difficult to tell someone that he has lost a competition when in the past, he was guaranteed a ninth place trophy where everyone was considered a winner of a medal for trying hard.

The superintendent of the New York City School District published a list of fifty words not to be used by standardized test makers. What were some of the egregious words prohibited? Dinosaur was prohibited because of concern over its association with evolution. The words poverty, divorce and cancer were also on the list as they could cause discomfort. How do you expect to prepare students for the cruelty of real life if you are overly concerned with protecting their feelings? Despite a graduation rate of around sixty-five percent, The State of New York Education Department reported that only 38.4 of the graduates of New York City schools were prepared for postgraduate studies or careers.

Dr. Drew Pinsky, the famous Hollywood psychiatrist, and author of *The Mirror Effect,* blames many of the narcissistic traits of today's culture on the adulation of both Hollywood and reality TV stars, who are placed on a pinnacle and adored for their success, despite never fulfilling any apprenticeship or earning their status. The movie poster from *Taxi Driver* embraces the narcissistic mindset with the quote, "On every street in every city in this country there's a nobody who dreams of becoming a somebody."

The confessional culture of today has accepted and even embraced the concept that it is all right to be a victim and not to take responsibility for one's actions. The workplace shooter is often described as being disgruntled at work and the implication is that it was the fault of the boss or the employer. The alternative would be to describe him as an angry, dysfunctional individual, who sought revenge at his place of employment.

The real problem with narcissists is that they can become ticking "I bombs." They do not handle criticism well, and they certainly do not handle adversity well. When there are speed bumps along the yellow brick road, they often stumble and have trouble getting back up on their feet. When a student who was always told he could be whatever he wanted to be suffers rejection, the reality that he will be denied his dreams can result in a crushing defeat, a defeat that he was not prepared to cope with, and he cannot adjust to in a more positive mindset. James Holmes, the Aurora shooter displayed many of these traits.

I often wondered how the generation that endured the Great Depression and the horrific battle experience of World War II was able to face adversity throughout life, overcome, adjust, and become productive. The road was not always smooth for them, but they possessed the grit and determination to endure hardship and overcome the challenges of life.

Bobby Bowden, the famed and retired football coach at Florida State University, was once asked what changes he had seen in football players over his coaching career. He responded that today's football players all wanted to play in the "I formation." That is, "I want the ball" and "I want this or that." Go back to the *Me Generation* of Dr. Twenge, in which she explains that society has difficulty teaching the youth how to overcome adversity in life. Narcissism is just another ingredient to throw into the volatile mixture that can produce an individual committed toward targeted violence.

Chapter 14
PTSD

The news has widely reported the effects of post-traumatic stress disorder (PTSD) in soldiers returning home from military service. Individuals who suffer from PTSD do not necessarily have to be soldiers of war or first responders. They can be those who have been suffering from an accumulation of prolonged repeated and unbearable stress over time. It can include those who have endured a significant traumatic event, such as the terrorist attack at the World Trade Center.

PTSD is a condition that can be managed and overcome with appropriate counseling, treatment and medication. PTSD is commonly characterized by flashbacks to the trauma-induced events, avoidance, detached personality, and irritability. When irritants are introduced, those afflicted with PTSD can suffer from violent outbursts and fits of anger. Due to the lack of anger management control, their violence is typically confined to that short outburst. Anger hovers near the surface and waits for the next stimuli to elicit a response.

Historically, subjects suffering from PTSD have not been inclined to engage in premeditated acts of violence. As this disorder is researched and more closely examined, studies may shed more light on the ramifications of PTSD. Depending on the severity of the trauma, the patient may always struggle with controlling his or hers emotions.

There have been assertions that some members of the military, who were thought to be suffering from PTSD, have engaged in premeditated attacks. Two noteworthy cases were Sergeant Robert Bales, who went on a killing spree in Afghanistan, killing sixteen civilians and Aaron Alexis, the Navy Yard killer. Although PTSD may have been a causal factor, there were much deeper issues.

According to Alexis's father, he reported that his son responded to Ground Zero on 9/11 to help and was suffering from PTSD. Perhaps he was, as many responders and survivors from that horrific day also developed the symptoms of PTSD. In 2001, Alexis would have been in the age range where symptoms of schizophrenia also begin to manifest. His bizarre behavior could have been blamed on PTSD, but in all probability, his auditory and visual hallucinations were associated with schizophrenia.

Bales was being deployed on his fourth tour of combat. He previously sustained a traumatic brain injury because of a vehicle rollover. Physical examinations cleared him for active duty. Bales had failed to graduate from college and became a registered broker at five different financial services companies that were interrelated. This relationship between the various financial service companies was reported to be a boiler room type operation. Bales moved to Florida, where he opened up another financial services company called Sparktina. It was here that Bales was accused of financial fraud and a civil judgment of $1.4 million was held against him. He left Florida and joined the Army. There was no subsequent enforcement of the judgment, as the plaintiffs had no knowledge of the whereabouts of Bales.

Bales also had some minor run-ins with the police. He was upside down in his house and the home was put on the market three days prior to the shooting. The listing price was $50,000 less than he paid for. There was reporting that he was also suffering from stress within his marriage. This is not unusual because of his financial hardships and combat deployments. On the night of the attack, Bales reportedly consumed alcohol, snorted valium, and he was abusing steroids. After his initial attack on the civilians, he returned to his barracks and confessed his crimes to one of his bunkmates. The soldier dismissed Bales' claims, and Bales exited his camp and engaged in a second murderous rampage. This is not consistent behavior with someone suffering from PTSD. Bales, who killed seventeen civilians and also wounded six others, pled guilty in return for a life sentence to avoid the death penalty.

Chris Kyle, who wrote *The American Sniper,* was killed along with another person by a military veteran suffering from PTSD. Kyle who gained fame as the most lethal sniper in U.S. history, was the victim of what appeared to be a spontaneous attack by his murderer. The PTSD patient shot Kyle and another at a rifle range and drove away in Kyle's truck.

Those who suffer from PTSD can feel a sense of isolation. Police officers enduring treatment for PTSD, could feel isolation and betrayal depending on the support provided by their respective departments. This wallowing in self-doubt, while considering the adverse impact on their future careers, could have negative consequences.

Many times, officers who have been diagnosed with PTSD will have difficulty returning to the street because of liability concerns if they were to become involved in a shooting situation. As a result, officers are reassigned to assignments that reduce their exposure to perilous situations. There is no current evidence that any law enforcement officer has engaged in violence because of PTSD.

Studies have not been able to attribute violence with PTSD. Those who are suffering from the illness are more likely to harm themselves than others. As in the case of Robert Bales, there could have been more significant issues in their lives than PTSD, which then becomes an easy excuse to justify the actions of a disturbed person. Those suffering from PTSD are more likely to commit suicide than engage in premeditated violence.

Chapter 15
Mental Illness Legalities

As law enforcement officers attempting to obtain the cooperation of mental health professionals and/or access to patient records, we are often inhibited by concerns over violation of HIPAA. Anyone who has visited a doctor has been asked to sign and acknowledge his or her privacy rights under the law. HIPAA stands for the Heath Insurance Portability Accounting Act. The act was instituted to protect the rights and privacy of patients from public disclosure.

Disclosures of mental health records are permitted in limited circumstances. The first is with the permission of the patient. Despite having the written permission of the patient, I have at times encountered challenges in obtaining access to records. I understand that many healthcare professionals are overly concerned that, in our litigious society, they might be sued. They are also genuinely protective of their patients and indeed, they should be. Medical employees are also concerned about bureaucratic oversight and being disciplined by hierarchy over the release of highly protected records. In all instances where I had a release from a patient, I was able to convince the care provider to provide access.

One difficulty I experienced was when a social worker said she would not honor the release because the individual was in a crisis mode and was incapable of making an informed decision. Since the subject was putting puzzles together in the day room with other patients, he was easily accessible to obtain a new release. When she capitulated and agreed to allow me to view those forms, I pointed out the hypocrisy that the individual was now heavily medicated, and could in fact, be suffering from a more acute impairment of judgment than he was during his crisis.

I never strong-armed these releases. I always approached the subject of my investigation from the mindset that we wanted to ensure public safety. I emphasized that my intent was to substantiate the position that no one should fear that the suspect was dangerous. One subject willingly told me that he felt our review would provide validation for his work and stability. Although, his grasp of reality was impaired.

The other area that is considered permissible on disclosures is an imminent threat. If the care provider is made aware that the patient presents an imminent threat, he or she may contact law enforcement authorities and release the information. The reading of the law does not require them to do such, but merely instructs the care providers that they may release the information to a law enforcement entity concerning an imminent threat. Once again reverting to this litigious society, we can see that hospitals that fail to report such a threat would be exposing themselves to a huge liability. No one would want to sit on information concerning a threat and not act upon this information. It all comes down to covering our assets. In my review of hundreds of medical records, I have uncovered direct threats that were made by patients, which were recorded in the medical charting but never forwarded to law enforcement authorities.

The third disclosure, concerns the location of violent fugitives. If the public safety at large is threatened by a fugitive, and the location of that fugitive can be determined by information held by either a patient or the facility, care providers can assist in the apprehension of that fugitive by sharing the information with law enforcement. Personally speaking, I have no experience in retrieving information through this disclosure avenue.

The last disclosure is as required by law, through court orders, warrants or subpoenas. Having always been in a position to use a patient release, I have not had to rely upon this method. Obviously, it is more time-consuming to have to go through the judicial process to obtain such an order, but the actions required are undeniable.

In addition, HIPPA also provides for a few additional disclosures to law enforcement: to provide and assist in response to a law enforcement official's request for information about a victim or suspected victim of a crime; to notify law enforcement of a person's death at the facility; if the entity suspects that criminal activity caused the death; when a covered entity believes that the protected health information is evidence of a crime that occurred on its premises; and in the instance that a care provider in a medical emergency not occurring on its premises, but deems it is necessary to inform law enforcement about the commission and nature of a crime, the location of the crime or crime victims, and the perpetrator of the crime.

When traipsing through the minefield of HIPAA, I would urge investigators to consult with legal authorities to ensure compliance. Some health care providers are overly protective and may not fully understand their legal standing. They are not confronted on a daily basis by law enforcement to examine records. I felt it was incumbent upon me to inform the administrator of the purpose of the examination and the release of information form I presented. I found everyone wanted to cooperate, but wanted to ensure protection of their facility.

I have heard other investigators complain of enduring challenges in this area. Individual hospitals sometimes required their own legally drawn patient release form had to be signed. You could imagine how difficult this would be to accomplish. I had some subject's who had been at multiple facilities and if each one required a different form, I would not have enough room in the trunk of my car for all the forms.

Another section that law enforcement should be aware of is FERPA, which stands for the Family Education Rights Privacy Act. FERPA covers the release of student records at an educational institution. Concerns over student privacy were evident after the Virginia Tech shooting. Despite significant evidence of mental illness impairment in Cho, his parents were never contacted by the school. The parents had said if they were aware of his mental health hospitalization, they would have withdrawn him for the spring semester and brought him home for treatment. They had previously provided their son with adequate treatment when he was in high school. At that time, he responded positively to the treatment method. Virginia Tech was criticized for an overly strict interpretation of the law, despite Cho's threats of suicide.

Under the provisions of FERPA, the educational institution must deem the individual student presents an emergency to the health and safety of the community. The law provides the same provision as HIPAA to warn of a threat to public safety. A legal order will also provide standing for the institution to release the records. Many parents are unaware that despite their students still being considered minors, and the fact that the parents are paying for the majority of the educational bills, they are not at liberty to access their child's student records. That includes academic records, as well as any mental health counseling records, unless there is a risk to public safety.

If you encounter a student at a college campus who becomes a concern, you may once again be obstructed by bureaucratic hurdles by individuals who are acting in good faith under the same guidelines of HIPAA, which includes liability concerns, management scrutiny, and protection of student rights and privacy.

Chapter 16
Mental Health and Violence

The one thing that must be made clear is that not all individuals suffering from mental illness will become violent or initiate targeted violence. There are many people who suffer some form of mental illness that are living among us, including friends, neighbors, relatives and coworkers. Thanks to therapy and medications, their conditions are managed and not a relevant concern to anyone. At the far extreme of mental illness are those who must be institutionalized. The vast majority of these individuals are not dangerous. I have spent untold hours in mental health facilities, and although I used caution, I never had a physical confrontation.

There are others who are of concern and are dangerous. In his book, *The Insanity Offense*, Dr. E Fuller Torrey asserts that only 1% of those suffering from mental illness are truly dangerous. If you base these calculation on the approximately 40,000 mentally ill who are housed in mental health facilities, then there approximately 400 people of concern. This number however, does not include the ten to fifty percent of incarcerated criminals suffering from mental illness. The American jails have become the modern day asylums. There are also countless homeless people wandering the streets who suffer significant mental health impairment. Dr. Torrey asserts that half of all murderous rampages are conducted by individuals who fall into this 1% of dangerous individuals.

After the Virginia Tech shootings, states were then mandated to report those prohibited from possessing firearms through mental illness to the FBI. As of October 2012, as reported by USA Today, one third of the states reported fewer than one in 100,000 of their population as having mental health hospitalizations. Alaska, Hawaii, Massachusetts, Pennsylvania, and North Dakota, were all benevolent enough to report only one person who would be prohibited from owning a firearm because of mental illness hospitalization. In the state of Rhode Island, they had zero entries. Apparently, no one in the state of Rhode Island has ever been hospitalized or committed for mental health disorders. Now in context, you have to consider that according to the National Association of Mental Health Institutes (NAMI), 1 in 17 Americans suffer from some form of mental illness.

Some of the problem with the reporting mental illness is related to budget shortfalls. Another reason stems from the fact that under federal law, only those who have been adjudicated mentally ill are prohibited from owning firearms. In many states, adjudication of mental illness comes only after a commitment by a judge. Despite being involuntarily committed by a police officer, in many states this would not be deemed adjudicated mentally ill. They will only consider an individual to be mentally ill after appearing in front of a judge who determined the subject was a danger to self or to others. This would occur after the initial assessment and when the mental health facility was seeking to extend that initial detention. The time frame for judicial review by a judge is dependent upon the laws of the individual state.

In the instance of Stephen Kazmierczak, the killer at Northern Illinois University, the state of Illinois has one of the strictest gun ownership laws in the country. If you have been hospitalized in a mental health facility within the past five years, you are prohibited from owning or possessing firearms in Illinois. Kazmierczak understood this law and intentionally avoided hospitalizations despite deteriorating mental illness. As a result, once he passed the five-year mark, he began acquiring weapons. He probably would have benefited from proper mental health treatment, but it appears he was reluctant to obtain such in fear that he would not be able to possess firearms. This is not an assertion that the Illinois law motivated him to avoid mental health treatment in an effort to obtain firearms. On the surface, the law was well intentioned; the lawmakers wanted to ensure that those who had mental health issues would be stable enough for an extended period in order to demonstrate responsibility.

With Kazmierczak, with his degree of intelligence, even if he could not legally possess the firearms he would have sought alternate means to acquire those weapons. He could have used a straw purchaser; (someone legitimate to buy the firearm for him), or he could have exploited other loopholes such as the Internet, gun shows, or merely stolen a gun from someone.

Chapter 17
Radicalization of Mass Killers

In light of the Boston Bombers, the term self-radicalization has been used extensively to describe the motivation behind a number of homegrown terrorists. This is a not a new phenomenon. This radicalization process has been occurring for over a decade. The 9/11 terrorists and Ahmed Ressam, The Millennium Bomber, are examples of this mindset. Despite Department of Defense's assertion that the Fort Hood shooting by Major Nidal Hassan was workplace violence, that theory has no substance and is an egregious atrocity. Hassan's own writings reflect his motives and his support of terrorism.

After the tragic events on September 11, 2001, the New York City Police Department had reached the breaking point of frustration in combating terrorism. Because of classification rules and bureaucratic obstacles, NYPD was frustrated with the lack of forthcoming information from the government concerning potential terrorists and their activities. The city, and the World Trade Center specifically, had now been the successful target of two separate terrorist attacks within a decade. As a result, NYPD utilizing intelligence consultants increased their own intelligence platform and produced a more robust and aggressive intelligence division.

NYPD had become concerned about the homegrown threat in America. Individuals who, despite being raised for the majority of their lives in the United States, become radicalized terrorists. There had been a number of incidents over the years and NYPD was searching for answers.

The NYPD Intelligence Division published a study entitled *Radicalization in the West: Homegrown Threat,* which identified four stages of the homegrown radicalized threat. The first stage was the pre-radicalization, which is the process of assembling like-minded individuals in a loose knit socialization structure. These individuals had moved from other countries or other parts of the United States in search of socialization and interaction with others with common interests. These interests could be based on common religion, political views, or recreational pursuits such as soccer.

This collection of individuals would start exploring the group and looking for a sense of meaning. This phase was called the self-identification stage. This is primarily the result of an external or internal crises caused by a religious, political, social or personal catalyst, and the result of real or perceived stressors in their lives. These individuals could be described as feeling disenfranchised or suffering personal trauma, such as the death of a loved one, lost economic opportunity, and so forth.

The next stage is the indoctrination stage, which is the acceptance and embracing of a belief system that provides a sense of purpose and belonging. You can see this in many areas of life where we want a sense of belonging and acceptance. The NYPD report focused on the embracing of the strictest form of Islam, which ultimately influences the group to adopt the radicalization stage and final stage, which is the participation as a jihadist attack with a desired outcome.

Many people find empowerment when they adopt a common purpose, whether it is a political platform, a particular candidate, or a social cause from which individuals can form an identity. We see many people go through those first three phases with no nefarious intentions. The desire for acceptance, belonging, and love can be found in the sixteen basic motivational desires published by Stephen Reiss from Ohio State University. The last stage of radicalization is one of concern. It is upon the acceptance of the last stage that those around the individuals notice a marked change in their behavior.

This study was based on Muslim extremists. It was based on the assertion that these extremists would find like-minded individuals and the jihadist stage would occur while attending daily prayers and activities at a mosque or a student association. That can still be the case today, but due to the Internet, you can essentially have a virtual mosque online. You no longer need the physical building of worship to attend. They can now assemble online in chat rooms and on discussion boards on websites. This interaction becomes a social community or group that becomes defined by this virtual house of worship.

One of the consultants for NYPD was Marc Sageman, a retired CIA case officer and forensic psychiatrist. Sageman studied over five hundred Muslim extremist groups that then engaged in terrorist attacks. Among the groups he studied were the Hamburg cell, which executed the 9/11 attack on America, the Madrid train bombing, and others.

What he found in these groups was that most of the terrorists were in their mid to late twenties, were college-educated, married, essentially had no prior criminal history and minimal mental health issues, if any.

Dr. Sageman identified common traits among these groups: they all felt a certain economical or political exclusion, and they were in search of an identity resulting in the formation of these groups. Many of these individuals were not particularly religious to begin with, but now they had of a sense of belonging. They found themselves attending daily prayer and congregating with their like-minded friends. Their networks were not hierarchal, as they were worshipping in a community and sharing moral outrage at the mistreatment of Muslims.

Sageman describes the three waves or phases of Jihadists. The first wave was Bin Laden and the first disciples. They were the elites, and well educated. They were devoted followers and trained mujahedeen. The second wave was primarily the expatriate community in non-Islamic countries. Most were students in higher education. The third wave is comprised of the "lone wolf" terrorists. They are essentially criminals and losers who are in search of an identity or affirmation of their beliefs.

I had a discussion with an Israeli intelligence officer a number of years ago. He said that the homicide bomber movement began on a foundation in Palestine, where not only were the individuals who martyred themselves famous and exalted hero status, but their families were also elevated to a higher status in the community. He said that you have to understand that they were indoctrinated with anti-Israeli rhetoric 24/7. They were under a constant barrage of indoctrination by various spheres of influence at the supper table, at prayers, on the radio and TV. Everywhere they turned, they were being indoctrinated with anti-Israeli sentiment.

As with the Israeli homicide bombers, mass killers can be indoctrinated and jihadisized in a particular belief or thought due to the fact that they are constantly exposed to the Internet in this essential virtual mosque or house of worship. There was evidence that the Fort Hood Texas shooter became jihadisized via the Internet and not from attending extremist-based mosques. Anwar Al-Awlaki, the Yemeni cleric who was educated in the U.S., has been cited by a number of homegrown terrorists, including Hassan, as being an inspiration.

As an alternative, there are examples of individuals who become radicalized, but not necessarily as Muslim jihadists. In 2012, Wade Michael Page launched a targeted attack on a Sikh Temple in Wisconsin leaving seven dead. While he was in the U.S. Army from 1992 to 1998, he was demoted and discharged due to excessive alcohol consumption. Looking for some sense and purpose in life, he was able to find a sense of belonging and self-identity in the white power movement. He became a member of the Hammerskins and was involved in the hate music movement. Outside of the band, his house was in foreclosure, and he had a deep-seated distrust of nonwhites.

Floyd Lee Corkins attempted to carry out an attack at the Family Research Council in 2012. Corkin, who volunteered at a gay rights advocacy center, was incensed by his perception of the anti-gay platform of the Family Research Council. His undisciplined and poorly planned attack was quickly halted at its inception by a guard who was wounded was able to subdue Corkin.

While I was interviewing an individual who had made threats against the president, he told me he had a successful business at one time but was now struggling financially. He was having marital issues and his wife had been undergoing treatment for cancer. He became consumed with watching a particular news station in the evening. He increasingly became more agitated over the content of the news broadcasts and felt a great deal of frustration and anger at what he perceived was a politically correct country gone astray. He attempted to self-medicate this building anxiety through the consumption of excessive amounts of alcohol. This only exacerbated his lack of coping skills. This anger resulted in him arming himself, and threatening the police and the president. I told him that he needed to unplug the television, stop reading the newspaper, and walk away if this was creating too much anxiety in his life. He perhaps followed my advice, because I never heard from him again.

In 2009, a radicalized Muslim convert targeted a recruiting station in Little Rock, Arkansas. Carlos Leon Bledsoe, aka Abdula Hakim Mujahid Muhammad, was raised in Memphis Tennessee. He worked at Chucky Cheese, played basketball, and was raised in the Baptist Church. While attending college in Nashville, Tennessee, he was arrested for carrying a concealed weapon. Looking for a sense of identity in his life, he began to enter a religious self-examination and experimented with a number of different religions.

While listening to speeches by Malcolm X and reading the teachings of Louis Farrakhan and the Nation of Islam, Bledsoe went through a religious conversion and became a Muslim. He attended a mosque in Nashville, which was administering to a large Somali community. To deepen his religious conversion, he moved to Yemen under the auspices to teach English. Embedded in the Yemeni Muslim community, Bledsoe studied the jihad. He married a Yemeni girl and remained in Yemen from 2007 until 2009. Bledsoe was inspired by the teachings of the former U.S. citizen and Yemeni cleric Anwar al-Awlaki, who also inspired the Fort Hood terrorist. In an effort to broaden his skill set, Bledsoe was told that he could obtain explosives training in Somalia.

His visa and immigration status were not in order, and he was jailed in a Yemen prison. He claims that his true radicalization occurred in jail as he listened to other jihadists continually espouse anti-American rhetoric and planted the thoughts that America had abandoned him. Meanwhile, his father, Melvin Bledsoe, was desperately campaigning for his release. The FBI interviewed Bledsoe while he was incarcerated.

After three months of detention, Carlos Bledsoe was released and returned to Tennessee, where his father operated a tour bus company. His father had initiated an expansion of the tour bus company in Little Rock, Arkansas, and hired his son to run the operation. While still in Nashville, Bledsoe was again interviewed by the FBI. Aware that could be under surveillance and that his actions would be scrutinized, Bledsoe was very careful in his movements. He had purchased a weapon at a Wal-Mart and waited to see if the purchase would initiate police interest. When no action occurred, he purchased additional weapons.

Believing his attack was justified under Islamic Law, he began conducting research and surveilling possible target locations. He launched an unsuccessful Molotov cocktail attack on the residence of a rabbi in Nashville. His plans to attack another recruiting station in Kentucky were thwarted when he found the center was closed.

Standing in front of the Army Recruiting Center in Little Rock were recent basic training Army graduates, Privates Quinton Ezeagwula and Andy Long. They had returned home for a short stay as hometown recruiters and stepped outside the recruiting depot to smoke a cigarette. Private Long's mother, who had driven him to the depot, sat in her car in the parking lot reading her bible.

Bledsoe drove to the depot, opened fire on the unarmed soldiers, killing Long and critically wounding Ezeagwula. Bledsoe fled, but he was subsequently arrested a short distance away. In his post arrest interview, he made some startling statements. The first was, "What I had in mind didn't go as planned but Allah willing He will reward me for my intentions." The second statement he made was, "Had I got this training my story would of ended a lot differently than it's going to end now. My drive-by would of been a drive-in with no one escaping the aftermath!" The last statement was in response to his lack of explosives training. Those statements made by a former all-American boy who worked at the neighborhood Chucky Cheese but transitioned into a jihadist terrorist determined to kill fellow Americans.

This terrorist attack was labeled as a drive-by shooting by the military and prosecuted in state court as a murder. Neither soldier who was targeted because they were in uniform received a purple heart. The tragic shooting united the father of the victim, Andy Long and father of Carlos Bledsoe to share their story in a documentary, Losing Our Son's.

The Boston Bombers provide an interesting dynamic. The older brother, Tamerlan Tsarnaev was a loser. He was a 26 year old washed up boxer. As an accomplished local boxer, who had won the Gold Gloves competition, he had dreams of becoming an Olympic boxer only to be derailed by the U.S. policy of banning non-citizens from participating. Considering most U.S. Olympic boxers are in their late teens or early 20s, Tsarnaev was past his prime.

Tamerlan had not completed community college and was living with his wife and child. His wife was providing the primary financial support for the family as the family's welfare support payments were reduced in November 2012 and their Section 8 housing subsidy was terminated in January of 2013. His parents had failed in their employment endeavors and returned to the country from where they had requested asylum. His mother had been arrested for shoplifting. He claimed to lack any American friends, thus increasing his isolation.

To his mother, Tamerlan claimed that he had the feeling that he had two people living inside him. Being concerned about his mental state, his mother encouraged his friendship with a Muslim convert, Mikhail Allakhverdov, known as Misha. The seeds of radicalization began at the kitchen table as Misha schooled Tamerlan in Islam. Those who knew him said he began to change as he became more devout. One of his former boxing friends became a victim of a triple homicide. After the killing bombing, Tamerlan became the prime suspect in the murders. The case remains under investigation. Another person of interest was killed by the FBI in Orlando.

As Tamerlan became a more devout Muslim, he was exiled by his mosque for radical and inappropriate rhetoric. He associated with Muslim extremists on the Internet and sympathized with their teachings. He spent six months in Dagestan living in the Muslim community. There is some indication that perhaps, he was viewed as an outsider by this group and not accepted by them either. About the same time of his embracing Islam, he befriended a disabled patient, who his mother provided home health care to named Donald Larking. The patient was a conspiracy theorist and shared his views with Tamerlan, who converted Larking to Islam.

Tamerlan Tsarnaev was a stereotypical third wave jihadist as described by Dr. Sageman. The third wave is primarily comprised of losers and thugs. Tamerlan clearly fits this profile. His brother Dzhokhar's radicalization path is not as easy to follow.

Dzhokhar appeared to be more focused on smoking pot than on his studies, and he was described by those close to him as being easygoing and not overtly religious. Those who knew him claim not to have heard him espouse any radical thoughts or behaviors. However, Dzhokhar did share with one friend that he felt terrorism was justified because of the U.S.'s military action. Despite being hailed as a good student, his grades in college reflected an uninterested student. He failed most of his classes, while compiling a large debt. His parents divorced and moved back to the same country from which they claimed asylum. His sisters lived out of state. His only deeply rooted social support system was his dysfunctional brother.

As with many new college students, there is a great deal of internal conflict and stress. For many students moving from home, adapting to higher academic standards and adjusting to making new friends can result in a great deal of anxiety. Many students have difficulty adjusting to college, especially those from out of town. It is during the first year of college that the new students feel the most vulnerable.

He was perhaps heavily influenced by his older brother, but Dzhokhar was not a reluctant terrorist. He willingly placed the bomb next to an eight-year-old boy and walked away. He attended a party the same evening at school, where the focus of the party conversation was on the Boston Marathon Bombing. The next morning, he worked out in the school gym. These are not the actions of someone consumed with grief or guilt.

This chapter was meant to provide an insight into the thought process of some of the lone wolf terrorists. Feeling rejected by society or consumed by their negative emotional vortex of life, they are desperately in search of an identity or an affirmation for these feelings. I discussed the concept of a virtual mosque or house of worship. This "virtual influencer" could be any political, religious or social cause that adds significance to their miserable lives. Recall, Timothy McVeigh in Oklahoma City, David Koresh in Waco, Jim Jones in Jonestown or Charles Manson and the Manson family commune in California. It does not matter if they are moved to action by their belief in an environmental movement, religious fanaticism, or political activism; they can use this belief system as substantiation for their path of violence.

Chapter 18
Domestic Mass Killers

In 2007, the Department of Justice estimated that there were 2,300 victims of intimate partner homicide throughout the United States. Many of these homicides were a product of what are described as crimes of passion. A spouse enters the residence to confront his or her partner in an intimate relationship with another individual. In an outrage and a response to the emotion of the moment, the partner reacts in a violent way, resulting in death. Other times, a domestic arrangement is in shambles and consumed with ongoing physical abuse. Some of these will escalate in violence, ending in homicide.

There are also the victims of the love-obsessed stalker. At any given time in the United States, there are three million victims of stalkers. We see where the victims of intimate partner homicides also fall into this category. An individual decides that if he cannot have his partner, then no one shall, and he decides to execute the focus of his desires. Quite often, this leads to suicide to accompany the homicide.

The ex-intimate partner who stalks the former lover can be quite concerning. If the stalking behavior increases in intensity and becomes concerning, it is best to obtain law enforcement guidance. There are many excellent books on stalkers, and I would encourage you to seek knowledge from those sources.

The line between stalkers and targeted violence in a domestic situation is sometimes blurred. We must return and examine the commonality among all targeted shooters: they are trapped in what they perceive to be a negative emotional vortex.

In 1971, in a large, upscale home in New Jersey, a family of five was found slain. The bodies had been decomposing for approximately a month. They were victims of a homicide committed by John List. If one were to look at his picture, the photo might resemble that of what you expect a mild mannered accountant to look like. In fact, that is how he made his livelihood. Except, he had lost his job and was now unemployed. He was an extremely devout Christian, and he was described by those that knew him as being extremely quirky and odd. Neighbors reported seeing him mowing the yard in a suit.

Unable to sustain his mortgage debt, he began siphoning money from his mother who was living in an upstairs apartment. He became even more troubled as his daughter had been caught smoking marijuana, and she was beginning to display interests in fringe movements and religious groups. On top of that, his wife was an alcoholic, and he had a dysfunctional relationship with her. List became obsessed with the notion that his entire family was destined to meet the devil in hell.

John List awakened on that fateful morning, walked up behind his wife while she was eating toast and shot her in the back of the head. He climbed the stairs to his mother's apartment. He kissed her and shot her as well. He returned downstairs and ate the rest of his wife's toast. He waited for his three children to arrive home, killed each one, and laid them out in the ballroom of the residence.

Apparently, there were some concerns within the family. The daughter intimated to her drama teacher that if all of a sudden, they withdrew her and her siblings from school on a short notice, long-term vacation, then they were likely the victims of homicide at their father's hands. This is not the idle chitchat of a teenage girl. This type of warning is screaming for attention.

This was not a spontaneous act. John List stopped the mail delivery and the newspaper for thirty days. He turned the heat off and in the cold January weather, this helped to delay the onset of decay. He also turned music up and left lights burning inside the house to project an appearance of activity. The drama teacher reacting to the concerns of his student and subsequent unexpected withdrawal from school, decided to check on the family. He noticed the lights and heard the music, thus assuming nothing was amiss.

He returned days later and called police about the same time that neighbors also summoned police over concerns that something appeared abnormal.

Thirty days after the killings when the bodies were discovered, John List's vehicle was located at the JFK Airport in New York. The assumption was that he had fled the country. When in fact, he remained in the United States, where he was a fugitive for the next eighteen years. It was the TV show *America's Most Wanted* that was instrumental in locating and apprehending John List, who by that time had remarried and was living in Richmond, Virginia.

When interviewed by Connie Chung, John List again reiterated his concern about his family's decline and the degradation of their moral foundation. He feared that they were headed for hell. He felt that killing them was the only alternative to save his family and preserve their path to heaven. He expressed his confidence that he would one day rejoin his family in heaven. When Connie Chung questioned why he did not commit suicide to join his family, he responded that he viewed suicide as a sin. I presume he did not see the sinful conduct in the execution of his entire family.

In 1985, during a dark and stormy night (and no, this is not the bad opening sentence to a mystery novel) John Markle, killed his wife and two children in Little Rock, Arkansas. While his suicide could have been forecasted, the murder of his family members could not. His employer, Stephens Investment Company, accused Markle of embezzling in excess of one million dollars, which he diverted into an account in his mother's name. When he was confronted concerning the crime, he was provided an ultimatum and told to repay the stolen funds.

In desperation, he went to his mother, Mercedes McCambridge, the Academy Award-winning actress, for financial relief. She turned down his request for financial assistance, essentially informing him that he was responsible for his own malfeasance. Having a doctorate in economics, he was now faced with paying back over $1 million, and the loss of his Securities and Exchange Commission License. He no longer had the funds, as he had been a free spender.

Being a detective on the case, I found a motive for John Markle's decision to kill his family. Markle had a close acquaintance who committed suicide the previous year. The friend's widow was so distraught over the loss that Markle hired an individual to look after her and provide companionship to the widow during her period of grief. Markle was deeply affected by the trauma to the widow. As a result, in an effort to spare his own family the agony and humiliation of not only a suicide but the publicity of his crime, he decided it would be best to kill them as well.

When Markle shot his family, he sedated them with Elavil, an anti-depressant. He donned a Halloween mask, so in the event his children woke up, they would not see it was their father. He wrote out a long suicide note, blaming his mother. He then called his attorney and told him to come to the house. After the phone call, Markle committed suicide with simultaneous gunshots to his head.

As you can see within the two previous examples, both Markle and List were caught in the negative emotional vortex. With Markle, his desperation is clearly understood, but the taking of the lives of his family could not have been anticipated. List, on the other hand, was clearly suffering from the vortex with his troubling family, but one would have expected that he would have taken his own life as well. Therefore, it is not always so crystal-clear when it comes to targeted violence in a domestic situation. In hindsight, we can always look at these events with crystal-clear vision, when in fact it is not always transparent.

Chapter 19
Workplace Violence

A Career Builder survey in 2011 found that one in four workers or approximately 27% of the respondents claimed they had been bullied at work. Bullying may not arise to the level of violence, but unfettered bullying can have unintended consequences. Those who are victimized could become so filled with anger and frustration that they view violence as an acceptable means of revenge. Especially if the company's responses to bullying claims are viewed as weak or ineffective.

According to a 2007, Employment Law Alliance Poll, nearly 45% of the workers claimed to have suffered from an abusive boss or employer at some point in their career. Have you? Studies reflect that approximately one in four supervisors display narcissistic traits.

There is significant disparity in the result of these bullying surveys, which can be dependent upon the definition of bullying or the manner in which the questions were asked. It is similarly difficult to determine the level of bullying in schools. If you ask an open-ended question, such as, "Have you ever been bullied?" the responses can be skewed toward the affirmative. If the response could be vetted requesting the respondent to recall specific examples, this could provide a more in-depth veracity to the legitimacy of the question.

The Department of Justice defines workplace violence as any form of conduct that intentionally creates anxiety or fear in a climate of distrust in the workplace. The Occupational Safety and Health Acts general duty clause section 5A1 requires employers to provide workers with a workplace free from recognized hazards that are likely to cause death or serious physical harm. This OSHA regulation was intended to ensure a workplace safe from hazards, such as known deficiencies in machinery. Lawyers have started using this regulation as leverage to combat workplace bullying and harassment, which can result in various personality and anxiety disorders, unintended health consequences, including death.

Dr. Sandy Lim, of the Singapore Management University School of Social Sciences and Dr. Lilia Cortina, University of Michigan Department of Psychology and Women's Studies, estimate the cost of bullying to American employers to be in the range of $64 billion to more than $300 billion. These figures stem from reduced productivity, increased welfare costs, disability payments, unemployment, and the subsequent impact resulting in workers who face eviction, foreclosure, homelessness, unemployment compensation, food stamps, hospital admissions and so forth.

Many books have been written on workplace bullying and you cannot have a discussion on workplace violence without examining the effects of bullying. Despite the business world embracing sensitivity in the workplace, too often the best intentions are not followed through. Many of these programs are delivered in an effort to ward off possible litigation in the future. Some companies may have written policies, but there is a consistent theme of limited enforcement.

The Centers for Disease Control (CDC) have documented studies establishing the relationship between job stress and common ailments like mood and sleep disturbances, upset stomach, and headaches. The American Psychological Association (APA) reported in 2011 that the nation is on the verge of a stress-induced public-health crisis. In the report *Stress in America, Our Health at Risk,* the APA surveyed 1,200 U.S. residents, of which 22% reported extreme stress. According to the U.S. Department of Labor's Bureau of Labor Statistics reports, workplace suicide in the United States increased 28% in 2008 over the previous year. All of these aforementioned studies provide evidence of the destabilizing impact of stress on the workers' mental health.

Our identity is the amalgam of all aspects of our lives. We often seek a great deal of our identity from our occupations and places of employment. When we are stripped of both our occupation and our place of employment, which can lead to a humiliating experience, frequently accompanied by depression and a loss of income. Termination of employment can also lead to a loss of status within the community. There is an inter-relationship between employment and stability at home. If the status quo is interrupted at either home or work, this often impacts the other.

When we are introduced at the neighborhood picnic or barbecue, the conversation eventually will get around to, "What do you do for a living?" or "What what line of work are you in?" It is a primary source of identity for many of us. For some, that identity from career overshadows all other aspects of our life.

The economic impact of losing a job can create cascading effects on one's entire life. Employment provides food on the table, the roof over our heads, and the clothes on our backs. When these essential elements of life are taken away, the consequence creates a tremendous stress not just on the individual, but also on the entire family.

As of the writing of this book, approximately 25 million people are either unemployed or underemployed. Only a handful will become so overwhelmed that they will be pulled into a negative emotional vortex and believe resorting to violence is an acceptable exit strategy for their devastating situation. Those who lack the coping skills, and who have impaired judgment because of either mental health issues or substance abuse issues, can fall into deep despair.

This is why so many people struggle with retirement. We often wish our days away yearning and looking forward to not having to go to work. There are many factors involved with retirement discontentment, including losing a part of one's identity and the socialization. The same holds true for those who become disabled, or are fired.

Our jobs provide food for the table, a roof over our heads, clothing for the family, and financial support for various hobbies including: attending movies, sporting events, going out to dinner or paying for Little League baseball, soccer, scrapbooking supplies and it also supports any vices.

Regardless of whether you lost the job through attrition, plant closing, for disciplinary purposes or even health issues, the effects can be catastrophic. Unemployment insurance can only support you for so long, and the constant rejections of job applications only increase the stress on the victim. I use the word "victim" because quite often they assume the personality of a victim of society's woes. They are unable to continue funding the activities, and difficult decisions must be made to stop participating in children's activities or family vacations. These have a cumulative effect, and as time goes on, you perhaps fall behind in credit card payments, mortgage payments and rent payments and next you are facing foreclosure or eviction.

I volunteered at Metropolitan Ministries, which is a charitable organization that provides support to homeless families. These are not hard-core homeless individuals but families that have fallen victim to events quite often out of their control. I enjoyed exposing my daughters to volunteering at Metropolitan Ministries so they could gain a sense of how fortunate we were and how normal these people were. These families looked and spoke no differently from us, but they were dependent on a charity because of unforeseen circumstances.

As the pressure increases on the individual, so does the despair, and he or she feels more isolated and abandoned by society. Especially if family members have also abandon them. An excellent illustration of this negative emotional vortex is demonstrated by the Jason Rodriguez case in Orlando, Florida in 2009. Rodriguez was an engineer at Reynolds, Smith & Hills and was terminated for a lack of performance proficiency. He was $90,000 in debt, his house was in foreclosure, and he was going through a divorce. According to family members, he was also suffering from mental health issues. He was having such difficulty in life that even as an engineer, he had difficulty constructing sandwiches at a local Subway sandwich shop, and he was terminated. He attempted to ram his car into the sandwich shop but was unsuccessful due to a barricade.

He entered the engineering firm located in a high-rise office building in downtown Orlando and began shooting. He killed one employee and wounded five others. After his arrest, Rodriguez stated that he felt like he had been, "Left to rot." His attorney, Bob Wesley, eloquently stated, "He was the compilation of the front page of the newspaper." Rodriguez claims that he is haunted by a device planted in his ear. The command hallucinations come from an individual identified as "sharp tooth." Prosecution experts dispute this claim.

After Rodriguez's, termination from the engineering firm, his life began to spiral downward. There is no indication that the firm fired him without cause, but obviously he believed his termination was unjustified, and all the negative events that occurred after his firing could be attributed to his dismissal. This is a classic demonstration of a "wound collector," a term coined by former FBI agent Joe Navarro.

Homicides at work account for 12% of workplace deaths. This statistic is not exclusive of workplace violence in which a former or soon-to-be dismissed employee exacts revenge. The statistic also includes those who are victims of a homicide pursuant to a robbery, as well as law enforcement officers killed in the line of duty. Health care workers are the largest group of victims of workplace violence, due to assaults by patients and family members.

Workplace violence can be a very complex dynamic. The acts are often attributed to the angry worker or former employee who wants to make a statement to seek revenge. Many times it also includes a domestic situation in which a spouse or ex-spouse or ex-significant other targets his or her former love interest. The estranged partner has the knowledge of an approximate time that his or her target will arrive and depart from work.

In November 2012, viewers were horrified at surveillance video capturing an attack in Grain Valley, Missouri. Amie Wieland exited her place of employment, Owner Operator Independent Drivers Association (OOIDA) Headquarters and walked to her car. Alan Lovelace, her ex-boyfriend was sitting in the passenger side of her vehicle waiting for her. He confronted Wieland over a child custody issue. She turned and fled. Lovelace, whose life was collapsing for multiple reasons, ran after Wieland. Video captured Lovelace firing a gun and striking her in her head. Miraculously, she survived the assault. Lovelace fled in Wieland's mini-van and committed suicide as police closed in on him in San Diego.

This attack would not be considered workplace violence as the assault occurred outside of the work environment, in the parking lot. Despite not being categorized as workplace violence, an employer could fall under civil scrutiny concerning security protocols for the parking facilities.

In February 2012, Alissa Blanton in Orlando was a former waitress at a Hooters restaurant and was stalked incessantly by a significantly older customer for two years. Despite seventy pages of documentation, a judge would not grant a restraining order against her stalker, Roger Troy. The suspect confronted Alissa in front of her place of employment after she returned from lunch with her husband. Troy confronted her outside the AT&T office complex, shot Alissa dead, and then committed suicide.

Although businesses want to segregate the personal turmoil from the corporate world, there is often spillage. Anyone who has experienced an acrimonious divorce or child custody battle will attest to the toxicity of personal issues contaminating the workplace. I personally have not experienced the trauma of an unstable marriage, but I have navigated the turbulent foster program as a foster parent. The wounds of divorce and child custody are visceral and leave deep and lasting scars. As I described earlier, two professors engaged in a tumultuous, ongoing divorce lasting seventeen years. This prolongs the healing.

The betrayal of infidelity can be humiliating and devastating on the partner. In April 2013, Scott Edgerton, 63, walked into the Boca Raton, Florida, accounting firm of Cbiz, Goldstein, Lewin, where his wife Sharon Bellingham, 56, worked. Edgerton was upset that his wife was having an affair with another man. He understood his wife wanted a divorce and that his marriage was over. Witnesses described him as entering her office in a trance, as he walked directly past the receptionist, who protested his appearance. Apparently, Bellingham had warned the receptionist that he might show up and cause a scene. The violence was limited to Bellingham, who was murdered in her office and Edgerton, who subsequently committed suicide. Fortunately, no one else was injured.

In the spring of 2013, Carie Charlesworth, a teacher at Holy Trinity School in San Diego for fourteen years, was the target of an abusive and stalking ex-husband. Despite, a restraining order, her ex-husband appeared in the parking lot of her school. The school took the appropriate step of going into lockdown mode and calling police. The Diocese of San Diego reacted by suspending Carie, not renewing her contract, as well as suspending her four children from the same school. The school took the position that despite the restraining order, the school's faculty and students were not safe. Lawsuits are being considered. This unfortunate situation only provides more power to her ex-husband.

When personal strife impacts the professional life, the employer can become affected not only by impaired work performance, but also by legal proceedings that can lead to an intrusion of the emotional battle into the workplace. Phone calls by a wounded and obsessive lover disrupt the continuity of the job performance. Unexpected and uninvited appearances at work can adversely affect not only the targeted employee but also customers, clients and other employees. A scorned lover or stalker can choose the business as a target location to carry out violence.

The place of employment is a controlled variable in the eyes of the attacker. The attacker knows when the employee arrives, leaves and where he or she is during the workday. Despite taking the stance that the problem is personal, it can easily impact the safety and security of the business operations. The examples cited above clearly demonstrate that the employer needs to take measures to account for domestic or stalker violence transitioning into workplace violence. I do not agree with the stance of the church, which has empowered an abusive ex-spouse.

Many of the workplace violence incidents started at home where the suspect killed his or her significant other before moving on to the current or former place of employment. I want to be clear that these murderous acts are the sole fault of the perpetrator. The workplace environment can exacerbate the decision to resort to violence, but is not the entire reason for the violence.

Chapter 20
Toxic Workplaces

There are toxic work environments as well as toxic bosses. According to one study, approximately one in four of all supervisors are afflicted with narcissistic personality disorder. Despite the best efforts to provide sensitivity training to the bosses, many times they fall short. I think most people have at some time during their careers encountered bosses that were difficult and toxic. When you throw a toxic employee in the same barrel with a toxic supervisor, the only thing you are missing is a match to set the fire.

I do not want to spend a great deal of time on management and leadership, as there are many books written to address the deficiencies and weaknesses of bosses. There are entire shelves at the libraries and seminars that specifically target how supervisors can effect positive change and become a more effective and positive mentor and leader. There is a great book I stumbled upon in a bookstore, titled *How To Work For The Idiot Boss: Survive & Thrive-Without Killing Your Boss* by Dr. John Hoover. This book provides insight into the struggles of employees who are working for the idiot boss and how best to overcome these challenges.

Steve Albrecht, who is a former San Diego police officer and a psychologist, focuses on the area of workplace violence. He wrote an excellent book titled *Ticking Time Bombs*. The information contained in his book, despite being written in the 1994, still resonates today. He described an interview with an individual by the name of Robert Mack who was employed by General Dynamics. Mack was suspended by his employer during the Christmas holidays. On the day after New Years, he received a notice in the mail to appear for a termination hearing at the factory. As you would probably agree, this was an insensitive manner in which to handle or manage an employee termination.

What further exacerbated the situation was when Mack appeared at his termination hearing, the human resources specialist was twenty-five-years old. Mack had been employed at General Dynamics for twenty-five years, and his longevity with the company surpassed the life span of the individual, tasked with his termination. Mack killed that individual, along with another employee before surrendering. Mack said in his interview, "Termination, termination was what went through my head, termination. I've lost everything, everything I've worked for is gone. I'm not going back to work. What will people think? How will I tell people?" You can understand the desperation and humiliation that Mack was experiencing.

What do you do when one of your employees begins stalking another? This occurred at Electromagnetic Systems Lab, Incorporated (ESL) in February 1988. Richard Farley was employed as a software technician at ESL and was a military veteran. In 1984, the thick-bodied thirty-six-year-old was introduced to a bright, athletic and personable Laura Black. Farley was quickly enamored by the energetic electrical engineer. Farley would later say, "I think I fell instantly in love with her."

Farley began making advances toward Black, who politely rebuffed him. Farley became obsessed with Black, and began an incessant campaign of inappropriate contact and stalking. He wrote some two hundred letters to Black, and through manipulative social engineering practices, he learned of her home address, and obtained keys to her desk. Through these breaches, he was able to ascertain a complete biographical profile of the target of his delusional affections. He continually left gifts on her desk and shadowed her moves outside of work.

In the fall of 1985, Black became more concerned about the obsessive and aggressive traits of Farley. Black, who was working in a male dominated field, was concerned about filing a complaint, and how she would be viewed by her peers. She reported his inappropriate conduct to human resources (HR) at ESL. HR initially was skeptical concerning the allegations and accused Black of smiling too much. As Farley's conduct became more concerning, the company took the appropriate steps and notified Farley that he would need to attend psychological counseling sessions and immediately stop harassing Black in order to maintain employment.

Farley was compliant with his therapy sessions however, his stalking and harassment of Black continued and intensified. He made a copy of her house key that she inadvertently left on her desk. He displayed the key and handwritten note on the windshield of her car to announce his ability to gain access to Laura Black at a time of his choosing. He continued stalking outside her condo and through late-night phone calls. The clerk at the 7-11 across the street from Laura Black's condo saw Farley in the store on a daily basis. As Laura Black continued to rebuff his advances, the language of his telephone calls and letter writings became more agitated and threatening. At times, Farley referred to his gun collection.

In 1986, Farley made overt threats to Black's life. He demanded that unless she relinquished herself to him, he would continue threatening her and other employees at ESL. Farley made threats to employees concerning his gun collection and his expertise with guns. Farley had bragged that if ESL fired him, they would no longer be able to control his activities. ESL terminated Farley in May 1986.

Farley continued threatening Laura Black and blamed his termination on her. He lamented the loss of his wages, the foreclosure of his home, and trouble with the IRS were because of Laura Black's complaints. For nearly two years after his termination,

Farley made Laura Black's life a living hell. He had placed her in a psychological prison.

In February 1988, Laura Black, obtained a temporary restraining order (TRO) prohibiting Farley from approaching within 300 yards and ordered him not to make any contact in any manner with Black. A hearing was scheduled for two weeks later. The day before the court hearing, Farley drove a rented RV into the parking lot of ESL and prepared for war.

Armed with a cache of weapons, a hunting vest filled with ammunition, Farley walked across the parking lot, where he shot and killed his first victim. Using a shotgun as a breaching tool, he shot his way through the locked glass doors. Farley had previously made inquiries with security personnel concerning security measures at ESL. He fired indiscriminately at fleeing employees until he reached the office of Laura Black.

Laura Black, hearing the shooting, closed her door, locked it and sought refuge. Farley fired a shotgun through her door and gained access to her office. Farley shot Black, critically wounding her with a shotgun blast to her shoulder. Miraculously, she survived and was able to flee the kill zone and escape outside. Farley's murderous rampage resulted in the death of seven employees and the wounding of four others, including Laura Black. He fired into computers destroying company property. After a five-hour standoff and successful negotiations with Lieutenant Ruben Grijalva, Richard Farley was taken into custody by police SWAT team members. In 1992, Farley was sentenced to death. He is currently on death row at San Quentin prison.

ESL after initially being doubtful of Farley's conduct appears to have made appropriate measures to modify Richard Farley's aberrant behavior. ESL eventually placed Farley on notice of the consequences of his actions that could lead to termination, and demanded mandatory mental health counseling. When he failed to abide by the guidelines, Farley was terminated. Unfortunately, after his termination, ESL provided a neutral employment recommendation to future employers. Farley was rehired by an employer who was blind to his previous conduct at ESL.

It is difficult to have control over employees after termination. The Employee Assistance Program (EAP) should have remained vigilant and monitored the harassment and stalking of their current employee Laura Black. A restraining order should have been obtained by the company to restrict his access to the grounds of ESL. It is highly unlikely that Farley's conduct would have been altered by the order, but the company had an obligation to seek all legal remedies possible. The escalation and intensity of both his stalking behavior and his threatening communications should have provided insight and deep concern for his future behavior. A spokesperson for ESL, said they had no warning of the attack and had no other reason to suspect Richard Farley was plotting an assault. Really?

It must be understood, that the Laura Black stalking case, as well as the stalking and slaying of actress Rebecca Schaeffer, so shocked the conscience of the legal system that the stalking laws in California were significantly tightened to provide more adequate protection for the victims of stalking. Farley's behavior had clearly indicated that his efforts to pursue his delusional relationship would never be altered by any other means short of incarceration. Richard Farley all but posted a neon billboard stating that he would not be stopped and his crusade would not end well. In an ABC news interview, Laura Black, who provided absolutely no encouragement to Richard Farley's delusions said the word "no" is a complete sentence. Denials of affection must be clear and unambiguous. I do not believe that a definitive "no" would have stopped Farley, who was delusional in his love affair with Laura Black.

Adam Lanza conducted research of the ESL shooting rampage by Richard Farley. Did Lanza take instruction from the manner in which Farley breached the locked door to ESL? We have seen this repeated behavior, where shooters research previous acts of violence to learn lessons. Farley had also conducted significant research concerning security measures at ESL.

Chapter 21
Disgruntled Workers

In this day, with economic and budgetary restraints on companies, businesses have placed additional pressure on employees and managers to be more productive with fewer resources. Often, employees who demonstrate a certain level of skills are promoted to management positions with little or no training in developing leadership skills and have become either horrible bosses or are inept at managing difficult employees. This lack of leadership merely exacerbates the situation and leads to increased conflict within the work place.

Most employees respond positively to adherence to a set of guidelines that are administered with fairness and equality. Supervisors should distribute both discipline and praise. This holds for children and training pets, but many employers have difficulty with this basic concept. For a troubled employee who feels he or she are under increased stress and scrutiny by an insensitive and unfair supervisor this can leave an employee feeling vulnerable and frustrated.

Every day across America, disgruntled workers trudge to the quarry to break rocks, look forward to the whistle at the end of the day, and slide down the dinosaur's back to return home.

For most of the quarry workers, they can compartmentalize their misery or learn to adjust and cope with the additional stress. For others, their anxiety spills out on the home front. Domestic instability is often linked to disharmony in the workplace.

Dysfunction at home or at work can become a destabilizing force for the others, but the two together can lead to a cauldron of emotions, which leads to a boiling over and the subsequent violence. Turmoil at home will often bleed back into the workplace, with an individual suffering from a host of productivity issues relating to his or her attitude, reliability, production, and coexistence with fellow employees. Likewise, the reverse is true; when they carry their burdens home, disrupting the status quo within the family.

Often employees become afflicted with what has been coined "employee disengagement." Gallup estimates that the cost to U.S. business is $300 billion dollars in lost productivity. Disengaged employees are more likely to pick up the telephone and call in sick or take a mental health day or display a lack of loyalty to the organization.

There is a term that I use in my class called NIMBY-ism "Not in my back yard." This term provides insight into the mindset of many in management of corporate America. For that matter, it also applies to many of the employees. Quite often, individuals either minimize conduct or attempt to deny that a problem exists. Many people would like to believe that an act of violence could never occur at their place of employment. Workplace violence is something that occurs at someone else's business and would never occur at our business. This is tantamount to the ostrich sticking his head in the sand and hoping the problem either bypasses them or will never occur. This is foolish thinking. Every corporate manager must practice due diligence in their best efforts to minimize the threat of violence to their employees, customers, or clients.

In 1987, David Burke was described as an angry man who was physically abusive to his former wife and girlfriend. In November, his former girlfriend filed for a restraining order. There were allegations that Burke was involved with Jamaican drug dealers and his lifestyle exceeded his income. Burke had worked for USAir for over 14 years. On November 15, Burke was arrested for stealing $69 in beverage receipts from the airline and fired.

On December 7, 1987, Burke returned to his former employer looking for the boss, Ray Thomson, who had fired him. Thomson was not in the office. Using his employee credentials, which he still possessed, Burke boarded Pacific Southwest Airlines Flight 1771 with a concealed pistol.

His former boss and the person who fired him, Ray Thomson, was also a passenger on the same flight. After boarding the plane, Burke wrote a message on an airsickness bag. It is unknown if he gave the message to Thomson, but the statement read, "Hi Ray. I think it's sort of ironical that we ended up like this. I asked for some leniency for my family. Remember? Well, I got none and you'll get none." Burke shot and killed Thomson, a flight attendant, and three pilots. The plane crashed in a mountainous region of California. All forty-three passengers were killed on impact. Among the passengers killed were executives with Chevron and Pacific Bell, which resulted in corporate policy reviews of multiple executives travelling on the same flight.

Companies often have a myopic view of the inappropriate conduct. The business must consider not only the impact on the other employees, but also the customers and clients. On the day he went on his killing spree, Burke returned to USAir looking for Thomson, who was not available. This should have caused some concern. If he had surrendered his credentials upon termination, this violent act could have been prevented.

Tony Hsieh, the CEO of Zappos, known for promoting and embracing a crazy corporate culture has said, "Not everyone is a fit. Businesses often forget about the culture, and ultimately, they suffer for it because you can't deliver good service from unhappy employees." His HR department conducts two interviews of applicants. The first is to determine experience and knowledge. The second is to determine if the applicant is a good fit for the culture. Leadership members are invited to company outings to determine how they would interact and embrace the weirdness culture of Zappos.

When assembling his team for the eventual Olympic gold medal in hockey, U.S. coach Herb Brooks said, "I am not looking for the best players, I am looking for the best fit." Brooks was able to assemble and successfully integrate a group of college hockey players, who for the most part had never played together. Brooks understood that overall team chemistry was a more important factor to success than individual talent. The 1980 U.S. Olympic hockey team upset a dominant USSR team and went on to capture the Olympic gold medal.

Failure to address problem employees results in high turnover, lost productivity, and poor customer-client relations, all in the interest of accommodating one bad employee/supervisor. A common analogy is cancer. You identify the tumor and you must monitor the growth to see if it metastasizes. If necessary, you can administer chemo and radiation. You may have to excise the growth and begin rehabilitation. Ignoring the tumor and leaving it to fester will lead to growing, metastasizing, and eventual death.

Chapter 22
Skeletons in the closet

The idea of managing a problem employee does not start with a referral to the Employee Assistance Program but begins with the hiring process. Too often in our litigious society, employers are reluctant to conduct adequate background investigations or to share adverse employment history with other companies.

According to HR.com, 81% of companies reported conducting background screening to some extent. Most of these screenings are somewhat limited in their scope, primarily due to cost, time and available resources. Once an individual is hired and becomes an employee, only 12% of the companies reported conducting periodic checks of their current employees. In order to maintain a government security clearance, a thorough background investigation is required every five years during employment. There are a number of legal liabilities that a company may encounter when confronted with the knowledge of criminal or civil transgressions by an employee. This would have to be judged on a case-by-case basis to determine the severity of the offenses and how this impacts the employee in his or her relationship with the employer.

Most companies reported they did not conduct background screenings of sub-contractors. While a company may have conducted an in-depth security screening of potential applicants, they allow service contractors unfettered access to their business. You are still responsible for those who gain access to your workspace or represent your company. In January 2013, Jason Smith, an exterminator, entered the residence of Philadelphia pediatrician Melissa Ketunuti and began arguing with her. Smith strangled the 35-year-old doctor and set her body ablaze. In December 2011, Rashad Hales; was employed as a door-to-door salesperson for an alarm installation company. Hales forced his way through the door of a Tampa home and savagely raped the homeowner.

From my own personal experience while conducting background investigations for the government, I found an increasing number of employers who would refer all employment inquiries to a central database that would only share the previous position and dates of employment. For an individual who was a problem child, who decided to either pick up his or her ball and take it home or were terminated for cause, this information will not be shared with potential new employers. This is essentially planting a land mine in a new fertile field. The new employer will not know the extent of the potential for damage until it is too late. When ESL fired Richard Farley, he moved to another company.

Many companies rely heavily upon networking and referrals to identify applicants. Sharing a beer with someone at the corner bar may not be the best means of identifying a potentially good employee. Additionally, previous coworkers sometimes have clouded judgment due to friendship with the applicant, and are unaware of the deterioration of the employee's performance at the applicant's previous employer.

Companies rely heavily on resumes, which are prone to inaccuracies, exaggerations and outright works of fiction. These situations are often exacerbated by telephone interviews that are of limited value in establishing and identifying credibility. Telephone interviews are only useful in scaling down a large pool of applicants to a manageable group for which personal interviews will be conducted. One financial company told me they were victimized by proxy applicants. The person who showed up on the first day of work was not the one who was interviewed on the phone.

One situation that was related to me concerned a potential employee who was going through the applicant process with a Fortune 500 company. He entered the process with a series of interviews with different levels of management. He was then told he and the other applicants would be assembled for a final interview. On the evening prior to the interview, the applicants were invited to a social gathering for a mix and mingle. As it turned out, this social event was in fact the final interview in which management could monitor and assess the applicants' interpersonal skills.

A story was related to me in which an applicant was invited to dinner by his potential employer. The boss excused himself to make some telephone calls and promised to return shortly. In fact, the supervisor wanted to monitor the interactions of the applicant with the server to judge social ability factors. Very few business entities have the luxury of conducting such in-depth interviews, but all businesses have an obligation to practice due diligence in the screening of applicants for employment. Some of us are old enough to remember the old Fram oil filter commercial in which the mechanic states, "You can pay me now or you can pay me later." It is always much cheaper to exclude a problem applicant than to deal with a problem employee who becomes toxic to the workplace, counterproductive, possibly leading to litigious ramifications or perhaps injuries resulting from workplace violence.

Background checks should include a database search to verify the validity of assertions within the resume. There are numerous such databases, CLEAR, TLO, Lexis-Nexis, and others. These aforementioned databases include criminal records checks. There is an ongoing debate over the reliability and accuracy of arrest records. On occasion, someone has used a false identity when being arrested. One individual I encountered on a traffic stop presented me the identity of a cousin. Unfortunately for this traffic offender, his cousin had a warrant for his arrest. Ooops. He quickly recanted the false name. Records can also become tainted because of keystroke errors and similar name confusion such as Smith or Jones.

If an inquiry results in an arrest record, it is incumbent for the employer to confront the applicant, and provide them the opportunity to explain or deny the allegation. Relevancy of the criminal record to employment has become more critical. An accountant who was convicted of bank fraud would be troubling to have around the financial records. A sex offender being hired where children are present would be a problem.

James Wolcott killed his family when he was fifteen years old. He was diagnosed with paranoid schizophrenia, which was exacerbated by sniffing glue. The jury found him not guilty by reason of insanity. After spending the next six years in a psychiatric facility, he was released and he legally changed his name. He returned to school and obtained a doctorate in psychology. Forty-six years after the murder, he was exposed as a highly esteemed college professor at Milliken University. He had not been in trouble since his arrest. Is this arrest still relevant? Legally speaking, no.

As a police detective, I obtained a warrant for the arrest of a financial fraud suspect. Several months later, I received a call from a police officer in Virginia. The officer said he had discovered that I held a warrant for his arrest. This was a shock to the officer. He was providing training to his rookie on how to conduct a warrant check on the computer. The officer instructed the rookie to input the training officer's name. The rookie informed his partner that he had a warrant for his arrest in Arkansas. It turned out that the boyfriend of the officer's ex-wife had assumed his identity. Like any records, the arrest history is not always accurate.

Confirmation of previous employment must be established, regardless of the limited information typically shared by previous employers. It is helpful if a current employee previously worked at the stated employer of the applicant. The employee can be utilized to conduct an inquiry with former associates to determine the credibility of the applicant.

Numerous states have passed legislation restricting the ability to conduct credit checks as a hiring screening tool. Because of the current state of the economy, many individuals have struggled to maintain financial integrity, as many homeowners struggle with the devastating effects of short sales, foreclosures and bankruptcies on their credit report. Credit reports often contain discrepancies that could adversely impact the appearance of an applicant's financial integrity. The real question is what view the applicant takes of his or her financial situation. I have known some individuals who took immense pride over failing to live up to their financial obligations and viewed their bankruptcy as a financial badge of courage. Many others had genuine remorse and embarrassment over their inability to maintain their financial obligations.

Normally, references are handpicked by the applicant who will parrot the reliability of the applicant. With all of the background investigations I have conducted, I cannot recall a single incident in which a personal reference provided a poor assessment. References are friends listed on the application who will provide a character reference. There were a few who were dated and had limited knowledge of the current status of the applicant. References often are reluctant to share adverse information, which could be detrimental to an acquaintance.

On a personal level, I was screening the background references listed for a potential in-home childcare provider. The two references provided insightful and damaging appraisals of the applicant who would be charged with the responsibility of caring for my young children. Apparently, the applicant must have assumed that I would not check her out-of-state references.

In today's active social media culture, employers should check the digital footprint of their applicants. This should include Twitter feeds, public Facebook postings and LinkedIn profiles. The 140 character Twitter postings can provide pithy insight into the applicant. The LinkedIn profile can be utilized to compare the consistency with the employment application and resume submitted. Facebook will provide an assessment of the individual's social skills and interaction.

In today's society, a lack of social media presence, especially among applicants younger than thirty years of age, should result in additional scrutiny to determine if the individual has recently scrubbed an embarrassing or damaging online persona, whether they lack socialization skills that could be of concern for an employer. James Holmes and Adam Lanza, Aaron Alexis all in the age group that embraces an online persona, but had a minimal digital existence on social media. This is similar to being a digital hermit. They may not have to be overly active, but they should have some existence.

Despite the best attempts by the federal government to conduct security background checks, there are periodic lapses in their efficiency to detect problematic applic2ants or current employees. The background investigation is only as good as the investigator. Every government agency has had scandal with a current employee, including the Secret Service. The CIA was victimized by Aldrich Ames, the FBI was victimized by Robert Hansen, the NSA was victimized by Edward Snowden and most recently, the Navy was victimized by Aaron Alexis. In the Snowden and the Alexis case, the contract background investigating company, U.S.I.S., is now the subject of a criminal investigation.

Background investigations are contingent upon the diligence of the investigator and available information. Background investigations can suffer from shortened time constraints, budgetary restrictions, and a lack of experienced investigators are necessary to conduct thorough investigations. Periodic quality control checks should be conducted by the administrator to ensure adequate investigations. When I conducted these pre-employment checks, I approached the investigation from the point of view that I may one day have to work with this individual.

Chapter 23
Wound Collectors

A number of characteristics and behaviors have been associated with pre-incident indicators to workplace violence. I want to first caution all investigators and those in the human resources environment not to focus on a single behavior as a precursor to potential violence. As we explore these behaviors, I want you to think about whether you personally have ever suffered or projected any of these behaviors.

Most of us at some time have been disgruntled over a perceived injustice and viewed ourselves as victims of an unfair system. The ones who will not let go of the grievance are what retired FBI agent Joe Navarro refers to as "wound collectors." For this individual every minor transgression is collected and becomes a cumulative anthology of injustices that can eventually reach the boiling point. I see no better demonstration of this conduct then by Christopher Dorner the fired Los Angeles police officer, whose manifesto was bleeding with the collection of wounds throughout his life.

A number of the suspects tend to be socially isolated, and this is primarily due to their own toxicity. Many employees prefer to avoid the toxic waste dumps of constantly espousing negative attitudes and injustices. These troubled employees begin to perceive the world as me against them. Because of their dysfunctional conduct in the workplace, many employees will distance themselves and limit contact to avoid being sucked into listening to a dissertation from their lectern on how unfair the company's practices are and how mistreated they are. This burden of inequity is often carried home to the domestic front, where loved ones and neighbors grow tired of the caustic and frayed relationship. As a result, these employees become more socially isolated and wallow in their own misery. Their social support, which provides a balance of ideas, deteriorates and vanishes.

For all of these individuals you will see a pattern of disconcerting conduct observed by those around them. Sometimes perhaps it is odd behavior, while other times there is a pattern of disciplinary issues as well as the continual disregard for policies, rules and regulations. After the incidence of workplace violence and before the suspect's name becomes public, typically those who are familiar with the situation will attribute the act to an individual employee who was of concern to not only the company but also to the fellow employees.

Social isolates erect a wall of insulation from interaction with others. This is often a self-imposed isolation. They may be socially awkward or inept. Other times, there are more serious issues, such as mental illness, that can obstruct social interaction.

The identification of the so-called "problem child" or problem employee is consistent with workplace violence. Other employees are either intimidated or concerned for their own safety and fail to report inappropriate contact to superiors. Management is, again, often concerned about liability exposure and do not want to exacerbate the caustic relationship with the employee.

In September of 2012, Andrew Engeldinger went on a shooting rampage at his employer, Accent Signage Systems in Minneapolis. His final paycheck for $968.46 was found on the office floor of John Souter, who along with Rami Cook, had notified the killer he was being terminated. Earlier that morning, Souter told his wife, "It's good I'll have the truck, because if he goes crazy, he won't recognize that I have a different car." Souter probably expected to be targeted in the parking lot. Although concerned about the subject's behavior, he never expected the subject to pull a gun and start shooting in the office.

Engeldinger could be described as a "problem child." The week prior to the killing, he was warned about chronic tardiness for thirty-five consecutive days. The supervisor who authored the reprimand, Rami Cook, was subsequently killed, along with the owner, Reuven Rahamim, Eric Rivers, Ronald Edberg, Jacob Beneke and UPS driver Keith Basinski, who was making deliveries. Engeldinger committed suicide.

Engeldinger had a history of mental illness. He had become estranged from his parents for nearly two years over his refusal to seek counseling and mental health treatment. After the shooting, his parents shared in an interview that he suffered from delusions and paranoia. In high school, he exhibited signs of depression. He was withdrawn and sought comfort in substance abuse. After completing a drug treatment program, he obtained a job with Accent, where he remained for twelve years. He never overcame the paranoid beliefs that invaded his thought process.

Other workers described him as being a loner, who ate by himself. He had difficulty getting along with other employees. Several people complained that Engeldinger made disparaging remarks and that his behavior may have caused several people to leave the company. He was removed from a leadership role and sanctioned for his disrespectful behavior toward other employees. He was a disruptive influence in the workplace, and it had been tolerated for too long.

Engeldinger was notified to report to the supervisor's office after his shift. It is believed he walked out to his car, retrieved a gun, and re-entered the business. After he was terminated, he withdrew the weapon. A struggle ensued and he shot the two supervisors before continuing his rampage through the rest of the facility.

A former employee, when learning of the news of the shooting, anticipated that Engeldinger was the suspect because of his prior conduct and odd behavior. A wrongful death lawsuit is pending against Accent Signage, in which it is alleged that it was "reasonably foreseeable based on the suspect, Engeldinger's past incidents of employment misconduct and his known propensity for abuse and violence."

In July 2003, Doug Williams, an employee at Lockheed Martin in Meridian, Mississippi shot fourteen of his coworkers with a shotgun, killing six of them, before committing suicide in front of his girlfriend. When he entered the factory grounds, he was armed with a 12 gauge shotgun, a mini 14 rifle slung on his back, and a bandolier of ammunition draped across his chest. This is a good indication that this was not a spontaneous attack in which he suddenly snapped.

Williams, who had been employed at the aircraft manufacturing plant for nineteen years, was described by one employee as being mad at the world. Hubert Threat, said this man had an issue with everybody. Lanette McCall, who was wounded in the attack, had said that she expected Williams to harm someone someday, and that he had made racist threats in the past. Jim Payton, a retired employee, said when he first heard about the shooting, Williams was the first person that came to mind.

According to the lawsuit filed against Lockheed Martin, that plaintiffs accused their employer of ignoring Williams' conduct. "Williams made such specific and unequivocal threats and promises to supervisory and other personnel of Lockheed that Lockheed had sufficient time to both stop him before he entered the premises with loaded firearms, and/or to warn plaintiffs and other employees of the imminent danger he posed." The lawsuit also alleged, "Additionally, Lockheed management were told, but ignored, that Williams was headed toward the plant with guns." This again provides evidence that if those around the individual are concerned about their own safety that this should cause alarm for closer examination.

Troubled employees will often become the bullies of the cubicle city that they occupy for eight hours or more a day. This can result in the other employees feeling miserable, concerned for their own safety, and decreased productivity as the focus of attention is constantly shifted away from the mission of the company and instead on the distracting, disruptive behavior of the problem employee.

I interviewed an individual who made some inappropriate and threatening statements while at his workplace. As I interviewed his fellow cubicle city dwellers, I learned that they were in constant fear of his intimidating and bullying behavior. He commonly displayed anger management issues and was unable to control or moderate his bursts of anger. He would listen to various talk radio shows that espoused political leanings and were not conducive to a harmonious workplace environment. He constantly injected his political beliefs from the sanctity of his own cubicle much to the dismay of his neighbors. Any of the coworkers who objected to his diatribes were immediately chastised and shouted down. Despite the fact that this conduct was well known, little had been done to moderate his behavior by management.

It was not until my involvement after complaints were made by employees that the hierarchy of management became involved. The subject was counseled, disciplined with a suspension, and prescribed a written set of behavior modifications and expectations for future conduct. If this approach had been utilized to begin with, it could have increased the productivity of the other employees and made them much more engaged. Keep in mind the cost of employee disengagement to corporate America. This is not all the result of workplace violence or bullying, but is often symptomatic of a hostile environment in one in which management displays limited empathy, fairness, and no enforcement of guidelines.

Many have written that those involved in workplace violence have a great fascination with firearms or military type operations. Although I will not dispute that characteristic, I would put little weight on its overall importance. It could provide some insight, but I believe this is a factor not worth getting wrapped around the axle over. Although I am no gun enthusiast, I know many people who spend huge sums of money every year on the acquisition of weapons, ammunition and memberships to various gun clubs and ranges. Of the people known to me that fall into that category, none has displayed symptoms of instability. I have known former military snipers who were some of the most disciplined individuals I have ever met.

If someone who has had not previously displayed an interest in firearms and marksmanship suddenly becomes highly interested in these hobbies, while also displaying other previously stated factors, then yes, I believe it can become a contributing factor to the overall assessment and determination of the dangerousness of the individual. Many of these attacks were the result of legally acquired and owned handguns and rifles. The handgun is the most often used in the killing fields of corporate America. There are approximately 300,000,000 guns in the United States, and almost no one owning a firearm will become a workplace killer.

The gun control debate is extremely polarizing and the two sides will never come to agreement. Despite carrying firearms as a tool of the trade, I have no interest is stirring the gumbo on this issue. My beliefs fall into a territory of neutrality. Those that are committed to violence or ending their life will find a way to carry out their intentions. I prefer to focus behavioral factors to violence.

The Minnesota killer, Andrew Engeldinger had 10,000 rounds of ammunition and two handguns. Because of his isolation, not many were aware of his fascination with weapons. John Huberty, the McDonalds killer, had an arsenal at his disposal. It has been well documented that Adam Lanza had access to a cache of weapons.

I want to stress once again that people do not just snap. They don't just wake up in the morning, pour the first cup of coffee and decide they're going to go to work and conduct a mass killing. This is an evolutionary process. Other employees can usually point out the problem employee and speak specifically to pre-incident factors and indicators that were ignored, never addressed, or allowed to percolate.

Chapter 24
Dismissed Not Forgotten

Every year, millions of employees will be fired or laid off because of a reduction in the work force. The economy is often the determining factor in the stability of employment and varies widely from year to year. Very few of these individuals will return to exact revenge. I have witnessed numerous friends and relatives, including my own father and father-in-law, lose their jobs due to corporate cutbacks. None of them ever contemplated resorting to violence. Most individuals who are terminated may have difficulty rationalizing their dismissal, but again most will not resort to seeking violent revenge. Some may engage in acts of sabotage or engage in a verbal outburst, but they will leave and never be heard from again.

A challenge for corporate America is to identify those individuals who, once they are terminated, will view their firing like an open wound for all future failures in life, both professional as well as personal. Quite often, that these individuals will return to their former employer with little warning. These so-called "late bloomers" are the most difficult to identify. Most of the associates of the former employee will limit future contact with a problem employee, which only tends to lead to isolation and misery. A source of monitoring their conduct and emotional state has now also been eliminated.

Over sixteen years during the 1940s and 1950s, New York City was targeted by an individual who was nicknamed "The Mad Bomber." The unknown subject left bombs in various public locations, including transit stations, famous landmarks, theaters, phone booths and so forth. The first attributed bomb the "Mad Bomber" left was at the Consolidated Edison (Con Edison) power plant headquarters. The device did not explode, but a note was found with the explosive device, which read, "Con Edison crooks this is for you."

Despite planting thirty-three bombs, only twenty-two exploded, resulting in fifteen injuries. Fortunately, there were no fatalities. The bomber did take a hiatus during World War II, and there were no bombings between 1941 to 1951. Throughout his bombing campaign, the bomber left notes in some instances, but he never provided a motive.

In January 1957, a Con Edison clerk, was searching the workmen's compensation case files for those that had been labeled as troublesome, and she discovered one file which had been marked with the words "injustice" and "permanent disability" which included some of the same verbiage printed in the *Journal American* newspaper by the bomber.

The file identified George Metesky, who had been injured in a plant accident in September 1931. After his arrest, he told officers that he had been gassed in the Con Edison accident and contracted tuberculosis. He claimed his motive for planting the bombs was because, "he got a bum deal." In the industrial accident, a boiler backfired and the hot gases filled his lungs. He collected twenty-six weeks of sick pay and then lost his job. Metesky claimed that the accident could lead to pneumonia and ultimately tuberculosis. He filed a workmen's compensation claim, which was denied, and three subsequent appeals were also denied. His deep-seated hatred for Con Edison simmered and boiled for five years. He was so filled with rage that his bombing campaign lasted nearly two decades.

Mental stability is a significant factor in workplace violence. These affected individuals displayed symptoms of mental health illness including schizophrenia, bipolar disorder, and depression. Others will also score high on the narcissistic personality disorder and have a strong sense of entitlement, difficulty dealing with adversity, and due to their own arrogance, believe all problems blamed on them are actually the result of someone else's incompetence. Remember that according to NAMI, 1 in 17 Americans suffers from mental health illness. When you subtract those individuals who are already in mental health facilities, at home on disability, incarcerated, or homeless, the percentage of mentally ill working in the corporate environment is much lower. That does not remove the possibility of an individual working in your organization that is currently under treatment and counseling for a mental health illness.

Some of these individuals also have a higher degree of paranoia where they feel isolated and think that everyone is out to get them. As they become sucked into the negative emotional vortex in both their personal and professional lives, depression is quite often a symptom of the process. As despair becomes a larger factor, they often have a lack of faith in life and embrace a pessimistic attitude. As suicidal thoughts creep into their brain, it is at this crucial precipice that they begin to contemplate an acceptable means of retribution. Violence is a way to put an exclamation mark on life. From their viewpoint, they force everyone to remember who they were and what a mistake was made in their firing. Their lack of mental health stability provides an inability to filter stress and to cope with life's challenges.

As in the case of the assassins, a number of those who engaged in workplace violence also displayed an unhealthy obsession with other workplace attackers, or other active shooter cases. Any time we have witnessed an outrageous attack, we were often obsessed by the ongoing press coverage of the event. It becomes a concern when someone no longer talks about anything else but that event, and even as interest wanes for most people, the act is still a topic of stimulating interest. This interest will typically be demonstrated by an unhealthy excitement in learning all of the facts and perhaps critiquing the actual attack providing suggestions as to how the killer could have been more successful, or identifying what mistakes were made by the assailant.

Those verbal renderings can provide insight into the psyche of the individual. For human resources staff, identifying oral statements becomes a challenge. An obvious trait is when an employee becomes obsessed with previous attacks, information that may be viewed through his or her Internet history on their workplace computer. Almost all companies provide employees with the knowledge that they have no expectation of privacy on business-owned computers. If a problem is identified, the Information Technology (IT) department can monitor computer activity including the Internet history of the employee. The results of the computer forensic investigation can be reported to the human resources department for follow-up.

To those arising to the level of police intervention it is always of benefit to conduct interviews at the subject's home. Many interview and interrogation techniques advise conducting these interviews in a neutral environment as opposed to a comfortable setting, such as the subject's residence. In a typical criminal investigation, I will not disagree. When conducting a behavioral threat assessment, I find the opportunity to conduct an in-residence interview of such evidentiary value that it overrides the limitations of concern.

The in-residence interview provides an opportunity to ask or to receive consent to search the residence. While conducting the search, you can look for weapons, see what kind of books and movies are on the shelves. You can ask who the subjects' cable provider is to identify what movies are being viewed. The individual may provide consent to conduct a forensic examination of his or her computers and to determine who is providing their Internet service. We may all read various books and review various movies that deliver violent messages. It can become a concern when a person develops an unhealthy obsession with a particular book or movie. This should give pause to investigators in their overall assessment of the dangerousness of the individual.

Chapter 25
The Problem Employee

When an employee's behavior becomes problematic and concerning to those around him, it is incumbent upon the company to intercede on behalf of the other employees as well as the company. Many companies utilize the Grote-Harvey discipline model to identify and manage problem employees. This model is utilized to analyze the problem of concern and assess its impact on the individual employee, coworkers and the employer.

In a closed-door counseling session, the employee will be notified of his transgressions, inappropriate behaviors, and positive alternatives will be discussed and outlined. It is important that empathy be displayed toward the employee and that he should be allowed to articulate his viewpoint. An open and civil discourse should be encouraged. If the employee feels that he is being talked down to, and his input is not desired or sought, he will never embrace the suggestions. At the same time, control of the dialogue must be adhered to in limiting aggressive language by the employee.

The alternatives and actions should be clearly defined in a document and signed by the employee, and a copy of this should be provided to the employee to avoid any possible misunderstanding. It will be up to the first line supervisors to monitor the progression and modification of behavior to conform to the clearly outlined objectives. Additional counseling sessions may be needed. If the employee continues to ignore the structured approach, termination may be the only alternative. If the employee who has been properly counseled continues to ignore the objectives and desired alternatives, the employer who continues to keep this person employed is only delusional to believe that the person may ultimately change. It is the due diligence to protect clients, customers, other employees, and the company image, so at that point, the employee must be removed and terminated.

There is a concept that I refer to as the puppy dog model. That cute little puppy that we take home from the pet store has no idea that it is not allowed to urinate on the carpet until behavior modification and structure is provided to demonstrate the desired outcome is to urinate outside. Children and adults are no different. We all need to operate in a framework or a structured environment where we know the expectations. We need a clear understanding of the positive results when we fulfill those obligations and the negative consequences if we fail to adhere to the structured discipline of the system. The employee, who fails to adhere to a method that is clearly outlined, has no reasonable objection to disciplinary scrutiny because of not complying with clearly defined and applied guidelines.

In attempts to achieve behavior modification, actions may be necessary to enlist the assistance of others within the organization. Not all organizations are large enough to have an EAP. The employee assistance program is intended to provide what I call a "group hug" for an employee who is enduring personal strife that may adversely affect his or her job performance, health and stability. The EAP can provide support and referrals pertaining to substance abuse, mental health counseling, and other social support systems that may alleviate stress in the personal life of the employee. They can also provide short-term counseling sessions to provide an empathetic ear for an employee. They are not there to provide in-depth, long-term clinical psychiatric counseling. There are times that there is reluctance on the part of an employee to seek the assistance of the EAP, as quite often they are housed under the same roof, and there are always concerns about confidentiality and impartiality. Many companies contract their EAP services with outside vendors.

Some companies, as well as many government agencies, have employee ombudsmen. The role of the ombudsman is to act as an impartial mediator between the employee and management. The mediation is only effective if both parties are open-minded and willing to compromise on a certain portion of their position. Typically, the ombudsman will listen to one side in privacy and consult with the other party in privacy. The ombudsman will attempt to mediate a solution to the conflict between the two adversaries. Many companies lack a full-time ombudsman and for most, it is an ancillary responsibility. The ombudsman is solely a mediator and has no binding decision-making responsibilities.

As with all positions, the effectiveness of these support groups is only as good as the dedication of the individuals participating and the training that they receive. One horror story I can relate, occurred to an individual who was enduring a traumatic health illness. During his initial medical treatment, he received an inappropriate inquiry from a supervisor. The employee, who was indignant over the lack of empathy, responded abruptly to the supervisor. As a result, the supervisor refused any communication with the affected employee for four months. This was despite working in a relatively small office, in which they would pass each other in the hallway on a daily basis. When the employee reached out to the EAP, he received a sympathetic ear. They ensured that the employee was receiving his proper medical treatment and asked if he felt the need for mental health counseling. The employee denied the assistance, asserting that the greatest stress he was experiencing was due to the lack of communication and hostility with the supervisor. The EAP recommended that the employee contact the ombudsman and seek mediation. The employee politely declined and explained that the problematic supervisor was also a designated ombudsman. It was only through the assertions of the employee that he was able to mediate a tenuous resolution, but the uneasiness in the relationship lasted until the employee transferred.

Chapter 26
You're Fired!

During a termination hearing, it is always best to have two individuals in the office making the notification. It is also advisable to have security personnel in close proximity to respond if necessary. The actual act of dismissal should be completed in a quick and concise manner. The decision has already been made to remove the individual from the premises. Deliberation and debate will not alter the outcome. You are to inform the individual that their continued status with the organization has been altered and their presence is no longer necessary. This is the same case when breaking up with an abusive or inappropriate relationship partner. Under no circumstances should you debate or waiver in your commitment.

The individual should be apprised of any separation benefits and respond to any questions succinctly. Avoid using the words "termination," "fired," and so forth and replacing them "separation," "your services are no longer needed," your employment will not be continued," "your status with the university or company will not be continued," and so forth.

If the individual becomes threatening, you must make it clear that this is unacceptable behavior and will not be tolerated. It does not matter whether the threat is direct in nature, such as, "I am going to kill you." Or an indirect such as, "I wish this place would blow up, and you would die." A veiled threat in which the employee says, "You better watch your back, you never know when an accident may happen," or, "if you fire me, bad things will happen." At the point of the utterance of any of these threats, the meeting should be immediately concluded and the individual should be informed that law enforcement authorities will be notified and their threatening behavior will not be tolerated. If necessary, you should pick up the phone and call 911 and/or someone in your security personnel.

Security personnel should not be utilized as part of the firing mechanism. I have seen and heard this used on numerous occasions. Using security either as the axe to drop the bad news or as a bodyguard with an intimidating gaze only tends to infuriate the individual and exacerbate a volatile situation. Security should be kept in reserve and used only when the subject becomes threatening.

I recently heard from a security consultant that their client wanted to fire the employee over the phone. This will only exacerbate a situation and encourage a troubled employee to seek revenge. Outside of the employee being incarcerated for an extended time, I could not envision any other reason to use such lack of empathy in the termination proceeding. This will only plant the seeds of discontent and revenge.

When a problematic individual is removed, whether it is from a campus or business environment, packing boxes should already be on hand to speed up the exit process. A member of administration should accompany the employee and monitor his or her behavior and removal of personal articles. Attempts should be made to assist them in bringing the individual's property to his or her vehicle.

George Clooney played the role of a hired gun who would essentially travel from company to company and conduct widespread terminations in the movie *Up In The Air*. As with any dismissal, empathy and sensitivity must be displayed. Despite this emotional salve, the severance of the relationship must be definitive. Security must be notified, and they should be in close proximity to where the termination hearing is being conducted. Security should not be in the same room where the termination is occurring, but nearby, to respond to a dangerous situation if necessary. Although the termination should be witnessed by a second individual, it is usually best to utilize supervisors who have not had previous conflict with the terminated employee.

One mental health counselor I work with is often called in to assist in layoffs at large companies. As the pink slips are being distributed, the company offers the employee the opportunity to speak with her. She provides an empathetic ear and assists with conflict resolution of the affected employee. Her counseling helps to diffuse any volatility.

The IT department should be immediately notified and coordinated in concert with the termination hearing. The involvement of the IT department will provide for the removal of the individual's access to critical systems. This action will reduce the chance of sabotage or extracting vital information that can adversely impact the competitive nature of the business.

All employees should be notified that the employee is no longer welcome on the property of the business. This will reduce the chance that an employee who is unaware of the termination, will allow an ex-employee to gain admission to the inner sanctum of the business, which could result in property damage, theft or violence. In addition, the terminated employee should be provided referrals to employment agencies and mental health counseling agencies as appropriate, to demonstrate the company's empathetic posture.

When I speak with businesses concerning workplace violence, I encourage executives to practice personal security. I urge them to ditch the elitist reserved parking spots. They tend to portray arrogance and are not conducive to developing empathy with employees. Another reason is that you have identified your cars location for possible targeting.

Every executive should practice a certain degree of cautious paranoia. Watch for cars following you or surveillance at your home. This includes your immediate family. Do you have monitored alarms at home and upgraded locks? Check the front door before answering, and be cautious of unexpected packages. Think this is extreme? Ask the victims killed and maimed by the Unabomber.

In September 2004, U.S District Court Judge Joan Lefkow presided over a medical malpractice case in which Bart Ross was the plaintiff, and she dismissed the case. In March 2005, Bart Ross, who was about to be evicted from his home, broke into the Lefkow residence in the early morning hours. Later that morning, Ross was discovered hiding in a utility room by the judge's husband. Ross killed the husband and the judge's mother and after fleeing the residence, he committed suicide during a traffic stop in Wisconsin.

In March 2013, Tom Clements the Colorado corrections director heard the doorbell at his affluent home in Colorado Springs. The person ringing the doorbell just before 9 P.M. was wearing a pizza delivery shirt and carrying a pizza box. Clements answered the door and was slain by the visitor. Two days later, Evan Ebel, a violent parolee and white supremacist, was killed in a gun battle with Texas authorities. In addition to Clements, Ebel had also killed a pizza deliveryman prior to the assassination.

Immediately following the murderous rampage of ex-Los Angeles Police Officer Christopher Dorner, the news media, in their efforts to push out news of the developing story, often mischaracterized his personality, conduct, and the behavior of the killer. He was described as being an affable soul, always with a smile, whose dream of becoming a police officer was sabotaged by an unfair and racist Police Department. He was also described as a highly skilled sharpshooter in the Navy.

Christopher Dorner was a failure in life and in his manifesto, he documented his highly narcissistic personality. He was unable to overcome the adversity that he faced. He projected a very clear definition of a "wound collector." With his narcissistic personality, he believed totally in a sense of entitlement and certainly displayed a lack of empathy towards others and an overpowering sense of self-worth that did not measure up in his lack of accomplishments.

Dorner's view of his failure to succeed was not through his own shortcomings but was a result of an orchestrated corruption of justice by an incompetent and unfair bureaucracy. At no point in his manifesto did Dorner even begin to accept any responsibility for his termination and lack of accomplishments in life. All the shortcomings were attributed back to the Los Angeles Police Department.

It is unfortunate in today's society that so many people were rooting for Dorner while he was murdering innocent people; he was viewed by many as some sort of Butch Cassidy and the Sundance Kid. Others viewed him as a hero railing against an unfair and racially discriminatory police department. The bottom line is that all of his victims had zero involvement in his termination from the police department.

Dorner targeted Captain Randal Quan, the man who was responsible for defending him during his disciplinary hearings, Dorner executed Quan's daughter and her fiancé. He then shot and killed one police officer and critically wounded a second officer both from a different police department. I believe this clearly demonstrates his detachment from reality. As a former uniformed officer assigned to a patrol car, he sighted in on innocent, uniformed police officers sitting in the same position that he had occupied years earlier. I know from personal experience how helpless you feel when you are sitting in the patrol car at a traffic light and have a gun pointed at you by a passing motorist. Every officer, has in the back of his or her mind, contemplated that he or she could become a victim of an ambush. Yet Dorner felt very comfortable coming in direct conflict with that ingrained fear, shooting officers wearing blue.

Dorner played college football as a third string running back at a small school. He enlisted in the Navy but academically was unable to meet his obligations and failed out of flight school. He did retain his commission in the U.S. Navy and he transitioned into the U.S. Naval Reserves. Despite the news media's assertion that he was a highly skilled sniper, I would argue with that claim. Dorner had the minimum skill necessary to carry a rifle. He was a certified marksman, which is the lowest proficiency rating provided in the armed forces. He was certified as an expert with a handgun.

There is no indication that he was ever engaged in an actual combat situation. He was in a higher risk assignment for Navy personnel, as he was assigned to an oil platform security team in the Middle East, but there is no indication or evidence that he saw action. His naval career ended just prior to his shooting rampage. This could have been the final catalyst in a long decline through the negative emotional vortex. He had been passed over twice for promotion, which is a kiss of death in any of the military organizations. An extension to his enlistment was not extended, and he was honorably discharged. It is unclear at this point in time the reasoning for him being passed over twice for promotion while serving in a reserve unit.

Dorner struggled with personal relationships. One previous girlfriend posted on a website that he was bad news, extremely paranoid, and she warned others to stay away from him. He filed a restraining order against her, but he failed to show up in court, and the restraining order was dismissed. She said in later interviews that he displayed extreme paranoia and had multiple firearms positioned throughout the house in the event of an unexpected assault on his residence. He was briefly married, and his former brother-in-law stated that Dorner's spouse physically ended the marriage eight hours after the nuptials. The divorce was finalized thirty days later. He also had a tumultuous relationship with another girlfriend in Las Vegas.

His career with the Los Angeles Police Department was filled with shortcomings. He struggled in the police academy, and for someone who was so proficient with weapons, he was disciplined during the academy for an accidental discharge of a weapon. He struggled during his field training. Evaluations by his training officer indicated that Dorner was substandard. He had been counseled for his lack of tactical awareness and officer safety skills. When he was on the verge of receiving an unsatisfactory rating from his training officer, he made an allegation of physical abuse by his training officer against an subject in custody.

Violating the civil rights of an arrestee is one of the most serious allegations you can make against a fellow police officer. The disciplinary board determined that Dorner had fabricated the story, and he was subsequently terminated. Dorner appealed this decision, which was reviewed by the court system and upheld. A subsequent review after the shootings by the LAPD Police Commission and Inspector General reflected the dismissal of Dorner was correct and appropriate.

From Dorner's perspective, you could see where his life was a complete failure. He was a marginal football player, failed at flight school, was dismissed from the Navy, all of his relationships ended in failure, and he was fired from the Police Department. At the age of thirty, he was still living under his mother's roof. His family appeared to be defensive, as this often is the case. They are protective of their loved one.

I throw this into the category of the scariest of workplace violence shooters. These killers rarely threatened targets directly and harbor deep-seated feelings of betrayal, despair, and the desire to exact revenge. In a number of cases, we have seen this type of behavior in which the perpetrator of the crime returns to the business after having fallen off the radar screen on the company's threat matrix. Dorner was terminated in 2008 and his final appeal was denied in 2011. He did not begin his rampage until 2013. Dorner would by definition be labeled as a spree killer, but he does possess the mindset of a mass murderer.

In 2012, there was a workplace related shooting that occurred outside of Hazen Imports near the Empire State Building. Jeffrey Johnson was a meticulously dressed artist and who had constant conflicts with the gregarious outgoing salesperson Stephen Ercolino. Johnson had been laid off over a year earlier, and from all indications, his departure was civil. He had a recent physical altercation in the elevator with Ercolino, which resulted in both parties making reports to the New York Police Department. This resulted in one of those he-said-he-said situations and no charges were brought.

Obviously, the hostility raged inside Johnson, who presented a fastidious and calm exterior to his neighbors, as well as others who knew him. He was a quiet person who kept to himself and engaged in limited social contacts. He dressed daily in a suit and vacuumed his apartment every morning. He was also an avid bird watcher. His mother related in an interview with the New York Times, that he was devastated over the death of his cat. Johnson had been informed that he would have to relocate while his building underwent refurbishment. He left the keys behind and told the building superintendant that he would not return after Friday, the day of the shooting.

Neighbors were unaware of the demons that Johnson was battling, which I attribute to the "façade effect." The "façade effect" is one in which the subject's neighbors and relatives are unaware of what goes on behind the closed doors. How often is a community shocked by the arrest of the local teacher or Little League coach or clergy for being in possession of child porn? The image that they projected outwardly was one of decency. In most situations, these people are described as being quiet, affable, always a smile and always willing to help. One of the most notorious serial killers of all time, Ted Bundy, was known for his charisma, charm and intelligence. We have seen with the Columbine killers, and now most recently with the Boston Bombers, that individuals are able to create bomb-making factories in the safe confines of their residences while concealing their deviousness from neighbors and even the closest loved ones who were sharing the same roof. The house of horrors in Cleveland, in which a depraved suspect held three girls hostage for a decade, went unnoticed by neighbors. In the Johnson matter, he was completely off the radar screen for over a year.

On the day the shooting, Johnson showed up outside of the office building, waiting for his former adversary, Ercolino, to arrive for work. Johnson stepped on to the sidewalk and shot the victim multiple times without warning. He calmly holstered his weapon and blended into the crowds populated by a tourist-centered area of New York. Fortunately, several construction workers followed him and alerted two New York City police officers who engaged in a close quarter combat which resulted in Johnson's death. This gun battle was witnessed by number of innocent people that just happened to be walking through the area. The two police officers survived without injury.

The Johnson case is troubling for those in the threat assessment arena. It is another one of those delayed onset shootings in which the offender was obviously tormented by an internal rage that percolated for an extended period. There may not have been a final catalyst that would have been recognized by those on the outside. Johnson was considered a very private person, and he may have lacked social support. He had been laid off, there was no source of income, he had to relocate, and his cat died. Yes, his mother in an interview said that he was deeply affected by the death of his most trusted friend and companion, his cat. There was no one waving the red flags in this case. This is one of the daunting cases where there are no easily recognizable pre-incident indicators.

In these delayed-onset-shooting cases, it would be incumbent upon friends, family or neighbors, who may be aware of inappropriate statements or behaviors, to report them not just to the employer but also to local law enforcement. Local law enforcement may not be in a position to make an arrest, but they can document the conduct for future reference. The police, if notified of threatening behavior, can conduct a welfare check on the individual to assess that individual's needs.

The police may be in a position to commit the individual to a mental health facility or make a referral to some other social agency that can mitigate the unbearable stress that the individual is experiencing. If those who are aware of disturbing behavior notify the former employer, they can be more vigilant and warn all employees of the ongoing dissatisfaction of a former employee, who may be directing his anger toward his former employer.

In the Navy Yard killing, the Police Department in Newport, Rhode Island, was called by Aaron Alexis to his hotel room. Alexis complained of hearing voices and paranoid beliefs that people were following him and beaming vibrations by microwave into his body. Despite the bizarre behavior, his conduct did not rise to the level of being a danger to himself or to others. He may have feared for his own safety, but Alexis provided no outward evidence of danger. The police appropriately notified the Navy in Newport, but sadly, no one addressed the notification. Twelve people died a few weeks later at the hands of Alexis.

Chapter 27
Workplace Response

All businesses must practice due diligence and should have a workplace violence plan in writing. The plan must be specific in its definition of what is not acceptable behavior in the workplace and the progression of disciplinary measures that will be invoked for violating the terms of the policy. It should also be spelled out for each and every employee what his or her response should be in reaction to workplace violence. We have to promote a sense of ownership in every employee of the company and stress that bad behavior will not be tolerated, as it undermines the safety and security of every employee. Inappropriate statements should never be taken in jest, and should always be reported.

An excellent video was developed by the Houston Police Department in cooperation with Department of Homeland Security. The video, which can be viewed on the Internet, is called *Run, Hide, Fight*. The video explores the options available, and shows that in each situation, the individual response should be assessed and determined according to the best course of action. Depending on the location of the threat and the location of the employee, running and fleeing from the scene may be the best course of action. Escape routes may not be a viable alternative because of the location of the threat. Therefore, seeking a hiding location may be the best alternative. Hiding under your desk may not be the best option. In the emergency plan, you should have already identified hard-rooms within the business environment that can provide some degree of security from the assault.

This hard-room, could be a bathroom that provides ample coverage from a threat but only if the entrance, can be secured. Most active shooters follow the path of least resistance. They look for entry doors that are unlocked and areas where potential victims are accessible. Moving targets will typically draw attention, but it should be noted that shooting a moving target is much more challenging than it looks. Playing dead only suffices after the shooting has commenced. In the Columbine shooting, the shooters taunted students who sought refuge under their desks and in some instances, the killers fired at their defenseless victims.

When you consider that half of the active shooter incidents are over prior to the arrival of law enforcement, it is even more essential that victims consider rising up and fighting back against the assault. This thought pattern takes tremendous courage and goes against the standard of "duck and cover" routine when someone is shooting at you. If the opportunity arises when the shooter is either reloading or experiencing a gun jam, which has happened in several instances, you may have an increased chance of survival by attempting to subdue the attacker and restrain him until law enforcement authorities arrive on scene.

No place is this more evident more than on the United Flight 93 on 9/11 that crashed into the field in Shanksville, Pennsylvania. Passengers were informed by loved ones that previous hijackings had resulted in the planes' demise and all the passengers were killed as they plummeted into strategic landmarks. A previously unassociated alliance of passengers rose up against their attackers and disabled the attack, thus preventing a much worse catastrophe.

Periodic training should be conducted. This does not mean sending an email to all employees or, as I would see on the government level, sending policies around, expecting employees to initial that they had read them. Many employees who were busy conducting required business had little patience to endure the bureaucratic requirement of reading these various policies, so they initialed the regulations without ever reading the documents. This procedure allows the government to claim legal cover with a signed document. The effectiveness of emails and written policies will be challenged in the legal community.

Employers should have semiannual meetings to reinforce the workplace violence policies and procedures. The meeting can be accomplished in less than fifteen minutes and it forces all attendees to emotionally prepare for a situation like workplace violence. Incorporate a video such as *Run, Hide, Fight* and perhaps analyze a recent workplace violence incident.

Training must also include periodic drills, during which an announcement is made to inform everybody that the threat is currently located at a certain location within the building and to initiate the workplace violence response, wherein every employee is required to react in some manner. Rally points should be established both on the property, as well as off-site at a more distant location. Distance is always a friend to a threat. The drills should incorporate the practice of actually mustering to these two different locations, where everyone can visualize where they are expected to show up. In the fog of a trauma, people often get confused, and it is only through visual experience that they will recall where they are expected to appear. New employees should be educated during their orientation period, as this training often overlooked for new employees, and that is inexcusable.

Rally wardens should be identified, and they will be able to take roll to identify any missing employees. This information should be reported to authorities. Under no circumstances should anyone search for the missing employee. Arrangements should also be made for those with disabilities. Buddies should be designated to assist those with mobility issues. This procedure can be easily overlooked if not practiced.

I have seen situations where security access stations had duress buttons, but when the panic alarm was initiated, there was no one monitoring the alarm status. Thus, it would be more beneficial for the personnel at the access station to yell and scream as opposed to pushing an inaudible alarm that is not monitored.

All businesses should recognize and identify their local law enforcement partners. Most police departments and sheriff's offices have a crime prevention unit or something similar. They can usually provide a certain level of advice to a business. In a larger business, it may be beneficial to have a diagram or layout of the business that could assist first responders. It is also essential to have a data system backup. Data storage should be backed up at an off-site location or in the cloud for all personnel records and business transactions. This is also essential during natural disasters, such as a hurricanes, tornados, and so forth.

Keep in mind that during these traumatic events employees may be experiencing tremendous stress. Employers should already have identified counseling services that can quickly respond and provide emotional support to traumatized employees. This sometimes can be achieved through the local religious community or as I witnessed at Ground Zero, the American Red Cross.

Communication with your core employees is essential. They should be updated on the status of the continuity of operations, injuries and the investigation so long as it does not compromise the judicial process.

It is essential during these times that corporate management provides a compassionate support structure to victims and families at their hospitals and residences. Personal appearances and phone calls will go a long way in developing respect and rapport, as well as diminishing the likelihood of litigious action. The support could be in the form of providing hotel lodging to visiting relatives and meals. Virginia Tech demonstrated a proficiency in this area, however, because of earlier actions, the legal sharks were already swimming in the blood stained waters.

While victims are recovering in the hospital, fellow employees can be organized to help shuttle relatives from the airport to the hospital, pick up children from daycare, provide meals to the family, mow their yard, take care of pets, and any other tasks that are so often overlooked. Lifting these burdens can be significant in demonstrating your compassion and sympathy toward a devoted employee. Companies often will say or use the moniker that we are all family, but often they fall short during a trauma situation. Too often, I have seen supervisors never pick up the phone to call an ailing employee or one who is going through personal struggles, and when they did reach out, the phone call was intended to find out when the employee would be returning to work.

I have witnessed the disappointment of some leaders who were expected to marshal the troops and organize relief efforts. Some were overcome and incapacitated with their own grief. When the bell sounded, their leadership abilities were absent. Meanwhile, others who you would not expect to respond not only took action, but also went above and beyond what was expected. They were pillars of strength in a chaotic situation.

A point person and an associate should be identified as the primary contact for all media interactions. In the hours following a dramatic workplace violence episode, the news media will be clamoring for information so that they can satisfy the 24/7 appetite of its viewers. This should be done in concert with local law enforcement and hospital spokespersons.

Another area often overlooked is crime scene cleanup. After the smoke clears, the ambulances have left, the news helicopters have moved onto the next story, and the crime scene tape has come down, the vestiges of the assault will be left behind. There are companies that specialize in crime scene cleanup. There could be bullet holes, blood traces, and discarded supplies left by emergency responders, such as bloody gauze pads, bandage wrappers and so forth. These traces can be a shock for those who are not expecting that scene when they return the next day. Along the same lines, security should be set up to maintain the integrity of the business as well as to keep overzealous looky-loos from violating the privacy and sanctity of the business and shocked or grieving employees.

At the earliest available opportunity, a meeting should be conducted with the employees. The essence of the message is to honor the victims and not allow the senseless act of violence to disrupt the progression of the business but instead to rise up and be strong during this difficult time. This is a very tender subject, and must be approached from the most delicate standpoint possible. This message can easily be misconstrued as having little regard for the victims and the misguided concern is for the business to return to profitability. You want to avoid delivering that type of message. You need to be empathetic and clearly define that the company's position is to provide support to the families and to the remaining employees. It should be constructive and anticipate the personal difficulty during the grieving process that many will experience.

You should also address the availability of counseling. It is essential to get back in operation as soon as possible to strengthen the mental health stability of the survivors. This goes back to the old analogy that the quicker you get back up on the horse, the better off you will be. If you are left to wither at home and deal with the roller coaster of emotions on your own, that can be destabilizing to your emotional health. Depending on the gravity of the situation, it may be necessary to find temporary space at another facility. These are concepts that need to be kept in mind.

Many employees will be emotionally unsettled at the one-year anniversary of the assault. There should be a consideration going forward in setting up a voluntary memorial service in recognition of the event. Ignoring the event at the one-year anniversary could hurt the business and your employee relations.

A dignified commemorative plaque, garden or tree could also be unveiled at the anniversary. I would like to share a cautionary tale. One facility had lost an employee in an accident. I lost track of the number of tributes within the office. There was a plaque greeting every visitor, the conference room was renamed in the employee's honor, and there were more plaques and mementos of the employee in the conference room. Some employees felt the abundance of tributes was to relieve the guilt of an uncaring boss, and became distracting. This same supervisor also wanted to install a memorial garden. There were no volunteers and the idea faded away. I observed at another facility that the plant bed for their employee, who had been killed at work, had turned into an overgrown weed patch. All the flowers had long ago died.

How the company responds to a trauma will be closely scrutinized by the Monday morning quarterbacks and law firms in the days following the assault. The lack of a written workplace plan and periodic training will expose the business to a huge liability. I have spoken with countless employees at Fortune 500 companies who have never received any training in this area. Those businesses lacking in protocols, training or practicing drills should set up direct deposit with the law firm of Dewey, Cheatum and Howe. It will make it easier to pay the huge settlement after the lawsuit.

Chapter 28
Postal and Hybrid Shooters

Going to the post office meant going to mail a letter or to buy stamps. Unfortunately, in the late 80s and early 1990s the U.S. Postal Service experienced a marked increase in workplace violence. These attacks included: Edmond, OK 1986 - 14 dead; Ridgewood, NJ 1991 - 4 dead; Royal Oak, MI 1991 - 6 dead; Dearborn, MI 1993 - 2 dead; Dana Point, CA 1993 - 3 dead; Goleta, CA 2006 - 7 dead; Baker City, OR 2006 - 1 dead.

As a result, the U.S. Postal Service became synonymous with workplace violence and the term "Going Postal," described not just workplace violence at the U.S. Post Office, but transcended to describe all workplace incidents and those suffering emotional instability. One of the postal shootings started at home with the slaying of a spouse and another killed a resident at their apartment complex. The U.S. Postal Service recognizing the issue of workplace violence, decided in 1993, that they would hire 85 workplace environment analysts. Their job was to assess the environment at the post office and to try to reshape the culture within the post office to make it a kinder, gentler and a more empathetic workplace.

A hybrid case that occurred at a school but was primarily workplace violence was the case of Professor Amy Bishop at the University of Alabama in Huntsville in 2010. No students were targeted. While in a department meeting, Bishop pulled out a gun, killed three faculty members, and wounded three others. The nation was initially shocked that a college professor would "snap," but an examination of her background provided insight into her behavior.

In 1986, she was accused of killing her brother, which was initially described as an accidental discharge from a shotgun. She had already discharged the shotgun in her bedroom. Bishop came down the stairs as her mother was unloading groceries. She claimed to have had problems unloading the shotgun. Her mother asked her not to point it anywhere, at which time the shotgun discharged striking her brother, Seth and killing him. She fled to a local car lot, where she attempted to commandeer a vehicle, but she was apprehended at the scene. This case has been subsequently reopened. There had been allegations made that there was undue political influence in the investigation of the shooting.

In 1993, while Bishop was a student at Harvard University, Professor Rosenberg received a mail bomb upon returning from vacation. Both Amy Bishop and her husband became the primary suspects. The Bureau of Alcohol, Tobacco and Firearms was unable to link the Bishops forensically to the explosive device. The motivation was believed to have been the anticipation of a poor evaluation of Amy Bishop's performance under Dr. Rosenberg, but this motive was never proven.

In 2002, Amy Bishop had an altercation with a customer at a local IHOP. The customer had picked up the last child seat available at the restaurant. Bishop became enraged that there were no more chairs left and confronted the customer, demanding that she give Bishop the lone seat, saying, "Don't you know who I am? I am Professor Amy Bishop." The local police were summoned to her house on at least five different occasions concerning ongoing disputes with her neighbors. It was reported that when the Bishop family moved, the neighborhood had a celebration.

When she was hired in 2003 by the University of Alabama at Huntsville, her resume contained a number of discrepancies that were not discovered until after the shooting. Reports from those that were in a position to assess her job performance indicated that her track record of published papers and laboratory management skills were lacking. She was known to be difficult to get along with by graduate students who worked in the lab with her as well as faculty members. They described an environment of hostility.

In 2009, she was denied tenure by the university. In the academic world, being denied tenure has grave consequences and makes it extremely difficult to find a teaching position at another university level position. She retained an attorney and filed an EEO complaint against the university. Her appeals were subsequently denied. One professor who was familiar with Bishop stated that she was crazy, and he would avoid contact with her outside of mandated contact within the campus environment.

It is quite apparent that she understood that her career was coming to a screeching halt, and she would be relegated to teaching at a community college or high school. She obviously had displayed an inflated view of her self-worth, a lack of empathy toward others, and a sense of entitlement. As Dr. Jeannie Twenge wrote about those who suffer from narcissistic personality disorder, they often have difficulty confronting adversity and will respond in an aggressive manner.

Her tenure appeal denied, Professor Bishop most certainly felt her life was ending. When she extracted the handgun, she intended to exact revenge on those who were now ruining her life. One of her first targets of her gun was a professor who had voted to approve her tenure. After her gun jammed, she disposed of it in one bathroom while discarding her bloody sweater in another bathroom. Not the actions of a person who was insane. Her initial statement to her husband in jail expressed concern over who would help the children with their homework. There was no remorse for the victims or the campus community.

Chapter 29
Blue Killers

While teaching this class, I have been asked by a number of law enforcement officers why there are no occurrences of workplace violence in the law enforcement community. In fact, there are physical assaults that occur in the law enforcement community. In 2011, violence escalated to a shooting that occurred at an Immigration and Customs Enforcement office (now known as Homeland Security Investigations) of the U.S. Department of Homeland Security in California. The supervisor, Kevin Kozak, was counseling an employee named Zeke Garcia, who was experiencing stress in the workplace as well as at home. At some point during the meeting, Garcia pulled his handgun and began firing at the unarmed Kozak, who despite sustaining multiple gunshot wounds survived his attack. Perry Woo, another agent, drew his firearm and killed Garcia.

Stress is extremely high in the first responder community. I have become associated with the Franciscan Center Post Trauma and Education Retreat at the Franciscan Center in Tampa, Florida. This in-residence program is focused on a holistic approach of healing and training for those who may be encountering unbearable stress related to incidents associated with or stemming from their duties as first responders.

Another program, the West Coast Post Traumatic Retreat has had a significant impact on more than 600 individuals who have undergone treatment at the center in California. Two of the founders of the West Coast program, Dr. Joel Fay and Mike Pool were emotionally moved after one of their fellow officers in San Mateo, California, committed suicide by jumping off the Golden Gate Bridge. This inspired them to start the program.

Police officers deaths by suicide outnumber deaths in the line of duty as a result of gunshots by approximately a two to one ratio. These statistics could be altered if you included intentional suicides that were classified as accidents including single car crashes or firearms mishaps. Typically, we have not seen those suffering from PTSD engaging in long-term premeditated targeted violence.

While workplace violence can become more spontaneous than other forms of targeted violence, there still is a thought process in the preparation stage, in which the killer or attacker makes a conscious decision to bring a firearm into the workplace. In the law enforcement community, the firearm is expected within the environment. A label of PTSD for a police officer could be viewed in a similar context as the lack of tenure for a college professor.

Due to liability issues, many police departments are reluctant to allow officers who have been diagnosed with PTSD to return to an environment where they would be engaging in enforcement activity that may result in using deadly force or even less-than-lethal force. As a result, many officers returning to the line of duty may be reassigned to what is commonly referred to as the "rubber gun squad" or "bow and arrow squad.' For those officers at home going through the recovery stage of PTSD, they will often feel isolated and feelings of betrayal and despair will naturally creep into the conscious mind.

PTSD is curable and a manageable illness. I have witnessed significant restoration of stability to those suffering from this stress illness. With group therapy, meditation, yoga, exercise, diet, and Eye Movement Desensitization Reprocessing (EMDR), I have seen miraculous results and healing.

Quite often in police work, and in all areas of employment, we fall victim to "out of sight out of mind." There are times we intend to check on a friend or relative, and we get busy with our day-to-day activities, pushing off a potentially calming phone call to the next day, or week, or the next month. For others, the lack of conduct is more overt. They have made a conscious decision not to maintain contact with the individual under treatment. This cements the concept of isolation in the patient's mind. Suicide has now become an acceptable alternative to ending the misery.

I no longer consider blue on blue violence as being impossible. I would still like to believe that most law enforcement officers abide by the moral and ethical convictions of their jobs and would never consider shooting innocent victims. In 2012, a Las Vegas Metro Lieutenant, Hans Walter, killed his wife and five-year-old son before setting his house on fire and committing suicide. There were reports that Walters was under stress because of his wife's chronic pain associated with a deteriorating back and upcoming surgery.

Hindsight is always 20/20, but so often critical factors are overlooked or ignored. Preventing workplace violence can be like Nik Wallenda walking the tightrope across the Grand Canyon. The business world is often operating under the shadow of legal oversight, in which a long line of attorneys is willing to sue for wrongful termination of a troubled employee. Companies must weigh the costs and consequences of not managing problem employees correctly and the resulting workplace violence.

Chapter 30
School Shootings

In 1999, the Department of Education in response to the recent spate of school shootings, asked the Secret Service if they could use the same model utilized in assessing assassins, attackers and near-lethal attackers in identifying common characteristics of the school shooters. In 2001, the U.S. Secret Service, along with the Department of Education published the *Safe School Initiative Final Report*.

For those hoping for a profile to hand out to all teachers and school resource officers they would be disappointed. Those interested in a myopic view of school shooters, the profile identified those in the age ranging between 11 and 21 years of age, over three quarters were white, all of those analyzed in this study were male and the majority came from two-parent families. Forty-one percent socialized within the mainstream community of the school thus discrediting those who say that all school shooters are loners. The initial reporting of the Columbine shooters was that they were loners and ostracized. As David Cullen wrote in *Columbine*, and Jeff Kass wrote in *Columbine: A True Crime Story*, that many of these reports are disputed. The study reflected that few students suffered from poor grades. Essentially, the profile could be reduced to angry white male students.

The 100% male model was slightly altered in 2001 when Elizabeth Bush fired a single shot in the cafeteria of a Catholic school. Her shot wounded one female student. Most people are familiar with the book *Men are from Mars and Women are from Venus,* which documents the differences in gender personalities. Females are typically more emotional and social with their emotions. Despite the fact that there may be more drama between females in school, they are more willing to share their feelings, especially among intimate friends. Boys, on the other hand tend to be more internal with their feelings and less expressive. Thus, any anguish they experience is internalized and the despair becomes disruptive to their personality.

Although over 60% of the shooters came from two-parent families, you must examine the depth and stability of that relationship. Just because a mother and father are living under the same roof does not mean that everything is harmonious. It also provides no indication as to the level of engagement of the parents in their students' lives. Many of the parents were clueless about the despair or conduct of their children.

Society has experienced a significant paradigm shift in family relationships. In the 1960's, we frequently ate dinner as a family and gathered around the television set to watch the evening TV shows on one of only five channels. Today, families tend to be over stimulated with organized sports, activities, the Internet, video games, and TV. These activities have not been conducive to solidifying family interaction, and they have had a polar effect where many times family members are running in opposite directions or finding stimulation through electronic media. Parents are less likely to detect personality changes and behavioral changes in their students. Often, they are delegating supervision to third parties and electronic media. I don't mean to use the same paintbrush to paint all parents in the same way. Most parents are still very active and very engaged in their children's lives.

Despite the fact that both of the Columbine shooters lived in two-parent families, the parents were unaware of the extensive planning and bomb-making operations going on within their own home. I conducted an interview of a set of grandparents of a student whose parents were no longer in the picture. Unfortunately, the grandparents because of generational differences were unable to relate to their grandson and allowed him to spend countless hours entertaining himself in his own bedroom. The bedroom windows were blacked out with black burlap and other exotic decorations, which should have been alarming to most parents. This individual assembled silencers and discharged his silenced firearms into telephone books in his own bedroom. His grandparents were completely unaware of this activity.

Although his grandparents were devout in their religious beliefs, this student proclaimed to me that he was agnostic. When I asked how a 16-year-old came to that determination, he stated that he had prayed for ten different items and that when God failed to deliver on any of those ten prayer requests, he concluded that there might not be a God. I explained to him that this was not like Santa Claus where we went shopping through the Sears catalog and put ten items on your wish list, but I could see that he was not open to my input.

In this students computer hard drive was a cartoon of two students walking along and the caption read, "Going on a killing spree would make me feel better, but I will settle for an ice cream." When asked about this cartoon, he said he thought it was just funny and dismissed it as nothing of significance. For the investigator, you have to understand that a picture like that resonated with him, and I realized he identified with the feelings contained in the caption to a certain degree. This particular student, I believe, was probably on the path to committing school place violence, but because of the vigilance and observations of the school resource officer, the situation was mitigated and effectively managed by social services.

With school shootings, we often discuss the concept of whether or not an individual socialized in the mainstream. We have to examine the school social network and identify what the mainstream is. Every school is populated by many cliques. Membership in any clique is somewhat exclusive, although quite often all of us can recall our relationships as we shifted from one group influencer to the next. Depending upon the activity or time of the day, we might associate ourselves with the jocks, the tech nerds, the science geeks and so on. The bottom line is most of these individuals interacted with one of the cliques. As in the Columbine students, they participated in the drama club and attended sporting events at the school. They may not have been in a popular group, but they had friends.

When we examine the characteristics of the individual school shootings, approximately three quarters resulted in the death of one or more individuals. Although the shooters may initially focus on an individual target or a list of intended targets, once the first shots are fired, the target list often changes rapidly with the changing dynamic within the chaos and ensuing pandemonium of fleeing and screaming students and teachers. Although in many of the school shootings other students may have aided and abetted the shooters, the majority of killers were carried out by a single perpetrator. The shootings in Jonesboro Arkansas and Columbine were the exceptions where two students engaged in a rampage. Others attacks that have been successfully disrupted did include more than one attacker.

As with other targeted violence killers, the school shooters are no different in that they do not snap. We use the concept of snapping as an easy default setting when we see children arming themselves and engaging in mortal combat at school. It is difficult to comprehend that a teenager could possess such evil thoughts that would go undetected.

Most school shootings, as well as other targeted violence incidents, are well planned. For most of the school shooters, the planning took place over at least a month and in the case of the Columbine shooters, was in excess of a year. Most had acquired and practiced with weapons.

None took their training as seriously as the Columbine shooters. They spent many hours out in the woods discharging their cache of weapons and blasting through boxes of ammunition. I saw one video in which T-shirts were being hurled at Eric Harris as he attempted to duck or avoid the flying garments and continue firing his weapon. Michael Carneal stole his weapons. Andy Williams removed the weapons from his father's collection, and in a number of other cases, we have seen the weapons removed from a legally owned collection of firearms within their own home.

As with the other mass killers, the school shooters only directly threatened their targets in 17% of the cases. Perhaps due to their adolescence and the feeling of wanting to share, in 81% of the cases other students were aware of their murderous intentions. In these instances, other students often dismissed the statements as reckless talk or jokes and assumed the student was not serious about the threats.

In Santee, California, at least two adults overheard Andy Williams discussing his intent to out-Columbine-Columbine. One of the adults confronted Williams, and he dismissed it as a joke. The second adult dismissed it as reckless speech. Neither adult followed up on the statements or brought the conduct to the attention of authorities or Andy Williams' father. The 2001, Andy Williams shooting resulted in the killing of two individuals and the wounding of thirteen.

In Bethel, Alaska, Evan Ramsey had shared his intent with enough other students that many in anticipation of the shooting, had assembled on the mezzanine level overlooking the lobby entrance to the school. One student, who was aware of Ramsey's intended rampage, had brought her camera to take pictures. As in previous targeted violence shootings, there was a behavior of concern displayed by the individual students who engaged in school shootings.

Mental health illness has not been thoroughly examined in school shooters, but I believe it does have a significant factor. Many of these students were experiencing despair and depression. For high school students this period can be the most difficult time during their entire lives. Stephen King wrote in *Guns*, "...high school sucked when I went, probably sucks now. I tend to regard people who remember it as the best four years of their lives with caution and a degree of pity." In three quarters of the school shootings, the shooters were identified as suffering from despair and having experienced a major failure. We must stand in the flip-flops of the students and view the world from their eyes.

The students are seeking inclusion. There is extreme stress placed on them for performance grades, competition for inclusion in clubs, as well as the selection process and application process for postsecondary education. They are changing, both physically and psychologically. Add in the influence of hormones, and there is a lot going on inside the body and mind of a high school student. Remember a number of the shooters were also in middle school.

The typical onset of bipolar disorder and schizophrenia starts to manifest itself in the late teens or early 20s. That is not to say that in some instances there is an earlier onset of mental health deficiencies. Michael Carneal, age 14 was so paranoid that he felt it necessary to cover the air vents in the bathroom to avoid people spying upon him. Kip Kinkel, age 15 claimed that the voices in his head told him to kill.

Their frame of reference is much smaller than that of an adult. What we might consider an insignificant event could be construed as a significant event in the life a student. An adult, might be deeply affected by the termination from a job, enduring an acrimonious divorce, health problems, financial ruin resulting in foreclosure, and bankruptcy. A teenager might be deeply affected by breaking up with his girlfriend of two days, he failed a geometry test, and he did not get the job at the local grocery store. In the grand scheme of life, these events are very minor, but for a teenager, these are major and significant events.

In most school shootings, the majority of the victims were preselected. Over half of the violence was directed toward faculty and administrative staff, and three quarters were based upon a preconceived grievance against the intended victim. Half of the shooters had preselected more than one target. However, keep in mind as in the military, after the initial contact with the target, all plans go out the window.

After the shooting at Sandy Hook, there was great debate that went on concerning the violent influence of books, movies, and video games. When the study was conducted by the Secret

Service, the majority of students did not have access to video games. In today's world, a recent Pew Research study showed that 99% of teenagers play video games.

The influence of violent video games is a much debated issue. This is where parents must take a much more active role in abiding by the age recommendations for the users. Parents often delegate babysitting to the video game console and have limited knowledge of the violence displayed on the screen.

A study by Ohio State University of a small sampling of approximately seventy college students in France indicated a higher ratio of aggression in those who played violent video games in excess of three hours. Another study conducted by Stanford University of elementary school students in the San Francisco Bay Area concluded that aggressive tendencies were decreased by over 40% in those students who had completely unplugged from electronic media. I am not aware of any studies indicating how long aggression is harbored after the conclusion of playing of violent video games. I am sure that studies being conducted to determine the longevity of aggressive tendencies after unplugging.

Millions of children play violent video games every day and will not become school shooters. However, what I will say is that these violent video games are a virtual training simulator that enhances shooting abilities and potentially desensitizes the effect of blood and gore upon the participants. This process occurs as they strive to achieve a higher body count, resulting in a higher score and bonus round. I can say that for the majority of my police career, I spent time shooting holes through stationary white paper targets that had limited movement. I never received any training that resembled the quality of the virtual simulation portrayed in the violent video games available to our teenagers.

Grand Theft Auto V has just been released and as in the case of earlier versions of Call of Duty, sales have eclipsed one billion dollars. Despite the indiscriminate violence in the video game perpetrated on innocent people on the streets, in airports, and hospital emergency rooms, while playing these video distractions, parents will lineup to purchase these games for their children. The long-term effects of these games have not been proven, but the increased shooting proficiency of the players has been established.

Dave Grossman is one of the greatest advocates against violent video games and movies. Grossman, a former Army psychologist and instructor at West Point, is one of the foremost experts on the psychology of killing. His books, *On Killing*, and *Stop Teaching Our Kids How to Kill, On Killing*, and the audio CD, *After the Smoke Clears* are widely read and listened to by his devoted base. Grossman holds up the case of Michael Carneal as a poster boy for limiting violent video games. Carneal, who was 14 years of age, had never fired a firearm in his life, but he spent countless hours playing violent video games. He entered his school in Paducah, Kentucky, and fired eight times at a prayer group. Of his eight shots, he hit 100% of his targets. The eight shots included five resulting in head wounds. This percentage is extraordinary when you consider that the average experienced law enforcement officer engaged in a shoot out, which occurs at the range of seven yards, has only a 20% successful hit rate. In other words, one out of every five bullets fired by a trained experience police officer finds its target, where Michael Carneal was able to fire and hit his target with all eight of his shots.

Many people in society have found refuge in an alternative three-dimensional virtual world of Second Life. In this virtual forum, you assume the alternate identity of an avatar. Many socialize in these venues for various reasons. Second Life provides those that are socially awkward an opportunity to exist and socialize without the scrutiny of the real world. Rejection in the virtual world allows an escape to another venue. The same holds true for those that find sanctuary in chat rooms and message boards. I have known many people who are more comfortable in these virtual settings than in direct human interaction. Adam Lanza displayed an interest in chat rooms associated with guns.

Over a third of the students in the study by the Secret Service wrote about violence in writings. We have seen this continually displayed by students involved in school place violence. The key-locked diaries have now been primarily replaced with computer journals and to a lesser degree, Facebook, Twitter and other social media platforms. In-depth leakage of violent thoughts will not typically be shared in the social media arena nearly as much as writing to their own personal journal on the computer or in some cases a written journal. If the investigator comes across either a handwritten journal or a computer-generated journal, this can be a treasure trove of insight into the mindset of the student.

Eric Harris and Dylan Klebold provided a wide-open view of their mindset and diabolical plot in their journals. Writing assignments in English class can often provide insight. The Virginia Tech shooter sympathized with the Columbine shooters in a high school essay that caused his English teacher to become concerned, and resulted in a referral for counseling. Cho's writing assignments in college were disturbing enough to raise concern among the faculty.

As educators become more cognizant of disturbing writings, countless individuals have been identified as having behavioral issues. School counselors and parents are included in an effort to determine the behavioral basis of the writer. Not all violent essays written in English class are an indicator that the student is considering violence, but a dark or disturbing essay should give pause to the English teacher, who must carefully consider what is being written. I refer to this as literary leakage. We often feel more comfortable writing our emotions as opposed to verbalizing our thoughts to others.

Both the Virginia Tech shooter as well as Eric Klebold from Columbine submitted writings that essentially were a blueprint for their subsequent shootings. In the Cho situation, the English department had loudly sounded the alarm and practiced due diligence. The faculty must have felt lonely and betrayed with the lack of response.

In the spring semester of 2006, Seung Cho submitted a paper to Professor Bob Hicok. The paper provides insight into the mind of the killer a year before his murderous rampage. It tells the story of a morning in the life of Bud, "who gets out of bed unusually early...puts on his black jeans, a strappy black vest with many pockets, a black hat, a large dark sunglasses [sic] and a flimsy jacket...." At school he observes "students strut inside smiling, laughing, embracing each other....A few eyes glance at Bud but without the glint of recognition. I hate this! I hate all these frauds! I hate my life....This is it....This is when you damn people die with me...." He enters the nearly empty halls "and goes to an arbitrary classroom...." Inside "(e)veryone is smiling and laughing as if they're in heaven on- earth, something magical and enchanting about all the people's intrinsic nature that Bud will never experience." He breaks away and runs to the bathroom "I can't do this....I have no moral right...." The story continues by relating that he is approached by a "gothic girl." He tells her "I'm nothing. I'm a loser. I can't do anything. I was going to kill every god damn person in this damn school, swear to god I was, but I...couldn't. I just couldn't. Damn it I hate myself!" He and the "gothic girl" drive to her home in a stolen car. "If I get stopped by a cop my life will be forever over. A stolen car, two hand guns, and a sawed off shotgun." At her house, she retrieves "a .8 caliber automatic rifle and a M16 machine gun." The story concludes with the line "You and me. We can fight to claim our deserving throne."

Professor Bob Hicok was concerned about the story. He sent Cho two separate requests to meet and discuss this submission, but Cho never complied with the request. Hicok discussed Cho's behavior with other faculty. Professor Hicok decided to keep Cho in the class as opposed to deferring the problem student to another teacher. Hicok gave Cho a D+ grade in the class.

Dylan Klebold's English teacher was alarmed enough to speak directly to him and notify his mother. His mother denied ever viewing the actual paper, explaining that the teacher did not have the paper with him. The teacher explained the paper was "disturbing." The Klebolds encouraged the teacher to share the paper with the guidance counselor. Susan Klebold reported she never received any follow-up from the teacher or counselor. If an English teacher notified me of a disturbing essay written by my child, I am going to ask some hard questions of the teacher and my child. When confronted by the English teacher, Dylan explained that it was just a story.

What was so disturbing about the story? Written in the first person of a bystander, Klebold described a 6'4" villain clad in a black trench coat, carrying a duffle bag along with an arsenal of guns and ammunition. Klebold would resemble the same image. The observer spoke of a sense of seeing the killer's anger growing. He described the laugh of the man. "The laugh would have made Satan cringe in Hell." The killer pulled out a detonator and exploded diversionary devices to draw the police away. The assault leaves nine high school "preps" dead. The last sentence read, "I understand his actions."

I'm sure if you went back to the writings of Stephen King while he was a student in high school, some if not many would be considered disturbing and by today's standards would probably warrant mandatory counseling and notification of his parents. I always stress the use of a holistic approach to threat assessments. Although a single English essay should raise a red flag, it should be taken into context and viewed in totality of other behavioral displays.

Speaking of the written word and Stephen King, one of his books has been often attributed to school shooters. *Rage*, was authored under his pen name of Richard Bachman. Michael Carneal the Paducah, Kentucky, shooter was a reader of *Rage,* as was another shooter, Barry Loukaitis, who killed two at his school in Moses Lake, Washington. Loukaitis entered his classroom and stated, "This sure beats algebra class doesn't it?" This quote has often been attributed to *Rage*, but the closest line to this is when the main character Charlie Decker said, "This sure beats panty raids." Through King's research, he identified two additional students who held their classroom hostage and displayed an interest in *Rage,* which is a fictional account of Charlie Decker a school shooter. Decker is disciplined for striking a teacher and in addition to killing two teachers, the shooter takes his algebra class hostage.

Stephen King wrote *Rage* as a junior in high school but it was not published until many years and many successful books later. The title of the book when he penned it was *Getting it On*. Was this underlying violence in the story much different from what Klebold or Cho wrote? Probably not. I will say that *Rage* was much better written, longer, and drilled down deeper into the psychology and frustrations of many students. I can see how anyone who attended high school could identify with Charlie Decker. You have to examine the entirety of the circumstances. Asking Mom and Dad to get under the hood to examine their child's intentions is a huge start. Too often, the parents become defenders for their offspring and fail to listen to the warning signs. Had King submitted this book in high school today, he would have been expelled and locked up in an asylum.

Although King does not feel that the book influenced the individuals or was a factor in the shootings, he did not want his work being attributed to the school violence. He asked his publisher to allow the book to go out of print. King did see the book as a possible "accelerant." As King correctly documented, these individuals all carried some significant baggage and had travelled far down the path of violence, with or without reading his work.

Another book that has been read by many shooters has been *Catcher in the Rye*. Many of them identify with the loneliness and isolation experienced by the protagonist, Holden Caulfield, who rails against the phonies in the world. *Rage* and *Catcher in the Rye* are not contributing factors in school place violence, however they both feature an emotionally troubled youth with who the reader can identify with and receive affirmation for the emotions that he or she is experiencing.

After the Aurora and the Sandy Hook shootings, there was an initial debate into the influence of violence in our culture, and specifically the influence of movies. Dave Grossman advocates that there is a desensitization of the viewers watching violent movies. As the audience watches indiscriminate killing and violence on the screen, they are often sharing these images with their social circle as well as munching on popcorn and popping Junior Mints. As a result, there is a positive reinforcement to the graphic images being displayed on the screen. Quentin Tarantino, who has a history of directing, producing, and writing violent movies, was questioned after Sandy Hook concerning the influence of violent movies. His curt response was that there has been violence in the theater going back to the day of Shakespeare. I would agree with this assessment however, we did not have school shootings in the 1500s. While millions of moviegoers and TV viewers watch violent images on a daily basis, very, very, few will ever be influenced to pursue an avenue of violence.

The real problem comes from an unhealthy obsession with watching the same movie repeatedly. The Columbine shooters were so enamored by the brutal violence portrayed in the movie *Natural Born Killers*, that they code-named their attack "NBK." It should be noted that Quentin Tarantino was credited as a writer of the screenplay for this movie. The movie, *Basketball Diaries*, starring Leonardo DiCaprio has also been attributed to Loukaitis and Carneal. In the movie, a dream scene portrays Jim Carroll, the heroin-addicted character wearing a dark trench coat and shooting fellow students with a shotgun.

Parents should be able to identify this unhealthy obsession and mitigate the fixation. Parental intervention on movie selection was clearly not the case with the Columbine shooters. We know that the movie *Taxi Driver* heavily influenced John Hinckley. There is also evidence that the Luby's cafeteria shooter, George Hennard was influenced by the movie *The Fisher King* in which Robin Williams plays a radio shock jock whose insensitive comments inadvertently motivates a fan to engage in mass murder at a bar. Kip Kinkel, the Thurston High killer was enamored by the modern version and violent remake of *Romeo and Juliet*. The soundtrack was set to continuous play when police arrived at his home and found the bodies of his parents.

Many studies have been conducted that will provide evidence for advocates on both sides concerning the influence of violence in the media. I do not intend to march off into those tall weeds. I believe it does provide some investigative insight as to what the subject's favorite movies are, and what he or she likes most about the movie, and how often he or she views it. The questions have to be asked delicately to avoid showing your hand.

The same holds true for music interests. You can always ask the subject what kind of music he or she enjoys, favorite songs and what do he or she likes about that particular song. If you are not familiar with the lyrics of the song, you can locate most of them on the Internet. I would caution against getting wrapped around the axle of one particular song which an individual is enamored and displays an unhealthy obsession.

I was preparing to interview a young student for threatening statements she made at school. He brother informed me that she had an interest in a German band. I researched the group, and their songs, and listened to a few. There was nothing alarming in the lyrics, but I used my new knowledge to establish rapport with the girl.

Not too long ago, I was surprised when giving this class when one of my students brought to my attention that a recent song called *Pumped Up Kicks* contained lyrics about shooting at a school. I admitted that I enjoyed that song and had downloaded it to my iPod, but had never paid attention to the lyrics. Therefore, it might behoove to ask what the lyrics say and if he or she pays attention to the words of the songs. The subject's music interests should be taken into context with the larger behavioral threat assessment approach.

Chapter 31
Bullying

Bullying has become a huge buzzword in the academic field. When I start this section of my class, I will typically ask the students how many were bullied when they were in school. The overwhelming majority will raise their hands. I would say that since the first days under the roof of the first schoolhouse in Boston in 1635, bullying has been taking place. Most of us have encountered some sort of bullying, and we were able to cope with the mistreatment and move on. The ability to cope with incessant bullying is dependent upon our family and social support systems. Those with higher narcissistic tendencies also have more difficulty dealing with the adversity of bullying.

In the days prior to the Internet, most bullying was confined to the school day. Now, bullying has expanded to cyberspace and impacting the victims being tormented in social media and through direct access on their cell phones. Victims of bullying suffer through tremendous humiliation and a lowering of self-esteem. Depression is closely correlated with those who are victims of continuous bullying campaigns. In the Secret Service study, 71% of the shooters claimed that they had been the victims of bullying. It was initially alleged that the Columbine shooters also suffered at the hands of bullies. This has since been debated. Although, they may have been picked on by the jocks, there is evidence that both also shared abuse and picked on others. This theory is supported by some of the writings of both Eric Harris and Dylan Klebold, who made references to picking on the "freshman's and fags."

Dr. William Pollock of Harvard University, author of *Real Boys: Rescuing Our Sons from the Myths of Boyhood,* has extensively studied the impact of bullying specifically on boys. His studies have led him to coin the term "boy code" which describes the inherent personality of most boys to internalize their emotions. Many boys are sad, lonely, and confused, although they may appear tough on the exterior. In interviews of previous school shooters, they often shared the feeling that they had no other choice and that they had no one to talk about their feelings. A mentoring, influential adult was missing within their sphere of influence. Pollock noted the importance of a maternal influence needed as a stabilizing force and to help mitigate the humiliating feelings experienced by bullying victims.

Schools have become much more aware of the negative impact of bullying on their student population, and many have attempted to address this issue. This includes having teachers that now stand out in the hallways as a force multiplier to be the eyes and ears and to help guard against bullying. New architectural designs have removed the doors to bathrooms to decrease the privacy for bullying attacks. Bullying will never be eliminated, but it is essential for school administrators to strongly enforce discipline and document cases of bullying.

Dr. Pollock estimates that every day, approximately 160,000 students will call in sick to school to avoid the effects of bullying. I have encountered victims of extreme bullying, and I can tell you that they have been tormented by their aggressors. They have difficulty sleeping, eating, socializing and they can suffer from deep despair, leading to the depths of depression. Parents should be interacting with their children to monitor these mood swings and to identify negative emotions that can adversely affect not only their psychological health but their physical health as well.

In 2013, twelve-year-old Rebecca Sedwick, jumped to her death in Polk County, Florida, after being tormented on social media. In 2010, Phoebe Prince was an Irish immigrant who had settled with her family in South Hadley, Massachusetts, where she attended high school. She had a fragile personality, which was further damaged by an incessant campaign of bullying. After many grueling days at school, she hung herself in her bedroom closet. In 2006, Megan Taylor Meier, a Missouri teenager, also hung herself after suffering from cyber-bullying. The horrible aspect of this case was the bullying was initiated by an adult.

The National Coalition for Parent Involvement in Education, the Center for Law and Education and the Center for Family and Community Connections with Schools all agree with the Parent Teacher Association concerning the importance of parental involvement. The PTA reported, "The most accurate predictors of achievement in school are not family income or social status, but the extent to which the family creates a home environment that encourages learning…"

Parents may not be able to prevent their children from being victims of bullying, but they can provide a nurturing and loving sanctuary for their children. Parental involvement is essential to your child's development. There are hundreds of good books on parenting to find solutions. I would advocate being engaged and involved in your children's lives. Have scheduled family fun nights, joint activities and chats whenever possible. Encourage children to talk about themselves, their friends and teachers. Ask if a younger sibling or a neighbor would enjoy their school. Disconnecting from the electronic world for a time helps, especially on commutes to activities. Many moms and dads delegate supervision to the surrogate parent of electronics.

In the aftermath of the Sandy Hook massacre, Richard Novia, the teacher of the audio video club was interviewed by PBS. Novia said he noticed Adam Lanza's lack of social skills and diminutive nature was a likely target of bullies. This teacher attempted to be a positive influence for Adam and to be a sort of guardian angel looking out for his best interest. I know of another high school teacher who provided refuge in his classroom prior to the start of the school day for two students who were being victimized by bullying. This was despite assertions by some fellow teachers that he must maintain neutrality and not become involved. That teacher demonstrated significant character and moral judgment in providing security to those who were the weakest.

Teachers have one of the toughest jobs in America. Alex Rodriguez, the now disgraced New York Yankees slugger, made more money every time he stepped to the plate, regardless of whether he struck out or hits a home run, than a teacher makes in year's salary. Alex Rodriguez's task was to hit a baseball safely thirty percent of the time. Teachers are responsible for molding and educating our future leaders. Unlike baseball players, teachers cannot tolerate a thirty percent success rate.

The days of having allies outside of the classroom have greatly diminished in today's society. Administrators often fail to provide the proper support expected of teachers. When a child is selected for discipline by a teacher, many parents are often running down the street to the Law offices of Dewey Cheatham and Howe. When I went to school, I would have been terrified of being disciplined by my teacher, and fearful that my parents would be notified of my lack of judgment. Many students today do not have these concerns, as they feel emboldened by assertions of their parents that "my child can do no wrong and how dare that teacher embarrass my student."

One episode illustrates this point. A student arrived late to the classroom only to find that the door was locked. The student then decided to drop his pants and moon the class through the window in the door. The students, of course, responded in disruptive laughter, but the teacher saw little humor in this act of disobedience. The student was taken to the principal and suspended. The parents, feeling that this could have an adverse impact on the student's future admission to college, quickly sought legal counsel in an attempt to alter the disciplinary action. I hate to keep invoking "I remember when...," but as a student, if I conducted myself in that manner, I can assure you I would have been grounded for a minimum of 30 days by my parents. My parents would have insisted that I apologize verbally to the entire class and write an apology to that teacher. Times have changed, and we just have to accept these changes for good or bad.

Chapter 32
College Killers

In April 2007, the entire nation was riveted by the news coverage of the massacre at Virginia Tech University in Blacksburg, Virginia. We were horrified to see that 32 innocent college students and faculty had been slain and an additional 19 wounded at the murderous hands of Seung-Hui Cho. Although this horrific act was shocking, there were numerous pre-incident indicators that should have identified Cho's aberrant behavior and steps could have been taken to mitigate and manage his behavior.

Cho moved from Korea as a young child. His parents worked in a dry cleaner business in Centerville Virginia. When I was assigned to the intelligence division in Washington DC, I lived in Centerville, Virginia, just a few miles away from the London Town Townhouses that Cho's family occupied. I used the cleaners that his parents were employed at and had I remained in that area, my children would've attended school with Cho.

In high school, Cho displayed early warning signs of aberrant behavior. He authored a disturbing paper on the massacre of Columbine High School. The teacher contacted his parents and he was referred for mental health counseling. He was diagnosed with selective mutism, which essentially indicates that he only talked when he wanted to speak. He was also diagnosed with major depression single episode and was prescribed antidepressant medications.

Cho exhibited evidence of antisocial behavior, in which he appeared to be more comfortable in a role of isolation as opposed to interacting with other students and faculty. He ate alone in the cafeteria and appeared to have no friends. The high school provided private testing for him as well as continued health counseling. He appeared to respond positively to the clinical treatment and was weaned off his antidepressants. Although there were some allegations that he was the victim of bullying, there was no evidence to support these claims. His sister advised that she was unaware of any bullying that occurred. One should not be surprised that some students might have made fun of his awkward social skills.

In 2003, Cho enrolled in Virginia Tech University, against the advice of both his family and his school counselor. They were concerned with the distance from his family, as well as the anxiety expected from a socially isolated student living in a large college campus environment. Cho was insistent on his selection of colleges and moved to Blacksburg, Virginia.

His first two years at Virginia Tech University appeared to be unremarkable. In 2005, he changed his major from computer technology to English. The puzzling aspect of this selection is that Cho struggled with English as his second language. He appeared to have found a newly unexplored passion in writing. This new-found passion would become quickly frayed as a manuscript that he had completed was rejected by either a publisher or agent. His sister asked to read the manuscript, and he refused her request. His sister noticed a behavioral change after this rejection. Even most successful authors today have suffered countless rejections from both publishers as well as literary agents. For someone who is delicate or has fragile self-esteem, this lone submission rejection could be devastating.

In the fall of 2005, Cho's behavior became more bizarre. In an effort to be more inclusive, his roommates invited him to accompany them to a female student's dorm room. From all accounts,

Cho had limited interaction during this social meeting, but at some point, he pulled out a small pocketknife and began stabbing the carpet. This is not the best way to make an impression. He also assumed an alter ego of "?". He changed his Facebook profile picture to one displaying "?". One can only assume that he was projecting an uncertain self-identity. According to his roommates, he fabricated a girlfriend who he called Jelly and who travelled in space. One day, he restricted access of one of his roommates to the dorm. He said he was making out with Jelly. As in high school, he was non-conversational and ate alone. He essentially placed himself in a self-imposed isolation and made no attempts to integrate himself into the campus community or social activities.

The noted poet and English faculty member, Nikki Giovanni, noticed that attendance in her class was beginning to diminish. She asked some students about the lack of attendance and discovered that the students were concerned about the bizarre behavior of Cho. He was attending class wearing hats, sunglasses and at times a Bedouin headscarf while surreptitiously taking photographs of other students with his cell phone camera from underneath his desk. In response to another student's essay, he vocalized, "I hope y'all burn in hell for mass murdering and eating all those little animals." Students became increasingly alarmed at his behavior and had stopped attending the class. Professor Giovanni demanded his removal from the class.

In an effort to mediate and intervene, Dr. Lucinda Roy, who was the chairperson of the English department, decided to intervene and reach out to Cho. He responded with an angry two-page letter ascribing blame to others. When he did appear in her office, he was wearing sunglasses, and Roy described him as displaying signs of depression, being lonely and troubled. She asked him to remove his glasses. He reluctantly complied. She said that his removal of the sunglasses revealed a naked distress. He claimed that his writings should only be construed as a joke. This is consistent with Dylan Klebold who dismissed his disturbing essay as "just a story."

Dr. Roy was concerned enough for her own personal safety that she informed her assistant that if Roy spoke the name of a now deceased professor, that this utterance would be the alert signal to notify and summon authorities to her office. Dr. Roy offered to meet Cho and to tutor him for the remainder of the semester. Dr. Roy notified the Dean of Students, judicial affairs, the Care Team, and requested a psychiatric review of his writings. The Care Team was developed to coordinate a response for troubled students and to arrange and provide necessary services to assist with conflict. There is no indication that the Care Team took any initiative or follow-up with these troubling events.

Dr. Roy emailed updates to administration voicing her concerns of Cho's depression in his writings that centered on murder and abuse of authority. She attempted to make referrals for mental health counseling for Cho, but he resisted those efforts. Despite the fact that he continued to wear reflective sunglasses, Dr. Roy introduced Cho to the works of Dickinson and Yeats in an effort to expose him to works that embraced empathy toward others. Roy evaluated his writing and Cho received an A in the class.

A female student alleged that she received an inappropriate email from Cho. The Virginia Tech Police Department was notified and made contact with Cho. The female student refused to press charges. His conduct was reported to judicial affairs; however, there was no follow-up. Cho apparently did call the Cook Counseling Center triage but apparently failed to follow up. A resident adviser notified campus housing through email of continued inappropriate instant messages sent to a student. In another instance, Cho, wearing a disguise with sunglasses and hat, appeared at a females dorm room and notified her that "I am '?'" I can only imagine the horror of the student as she slammed the door.

Another complaint was made with the Virginia Tech Police Department over the instant messages sent to the female. Cho failed to keep an appointment with Cook Counseling Center. In the post-incident review, many of the records pertaining to Cho were missing or were never maintained because of sloppy record keeping. A psychiatrist contacted by Dr. Roy, concerning Cho's behavior prior to the shooting, recalled the telephone conversation but had limited memory and apparently took no notes.

The female student, the same one who Cho had initially visited with his dorm mates and stabbed her carpet, began to receive instant messages and Facebook posts from Cho. Outside of each dorm room were small white boards in which students could leave messages for one another. On the white board outside of her room she found a quotation from Romeo and Juliet which stated, "*By a name I know not how to tell thee who I am, My name, dear saint is hateful to myself, Because it is an enemy to thee, Had I it written, I would tear the word.*

The Virginia Tech Police Department was notified and warned Cho of his inappropriate communications. This initiated an email stream between residence life and judicial affairs, but again there appears to be no action taken. After the police department left his dorm, he sent an instant message to his suitemate, threatening suicide. The roommate alerted Virginia Tech Police Department again. They responded, and he was transported to New River Valley Community Mental Health for an assessment.

Seung-Hui Cho was deemed to be a danger to himself or to others. A magistrate was contacted by telephone, as was standard procedure, and a temporary detention order was issued. In the state of Virginia, a commitment through a temporary detention order dictates that the patient must be assessed within four hours after admission by a clinician, and cannot be kept for more than 48 hours without being provided judicial oversight.

Cho was transported to Carilon St. Albans Psychiatric Hospital. His mental health assessment at the hospital detected no homicidal or suicidal tendencies. He was diagnosed as having a mood disorder of nonspecific origin. He was seen by the judicial officer and despite the absence of police reports or the initial triage assessments from Virginia Tech, Cho was released with an outpatient referral to Cook Counseling Center. His defense attorney for the judicial hearing was representing four individuals that morning, and had no individual recollection of Cho. This is indicative of the normalcy of the mental health system in

America today. Most facilities are understaffed, under budgeted, and overcrowded. It almost takes on a factory-like environment of quickly trying to process patients in and out. Only the most dangerous individuals who can be identified are kept in seclusion.

For the third time in fifteen days, Cook Counseling Center telephone triaged Cho. There was never any follow-up, and once again there was a lack of records which is primarily blamed on the lack of funding and cutbacks. Despite the ongoing mental health instability of Cho, his family was never notified of his bizarre behavior. They apparently spoke to him on a weekly basis on Sundays. Those telephone calls apparently provided no insight into his personality struggles. After the shootings, the parents said that had they known about his mental health commitment, they would have removed their son for the semester and obtained mental health counseling for him back in Centerville, Virginia. They had previously provided him counseling while in high school. One can only assume that had they been provided the opportunity, his parents would have been looking out for the best interest of their son's mental health and obtained the necessary counseling.

In the spring of 2006, Cho submitted the disturbing fiction paper to Professor Hicok, which I discussed earlier, concerning the literary leakage that can occur in the story he wrote about *A Day in the Life of Bud*. Professor Carl Bean, another English teacher opined that Cho's form of speech was so soft that he used his speech as a tool to manipulate power. Bean described him as being a poor writer. Cho submitted a paper on Macbeth and serial killers. Professor Bean dismissed Cho from his class and had a loud confrontation with Cho concerning his removal.

In the fall 2006 semester, Professor Lisa Norris was disturbed enough by the writings of Cho that she notified the Dean of Liberal Arts, who claimed that Cho had no previous record, despite Dr. Roy assertions to the contrary. Professor Norris volunteered to accompany Cho to a mental health counselor, but Cho refused the offer. In another incident, Dr. Edward Falco received two plays that were so laced with profanity and violence that other students refused to read them or provide input. Dr. Falco also conferred with other professors concerning the ongoing alarming behavior of Cho.

The final Virginia Tech report singled out the failure of the Care Team to intervene on an obvious display of aberrant behavior and to include other administrative offices because of an overly complex interpretation of HIPPA/FERPA. It also concluded that the continued rejection of his English passion by both fellow students and authorities caused him a great deal of anxiety and despair.

In the fall of 2007, Cho began making his gun purchases and practicing at an indoor pistol range honing his skills that would be ultimately used in the bloody massacre. He also began recording his manifesto. One part of his manifesto provides insight into Cho's thought process. While he was unable to verbalize to others, he could talk to a camera. He said, "*You have vandalized my heart, raped my soul and torched my conscience. You had a hundred billion chances and ways to have avoided today*," he said. "*But you decided to spill my blood. You forced me into a corner and gave me only one option. The decision was yours. Now you have blood on your hands that will never wash off.*"

Prior to the murderous rampage, there were a number of bomb threats at various buildings on campus. It is unclear or unknown whether these calls were made by Cho to assess and monitor the response by law enforcement authorities. There was a report of the doors to Norris Hall being chained, which would indicate pre-incident conduct.

On the Sunday before the shootings, Cho had his weekly phone conversation with his parents. He provided no indication that he was troubled or considering a path to violence. The next morning and the day of the killings, his suitemates observed him brushing his teeth and applying acne cream. Both of these activities would be bizarre for someone that was contemplating mass murder and suicide.

For many of these shooters, they have a moment of clarity and look at the actual act as being cathartic. The autopsy of Adam Lanza showed no evidence of alcohol or drugs in his toxicology report. Perhaps he needed to be on prescribed medications and was not. Eric Harris was alcohol free and had a therapeutic level of Fluvoxamine, an antidepressant drug. Dylan Klebold's autopsy indicated no substances. Cho was also drug and alcohol free. One exception was the University of Central Florida (UCF) shooter, James Seevakumaran, whose blood alcohol content was three times the legal limit.

At 7:15 A.M. on that fateful April morning, Emily Hilsher and Ryan Clark were killed. No association has ever been established between Cho and Emily. Ryan Clark was a resident adviser in Emily's dorm building. It appears that Clark was either visiting with Emily or responding to a disturbance. A friend of Emily's found the two dead students and alerted authorities. The Virginia Tech campus, the City of Blacksburg, and the surrounding area is primarily rural and free of violent crime. Murders are almost nonexistent in this area and the homicide of two students on a quiet campus became big news. The initial focus of the investigation was one based on a domestic motivation of a jealous boyfriend of Emily's. This is primarily due to the fact that Emily's boyfriend owned a gun. An alert was put out in an attempt to locate Emily's boyfriend, and all efforts were focused on this theory of the investigation.

Shortly after 9 A.M., Cho mailed his manifesto to NBC and a letter to Professor Carl Bean concerning his removal from the class and subsequent confrontation. At 9:26 A.M., the first email was sent to students by the policy group that notified them that there had been a shooting at a dormitory. At 9:40 A.M., Cho entered Norris Hall and began shooting. One minute later, Blacksburg Police Department received the first 911 call and immediately notified the Virginia Tech Police Department.

Within five minutes after the first shots were fired, police arrived at Norris Hall. Because of the heightened alert status over the shooting in the dormitory earlier that morning, a number of blended tactical teams from various agencies responded quickly to the scene. They attempted to gain entry into Norris Hall, but the doors were all sealed and locked with chains. The police were unable to breach these doors. They found a fourth door that would provide entry into a janitor's closet. Utilizing a shotgun-breaching round, police entered the janitor's closet, which then gave them access into the building's interior. It was at this time that Cho ended his killing spree and committed suicide. The entire incident lasted no more than 11 minutes from the first shot until the final shot of suicide.

By all indications, the police response to Norris Hall was appropriate and quick. They faced a number of challenges due to the chained doors and narrow first floor windows. The windows located on the second floor, which were 19 feet above the ground, would have slowed the process of entry. The tactical teams would have had to respond with fire personnel and/or ladders to access second floor windows. They did not have bolt cutters, which could have been used on the chains, but this would have been an unanticipated scenario in a school environment. Initial reports indicated that Cho was utilizing multiple weapons and initially provided an impression that there might be multiple shooters. The tactical teams cautiously cleared each and every room in Norris Hall. The only criticism of the tactical entry into Norris Hall was the limited communications between the tactical teams and officers posted on the perimeter. This can be expected, as tactical operators are focused on a chaotic situation, dealing with at least one gunman, and ensuring their own safety. There was also a great deal of unknown: the officers did not know who the attacker(s) was. This was a similar situation to Columbine where arriving police officers were faced with a chaotic situation and a stream of students attempting to escape.

Lessons learned from the victim's were that the response is consistent through all school shootings. That is to barricade doors utilizing whatever means possible. All the students who were able to secure the doors survived. One group was deposited by a professor in a storage room, and they all survived the carnage. The professor did not, as he went to investigate and was subsequently killed by Cho. The report cited the calm demeanor displayed by the students as a whole, and that no one acted irrationally. Some were able to escape out of the second floor windows and dropped out to the grass below. Others were unable to do so, as there was a cement courtyard below them and in all probability a jump would have resulted in injury and impeded their departure to safety. Some of the students played dead and apparently, they were ignored by Cho's gunfire. Some students sustained multiple gunshot wounds. This could have been the result of Cho's rapid firing.

Virginia Tech University was heavily criticized for their lack of communication within the campus community. On the day of the shooting, the emergency notification systems on the campus were limited. The school primarily relied upon an email notification system. The associate vice president for university relations had the authority and ability to distribute campus communitywide email alerts. The problem with email alerts is that quite often emails are either not checked on a routine basis, or are ignored. Having spoken to students in college settings, they have often complained about being spammed by university email communications. The students begin to ignore emails from the college campus. I have seen this in some cases, when with the best intentions, overzealous communicators hit the send key all too often and as a result, their messages are ignored.

The mindset of college students, or for that matter, even high school students, is they become consumed with their own world and their frame of reference is extremely narrow. The vast majority are not overly consumed with geopolitical forces or world events that are occurring outside of their individualized world. Beside the fact that college communications can sometimes become overwhelming in volume, they can also be viewed by the students as a nagging parent and quickly dismissed. Students live in a cloistered environment on campus that tends to promote peace and sanctuary from the outside world. Despite the efforts of most universities to push out emergency notifications to the campus community, there will always be students who either ignore the communications or are perhaps in a cone of silence in a lecture hall or the library, cramming for an all-too-important exam, and as a result, have unplugged from the electronic world.

It was surprising to hear that one of the leading universities in the field of engineering and computers was lacking a robust emergency notification system, but there are limits to mass communication. At that time, a high school that my children attended had such a notification system. Most students entering the university are provided an opportunity to participate in the emergency notification system. There are two problems with this concept. One is that students will on occasion change telephone numbers and will rarely consider updating their contact information with the emergency notification system. The other is because of the fact that some cell providers charge an individual fee for text messages, the college cannot force compliance and participation with the emergency notification system and as such, provides an option to not participate.

The ability to push out a voicemail messages can be challenging due to volume restrictions. Virginia Tech was in the process of installing an audible speaker system, but the project had not been completed. Most university campuses have installed such audible notification systems. One challenge in most university environments is the inability to communicate directly with each and every classroom through a public address system. While most high schools have a system, many colleges do not. This public address system was instrumental in alerting classroom teachers at Sandy Hook that a crisis was in progress and to take emergency action.

The public announcement system must now differentiate between fire, hazardous material spills, or armed intruder. Hospitals utilize a system of code words, such as code red for a fire, code blue for the crash cart, doctor quickstep for security. Whatever code words you use, must be known to all faculty, staff and security. A teacher who observes an armed intruder in the parking lot could call Mr. Danger in the faculty lot. This alerts everyone to take action and lockdown the school.

One of the largest deficiencies in the Virginia Tech emergency notification system was despite the fact that the campus police had the authority to send an emergency message, they lacked the technical means to deliver the content. At that time, only two individuals had that ability to send campus wide notifications, the associate vice president for university relations, and the director of news and information. The police had no access to the alerting system. When the shooting occurred, the protocol for sending emergency messages was dependent upon convening the policy group and deliberation of the content to be disseminated. The policy group was comprised of nine vice presidents and support staff. The campus police was not a member of the policy group.

University campuses are controlled by academics and often they do not hold the campus police in high regard. The campus police are often viewed as a tolerable and necessary evil. There is an ongoing conflict between many campus police departments and the university bureaucracy concerning safety protocols and enhanced security systems. In 2013, at the Entz Elementary School in Mesa, Arizona, a police officer was asked by the principal not to wear his uniform and gun while dropping his daughter off at school. This story illustrates the disconnect that can occur between administration and law enforcement.

The University of South Florida located in Tampa, Florida, has seventeen entrances to its campus. When the school became criticized for a growing crime problem, school security was examined. The understaffed and underfunded campus police department was augmented with unarmed private security guards. When discussions were held concerning the closure of some of the entrances onto the campus during the overnight hours, in an effort to monitor and control access to student populations, the discussion failed to generate enough support to enact. Eighty percent of crime on college campuses is perpetrated by students.

Fortunately, the Virginia Tech Police Department was well trained, professional, and armed. They integrated training with local departments, which increased their efficiency and response to the crisis on April 16, 2007. Their quick reaction no doubt impacted Cho's ability to carry on his rampage without the threat of resistance. He committed suicide once they gained entry to Norris Hall.

There is still a debate in institutions of higher education concerning arming their security staff. In the state of Florida, all public institutions have an armed police force that is comprised of certified law enforcement officers with arrest powers. In May 2013, Rhode Island voted to allow their public universities the option to arm the campus police. The faculty was not supportive of this measure. This hubris might have been different if they had experienced the carnage at Virginia Tech. Princeton University is another large school that relies upon a highly trained but unarmed security force. According to the Bureau of Justice Statistics, in the 2004 school year, 67% of all institutions of higher education (IHE) had armed security. According to the National Campus Security and Safety Survey, 75.9 % of the responding four-year institutions reported having an armed security force.

While being interviewed by a private institution, my blunt assertion was not well received. During the interview, I was asked what my position was on armed versus unarmed security. I stated that the security apparatus for the school was the first line of defense for the school community and that if they were not armed, they would merely be witnesses and note-takers to the event. I meant no disrespect to the dedicated and courageous security officers.

In July 2013, the campus police at the University of Washington conducted a high-risk traffic stop of a suspected stolen vehicle. The driver, a self-avowed anarchist, was armed with a hunting rifle, a shotgun, Molotov cocktails and body armor. I am glad the officers were armed as opposed to pointing flashlights and pepper spray. I admire the courage of unarmed campus security officers, who routinely place themselves in harm's way to protect the college community.

In 1992, at Simon's Rock College, Wayne Lo engaged in one of the earliest shootings on a college campus. A package had been intercepted by the campus postal service. The parcel originated from Charter Arms, a gun manufacturer, and it was addressed to the student, Wayne Lo. This package was of concern to the university staff and deliberations took place as to the proper procedure in maintaining safety on the campus. There appeared to be a lack of concise communication at the meeting, and the package was subsequently delivered to the student. He opened the shipment in the privacy of his dorm room.

The resident adviser attempted to confront Wayne Lo, but the student invoked a policy that required two staff members must be present to monitor him opening his personal mail. Eventually he allowed the staff to view the contents of the package, which appeared to contain parts of a firearm, but he dismissed this, saying it was a Christmas gift for his father. By the time this inspection occurred, Lo had already opened the parcel in private.

On the evening of the shooting, an anonymous phone call was made by a student. Subsequently, it was learned that the anonymous call was made by a friend of Wayne Lo, who had become concerned about his friend's behavior. He attempted to call the security office, but reached an answering machine that notified him to leave a message after hours. The student then called a resident assistant and informed her that they suspected Wayne Lo to be contemplating a violent act the next day, and that she perhaps could be a possible target.

The dean was immediately notified and the resident assistant, along with her family, were relocated from the dorm and moved to safety. Forty-five minutes after the warning telephone call, Wayne Lo shot and killed a professor who was returning to campus, critically wounded an unarmed security guard, and killed another student. The dean never notified either campus security or local law enforcement. The director of security had an impressive resume as being a former Los Angeles Police Officer and a former Marine. At no time was the director of security ever consulted during this alarming conduct and behavior. Was this once again the hubris detachment of the academic world from the law enforcement community?

Chapter 33
School Safety

Dave Grossman, the expert on the mindset of killing, advocates that schools must embrace a new culture of security consciousness and vigilance. Grossman points to the fact that over the last fifty years, we have not had a single student die because of a fire. Now, despite a significant increase in school place shootings and deaths, there has been a lack of action on the part of school administrators to address adequate response to an armed intruder. Fire drills are practiced on a routine basis and now lockdown drills have become more common. Although the sensitivity of children must be considered, preparation and drills are necessary to respond to an armed intruder. During the cold war, schools practiced air-raid drills.

In 1958, there was a horrendous fire at Our Lady of the Souls Catholic School in Chicago. Nearly one hundred children perished in this fire. Because of this tragedy, schools all across the nation began to re-examine fire safety and as result, fire codes for schools were significantly increased, as were mandatory fire evacuation drills.

The Columbine murders were a wake-up call to schools across the country. Many assessed the need to elevate their security standards. The Virginia Tech shooting was again another shock to the conscience and demanded action by university campuses. Many colleges ignored security protocols for years. Now, in light of the shooting at Sandy Hook, active shooter drills at schools have become trendy. Planned active shooter drills at schools on days where students are not present and where faculty have been briefed and made aware of what will occur is positive training. Local law enforcement and first responders should be integrated in these drills for realistic training purposes. This integration provides a thought process for faculty and staff to contemplate in determining the mindset for a proper response and procedures in the midst of a crisis.

Unannounced active shooter drills are ill-advised and can have detrimental consequences. Despite prohibitions for carrying weapons on campus, some faculty willingly or unwillingly have a firearm in their possession. When Luke Woodham engaged in a shooting at his school in Pearl River, Mississippi, his principal retrieved a gun from his car and took Woodham into custody. Every day across the United States, the transportation security administration will detain flyers who fail to remove firearms from their belongings. During an unannounced active shooter drill, a teacher who intentionally or who unintentionally failed to remove a weapon from their purse may attempt to arm themselves and try to defend themselves against the fake attacker. Meanwhile, other faculty members could hurt themselves while attempting to dive under desks. Others can suffer heart attacks or no doubt suffer from post-traumatic stress. Subsequent worker's compensation cases could occur. I could see more than one attorney licking their chops at filing suit for this undue and unnecessary stress. I do not recommend unannounced active shooter drills.

These active shooter drills are often performed in front of the local television cameras to share with the community. The presence of cameras will alter the reality of the training. Although it is important for the community to be aware of the training, it can have an effect not considered. The sight of a SWAT team weaving through the hallway could provide an excitement factor for the potential shooter. Going out in a hail of gunfire at the hands of a SWAT member can be the final thrill for someone determined to die and claim his or her fame. Press releases can inform the public, while not disclosing the tactical procedures the police will employ.

Another unattended consequence of these ongoing drills is the increased anxiety experienced by students, faculty and parents. In a Gallup Poll conducted and released in August 2013, thirty-three percent of parents say they fear for their oldest child's safety at school. This percentage is unchanged from the poll conducted in December after Sandy Hook and higher than the 25% at the start of the 2012 school year. One would assume that after eight months, heightened concerns would have abated. The concerns of parents escalated after Columbine to 55% and then leveled back to around the 25% range.

More schools are installing video surveillance systems that become a force multiplier in the security apparatus. Although civil libertarians will often argue over the intrusion into privacy and freedom, the positive aspects of surveillance systems cannot be understated. Technology has increased the resolution and capability of these cameras.

Motion analytics installed into the surveillance platform alerts those who are monitoring the system as to activities in certain defined fields within the viewing landscape. The analytics can differentiate between people, cars, packages, animals, and so forth. You can install interactive systems with speakers where you can verbally engage a person acting suspiciously. The resolution of these cameras is clear enough to identify a four-inch lizard running through the viewers screen.

Camera systems are also essential as a historical database to identify problematic and recurrent issues. Sophisticated camera systems are ineffective if there is no one tasked with monitoring the activity. A fulltime staff member may not be financially feasible. There should be someone charged with viewing the footage during critical times of student activity, while analytics can be used to alert staff at other times. The school resource officer should be out on patrol, interacting with the school community and not sitting behind a desk watching a computer monitor.

I heard one administrator boast that they were installing a 50-inch monitor. That is great. Who is watching? If the staff member steps out for a potty break, is there someone to step in with his or her eagle eye? Are they also tasked with answering the telephone or greeting visitors?

After Sandy Hook and other school shooting incidents, there will always be a mad rush of experts and vendors rushing to provide assistance. School administrators and parents will dash to embrace constructive improvements and as a result, may rush to judgment immediately following an incident. As with any purchase, I advocate careful consideration of available options.

I have heard of computer modeling programs for conducting threat assessments with hefty price tags. What guarantees do they offer if their program miss-identifies a problem student or does not identify a student who engages in a shooting event? One school purchased ballistic handheld whiteboards. They are effective if you are the one holding the board. Having been shot at in the past, I would have not felt comfortable seeking refuge behind a small 18' x 20" handheld white board that costs about $300 apiece. Multiply that by the number of classrooms and that expenditure must be weighed against new textbooks and teacher salaries.

Parents seeking emotional comfort have purchased ballistic backpacks for their children. These book bags have limited value and at $300, are a significant expenditure. Most schools prohibit backpacks outside of the locker or homeroom because of the ability to conceal contraband and weapons. Students faced with an emergency must react quickly. There is no time to seek your bulletproof backpack that protects a limited surface area. The head and legs are still exposed. Save yourself $250 and go to Target or Wal-Mart to buy a conventional backpack for less than $50.

College campuses are nearly impossible to lock-down. The footprint of the college campus is typically enormous and fencing the perimeter would exceed the financial benefits. Most college campuses are spread out over hundreds of acres and it is not possible to secure the perimeter during a crisis. Larger schools have roads that dissect the campus and cannot be restricted.

There is an ongoing debate in the security world concerning the locks on classroom doors. Classroom doors are commonly locked from the outside so they can be secured when no one is present. As we have seen in a number of school shootings, barricaded doors prevented or provided enough of an obstacle to prevent the shooter from entering. Locking the door from the inside would assist in providing an extra layer of security.

One concern is that after school hours, or when the student population is at a minimum that an attacker could launch an assault and drag the victim behind a closed door. This would assist in concealment or delay a security response. These considerations will have to be weighed by school administrators. A double locking keyed deadbolt preempts this argument. Locks can be partnered with proximity keys or key cards to address the security concerns of the school. Security and lock consultants can assist in the decision making process.

High schools are easier to secure. Their footprint is typically smaller and therefore the perimeter can be fenced. This not only inhibits or slows the movement of unwanted visitors but also provides a clear territory of ownership by the school community. When the student's faculty and staff have a common cause of safety and security, they are more likely to raise the alert when an unwanted visitor has breached the outer perimeter. In August 2013, an armed suspect entered a school in Decatur, Georgia; the students were trapped in a concentrated area against the fence less than a hundred feet from the school building. The fence had to be cut open to allow for the students to escape.

All access points to school property should be controlled and monitored. The minimum number of access points should be open during the school day. Most schools maintain a visitor access system in which visitors are screened and badged. Despite these systems in place, no school will ever be 100% safe. In spite of the fact that the Virginia Tech Police Department had a professional and highly trained and armed police department and they were in a heightened state of alert, Cho was not deterred from engaging in a horrendous act of violence. An armed school resource officer engaged the Columbine shooters and exchanged gunfire. Neither Harris nor Klebold were discouraged. Despite an enhanced security apparatus at Sandy Hook Elementary, Adam Lanza breached the security and launched a bloody rampage. The White House is one of the most heavily fortified and secured properties in the entire nation. Numerous individuals have scaled the fence of the White House or engaged in an armed attack. Yet we have no alternative but to raise the security standards and expectations of all schools.

Chapter 34
School Threat Assessments

It is incumbent upon all schools to have a threat assessment apparatus in place. Due to legal liabilities, schools may prefer not to name their unit as such, but the intent must be the same. That is to identify potentially troubled students and channel them into resources that can mitigate potentially dangerous conduct in the future. In a middle or high school setting, this is a much more achievable target. Students are more intimately known by the faculty staff and other students. This becomes a significant challenge on the college campus environment. There are often hundreds of students in individual lecture halls, and quite often tens of thousands of students transiting the campus on any given day. Many troubled students will operate under the radar screen and fall through the cracks in the college environment. The college community has no choice but to attempt to engage the due diligence of identifying troubled students. Once a student is identified as displaying behavioral concerns, one of the challenges determining is what recourse the school has to remove that student from the campus environment.

Jared Laughner, who engaged in a public shooting in Tucson, Arizona, where Congresswoman Gabby Giffords was critically wounded, was removed from the Pima County Community College. Campus security served a suspension notice in person to Laughner and his family. James Holmes, the Aurora Colorado shooter, raised concerns at the University of Colorado. The behavioral assessment unit at the university was aware of his troubling behavior. From news leaks, the possibility exists that his psychiatrist, who was also the founder of the behavioral assessment unit, notified campus security of Holmes' homicidal ideas thirty-eight days before the shooting. His access key card had been disabled, but there is no report that he was made a do-not-admit to the campus and it does not appear that local law enforcement was notified.

When a student's conduct becomes alarming, enough that administration feels compelled to notify the student's family, this alone can bring upon its own problems. With Seung-Hui Cho, his parents appeared to be supportive, and they would have been willing to remove him from the campus and obtain the necessary mental health counseling. Not all families are as supportive, and some become defensive and protective of their children to the point of not obtaining help when needed. The shooter in the dormitory at the University of Central Florida, James Oliver Seevakumaran appeared to have had limited contact and was estranged from his family. His family made a brief statement to the press identifying him as a loner.

The Northern Illinois University shooter did not rise to the level of concern to the campus community. Stephen Kazmierczak appeared to have lived a double life. He was a highly functioning and high-achieving psychology student, but had a deeply disturbing and dysfunctional personal life. He successfully compartmentalized these two distinct aspects of his life.

Another aspect to keep in mind is that as students move from high school to college they become more autonomous. There is less parental involvement and oversight. Students may be attending school at a considerable distance from their immediate family and social support system. As someone who has relocated numerous times through his professional career, I have always advocated that any move, even the ones that we're looking forward to the most, still incur a considerable period of transitioning. In my experience, it typically took a year to become fully acclimated to my new surroundings.

An 18-year-old that is attending college is not only leaving the security of his or her family nest for the first time but is quite often separating from close friends. Add to this the increased rigors of college academic standards while also contemplating future career decisions. Many students become conflicted when perhaps their first choice of disciplinary major was incorrect and results in altering their plans, changing majors, and lifelong dreams. All of these factors increase the emotional stress for college students.

It is also a typical time for the onset of certain mental health illnesses especially schizophrenia and bipolar disorder, which begin to manifest in the late teens and early 20s. According to Dr. Jeannie Twenge, narcissism affects approximately one in four college students. This overinflated self-value can significantly undermine the personal stability when confronted with the realities of life. Many students who have difficulty socializing in the mainstream can quickly feel isolated in a large campus environment and struggle to keep from being sucked into the negative emotional vortex.

Launching into a speculative mode and viewing life from the point of view of Cho, you can see the mounting anxiety that he faced. Despite the fact that he had practiced a self-imposed isolation from an early age, he was a loner wandering this earth with no social support system. Any attempts he made to reach out were awkward and inept. In his socialization attempts, he was rejected by the manuscript publisher, fellow students, and faculty. He was about to graduate and would be once again forced to move home and live under the roof of his parents. He understood that the expectations would be for him to move on in life and obtain gainful employment utilizing his college degree as a foundation for future development. This was never to be for Seung-Hui Cho. He would have always had challenges in his future, as he attempted to achieve stability in employment and his personal life.

In 1998, the Jeanne Clery Disclosure of Campus Security Policy and Campus Crime Statistics Act, better known as the Clery Act was passed in memory of Jeanne Clery, who was brutally raped and murdered in her dormitory room at Lehigh University in 1986. The Clery Act mandates colleges and universities to be forthcoming with the reporting of on-campus crime. Many times with crime reporting statistics, individual reporting parties become creative in their definition of particular types of crimes. For example, an armed robbery could be written as a theft. I believe most universities are cooperative and honest with the reporting. After Virginia Tech, Congress added a mandate that a campus emergency response plan be implemented. It requires that universities immediately notify the campus community as soon as an emergency is confirmed on campus unless a notification would undermine the control of the situation.

The cost of the Virginia Tech massacre was $48.2 million. The university had to invest $11.4 million in public safety upgrades and staffing. An argument could be made that some of these upgrades and staffing would have occurred anyway, but the shooting demanded immediate action. Another $6.4 million was spent on the cleanup and renovations of Ambler Hall and Norris Hall where the majority of the shootings occurred. The same deliberations are currently underway at Sandy Hook Elementary School. The massacre at the San Ysidro, McDonald's in 1984, resulted in the closing of that location. Many do not consider these ramifications in response to a traumatic incident.

Included in the renovations at Virginia Tech was the installation of anti-barricade locks. After Cho's diabolical plot, even the standard for door locks was forever altered. The crash bar type exit locks were installed as opposed to the push down arm type of locks that Cho chained together. The university made the decision to hire a public relations consulting firm to assist with image control and communications. This cost the school another two and half million dollars. In an effort to finish the installation of the Virginia Tech alerts system for emergency notifications, the school spent one million dollars. The school spent $4.79 million in legal costs and $324,258 archiving documents related to the shooting. Another $2.7 million was spent to provide support to the survivors and families. This expenditure included the costs of housing, feeding and transportation for the survivors' family members. The $7.4 million was spent on increasing mental health services on campus. Another $3.7 million was spent on operational costs associated with the expenditure of lifetime health insurance for survivors as well as the construction of a Peace Center.

Schools often walk a very fine tight rope of trying to balance the needs and concerns of an individual student versus the safety and concerns of the entire community. They often must deliberate over defending themselves against possible legal action of singling out a particular student for behavioral concerns versus the unlikely enormous expenditures that Virginia Tech faced in light of their deficiencies of addressing Cho.

In 1996, at San Diego State University, Frederick Davidson, a graduate engineering student, engaged in a shooting. He had failed his thesis dissertation and was appearing in front of an appeal review panel of three professors. Also present were several students who were spectators to the appeal process. Unbeknownst to those in attendance, Davidson previously concealed a firearm in a first aid kit attached to the wall in the room. He entered the room and before completing his appeal process, he no doubt understood the likelihood of an unsatisfactory final decision. Davidson walked over, reached into the first aid kit, extracted the firearm and began shooting. None of the student spectators were targeted, but all three of the professors were gunned down. The shooter unable to muster the strength to commit suicide, pleaded with the police to kill him. Davidson was taken into custody and serving three life terms.

The Columbine High School shooting in 1999 rocked the United States and the world. The attack was launched by two students, Eric Harris and Dylan Klebold. Eric Harris was described as being smart, cool and confident. From his journals, one can make an educated guess that he was also a psychopath devoid of any conscience.

Dylan Klebold, although smart was awkward and had a depressed disposition. He identified with *Downward Spiral* sung by Nine Inch Nails. The song's title adequately describes the content of the lyrics. The title also describes Klebold's thoughts. He also had in an interest in the movie *Lost Highway*, a cryptic thriller about confused identities. Klebold and Harris both loved *Natural Born Killers,* the graphically violent film. The two students were considered analytical, had interests in science and math, and they were computer savvy. They were both socially engaged in high school activities and were members of the drama club and spectators at sporting events.

In February 1997, Eric Harris began a journal, and his writings gave a very clear indication of his narcissistic point of view. He considered himself superior and had little tolerance for others, viewing everyone else as inferior. In March 1998, Eric Harris had a falling out with his good friend Brooks Brown. Some incidents occurred between the two students that resulted in Brooks's mother, Judy Brown confronting Eric Harris and bringing the conduct to the attention of the Harrises. Eric Harris was highly manipulative, and he utilized skills to lie and cover up his deeds with his father, who deemed Judy Brooks as overreacting to a minor incident.

This would not be the end of the turmoil between the two former friends. The Browns became aware of a website created by Eric Harris that was twelve pages in length. They brought these pages to the attention of Deputy Mark Miller of the Jefferson County Sheriff's Office. Miller's report recommended that copies of the report should be forwarded to the investigations bureau and the Columbine School Resource Officer Neil Gardner, who would eventually exchange gunfire with the two suspects.

The website pages contain violent threats directed toward students and teachers of Columbine High School. Other material on the website included blurbs Harris had written concerning his general hatred of society and his desire to kill those who annoyed him. Harris had noted the completion of the construction of pipe bombs, mentioned a gun count, and compiled a hit list of individuals he wished to target. Harris stated on his website that he was not only in possession of explosives, but had detonated at least one. This twelve-page manifesto is a clear indication of Harris's elitist attitude and his belief that he was above the law.

The Jefferson County Sheriff's Office was notified fifteen times by the Brooks family concerning the conduct of Eric Harris. The Browns, concerned about retribution wanted anonymity. The Browns must have felt like they were screaming into a mountain canyon and never heard. They only heard the echoes of their own voices.

Detective Mike Guerra had a dual assignment: he was a detective assigned to the bomb squad as well as a detective assigned to investigate general crimes. This apparently caused a conflict with his lieutenant, who had become frustrated with the detective's dual assignments. Guerra prepared an affidavit to conduct a physical search of Eric Harris's home. Guerra was also aware of an explosive device that was detonated approximately a mile and a half from the Harris residence that appeared similar to the one described on Eric Harris's website. The SRO, Neil Gardner, was also consulted by the detective. Gardner dismissed the two students as no big deal and kind of misfits. Guerra prepared the affidavit. There is confusion as to whether his supervisors read the affidavit or were briefed about the contents. That approval was denied and Guerra was apparently told that the affidavit lacked probable cause. The detective moved on to other investigations.

I do not pretend to be an attorney, but I can tell you that with over thirty years of law enforcement experience this denial was incorrect. Having knowledge that a 16-year-old bragged about possessing an explosive device, a similar pipe bomb was located near the residence, Harris displayed a general hatred of society and expressed homicidal thoughts and specifically named targets, I would have concluded that an affidavit should have been brought to the attention of the Jefferson County District Attorney's Office for review. If the district attorney's office or a judge had concluded, that, there was insufficient evidence of probable cause, than that decision would have rested upon the district attorney or judge and not on the sheriff's office. It is never a good combination to have an adolescent willfully bragging about detonating explosive devices, displaying the knowledge to assemble bombs and making direct threats toward individuals within the community. This is alarming behavior.

It is unknown why there was never any additional follow-up by the sheriff's office. There appears to have been some personality conflicts. This may have obstructed the clarity of the investigation, but beyond that, their inaction would be speculation. Even with the inability to obtain a search warrant for the residents, investigators could have contacted Eric Harris's parents and requested consent to search the residence. It is possible that the parents would have denied that request, but it is more likely they would have consented to a search. At a minimum, the parents should have been notified of the findings of the investigation to that point, and an interview with Eric Harris and Dylan Klebold should have taken place. Hindsight is always 20/20, but I believe the chances of disrupting this diabolical plot would have had a high chance of success. One could surmise that Eric Harris would have denied the accusations and attempted to shift blame to others, declaring a conspiracy against him. It is also possible that his parents would have defended him and circled the wagons. This attempted interview would have put both Harris and Klebold on notice that the police were aware of their actions.

After the shooting, the Jefferson County Sheriff's Office conducted a meeting at a facility in charge of managing county properties. What exactly was said at that meeting is unclear but it was obviously a strategy meeting to deal with the consequences of not properly investigating and possibly altering the outcome of the Columbine shooting. The case file by Detective Guerra was misplaced and subsequently lost. The under-sheriff's assistant claimed to have possibly shredded some files related to Columbine. Digital files were also deleted. In September 2003, a brief report was found that located a previously misfiled report dated August 7, 1997, which contained eight pages from the webpage, *"I Hate,"* which was Eric Harris's webpage.

Harris and Klebold had previously been suspended for hacking locker combinations and breaking into school lockers. Mr. Harris discovered a pipe bomb in the residence and confronted Eric, who swore that he would never do it again. Harris, in one of his papers wrote that it was easier to bring a gun than a calculator to school. We discussed Klebold's literary leakage earlier in his macabre tale of the killer of guns down the "preps."

In January, the two boys were arrested for breaking into a car and stealing a laptop. They were both placed on probation. In his journal, which he described as the *Book of God,* Harris wrote about his arrest, "People are stupid. I'm not respected. I feel like God. I am higher than almost anyone in the fucking world in terms of universal intelligence." He believed in natural selection and survival of the fittest. He said, "I know I will die soon so will you and everyone else."

The two students planned for over a year for their final assault. Harris and Klebold conducted significant computer research, devised utility belts, and attached match strikers to their clothing so that they could ignite their explosive devices. They practiced hand signals with each other understanding the difficulty of verbal communications with the noise of alarms and screams. They also planned to deploy diversionary devices that would be utilized to draw law enforcement responders away from the school. These bombs, used to distract first responders would allow the killers free reign to perpetrate their hideous acts upon the school.

The killers engaged in considerable target practice in the woods, even using a bowling pin strung from a tree. Eric Harris, upon examining the holes in the bowling pin, talked about imagining the pin was someone's head. They fired so often with the sawed-off shotgun that their hands began to bleed. Some of the target practice included ducking shirts being lobbed at them to enhance their focus and target acquisition.

Eric Harris, in his journal, included detailed surveillance notes of the cafeteria. He indicated the times and the estimate of the student population in the cafeteria. According to his estimates, at 11:15 A.M. the student census would be in excess of 500 students. In his final journal entry, he wrote, "Walk-in set bombs at 11:09 for 11:17. Leave. Drive to Clemente Park gear up (note that the park was where the diversionary devices would be set to explode). Get back by 11:15. Park cars. Set car bombs for 11:18 get out, go to outside hill, wait. When first bombs go off, attack. Have fun!" Have fun? What kind of depraved mind thinks of exacting an enormous body count on innocent high school students as having fun?

I don't believe Dylan Klebold would have participated in this violent act without his friendship and the influence of Eric Harris. From Klebold's writings, it appears that he takes on a more melancholy approach to life, and he probably would have been more prone to committing suicide as opposed to homicide. He was a willing participant and was provided an opportunity by the teacher who confronted him about his ghastly essay, but he chose to minimize this insight into his mindset.

In his notes, Klebold had written a page titled, "Do shit for NBK." He drew a diagram of the tactical positioning of his gear and weapons on the body. He wrote a list, "buy suspenders, cargo pants, Adidas soccer bags (which were used to carry the propane bombs), workout carrying gear, tech nine (which was a gun), knife, get bullets/shells – double ought buckshot, and practice in-car gear-ups." This is particularly telling, as it really demonstrates the preparation and planning that took place for this attack. Many adults would not have planned to practice gearing up in the car. There are inherent challenges to putting the gear on in the confined space of a car. This is highly intellectual thinking for a high school student.

It is hard to fathom that the parents of Eric Harris and Dylan Klebold were unaware that their homes were bomb-making factories or bomb storage depots. Among the explosive devices were two diversionary backpack bombs containing two 20-gallon propane bombs that were placed in the cafeteria but did not explode, 4 additional propane bombs, 30 exploded cricket devices that caused minimal damage, 46 unexploded devices, 13 explosive devices found in the subjects' cars, and 8 additional devices located in the residences. Six were found in the Klebold home and 2 located in the Harris residence.

A design flaw prevented the propane bombs from erupting in the cafeteria. Had they exploded as planned, Eric Harris would have properly estimated the fatalities to be in excess of five hundred students. Their intent clearly demonstrated how evil their plan was.

The basement tapes were the types of videos that many students will make in a sophomoric attempt to be humorous with one another. However, in this case, the videos provided insight into the deranged minds of the two killers. The two shared an internal rage against the world and they both felt they were victims of society. Harris complained of moves associated with military relocations and always having to start out on the bottom. Klebold collected wounds of mistreatment from as far back as nursery school. Harris said, "Isn't it fun to get the respect that we're going to deserve?"

They said goodbye to their parents and discussed how directors will fight over the movie rights. Eric Harris left a final message for his parents on a cassette player. On the tape, he recorded his final words, saying, "People will die because of me. It will be a day that will be remembered forever." Neither one of the two boys said a final goodbye to their parents. They merely walked out of the house for the last time never giving a kiss or a hug goodbye to Mom and Dad. Susan Klebold heard her son dash out of the house earlier than expected, uttering a single, "Bye."

There was a great deal of criticism toward the police response to the Columbine shooting. One must understand that in 1999, the standard procedure for an incident such as this was to set up a perimeter, approach with caution, extricate the children, and advance until you could isolate the shooters so as to either negotiate a surrender or to neutralize the threat. No one had ever been faced with a shooting of this magnitude before. This incident completely altered the future of police responses to active shooters. Valuable lessons were learned and refined. These lessons are utilized in training scenarios that prepare police agencies to respond to future school shootings. The Sandy Hook shooting has renewed an interest in active shooting scenarios at schools and on school busses.

Forty-seven different agencies responded to the Columbine campus. As a result, communication challenges existed. Emergency communications and shared frequencies have dramatically improved since 1999. The active shooter scenario inside the school required the formation of ad hoc entry/SWAT teams. These blended teams were comprised of different police departments and not all members were tactically equipped. There were numerous reports coming in of multiple shooters of varying descriptions inside and outside and on the rooftop as well. Upon entry into the school, the sprinklers had been activated and an audible alarm was piercing through the hallways. The school building was large, housing over two thousand students, and the school had a major remodel four years earlier. Students had to draw maps for the responding police officers. As the officers made their way through the hallways, they encountered numerous backpacks, which had to be examined to determine if they were explosive devices.

Having viewed the surveillance footage from inside Columbine High School, I have shared that video with students in my classes and among hardened, experienced, and seasoned police officers. The graphic images are very disturbing. Harris and Klebold riled in excitement and terrorized their intended targets. At times, they taunted those who were trapped or wounded. Other times, it almost appeared that they were bored and had lost interest in killing. Their final deaths were captured and even their suicide appeared to take place with little thought or consideration. They conferred with each other and agreed that on the count of three, they would execute themselves. In their deaths, school security would be forever changed.

School busses are a concerning weakness. In November 1995, Catalino Nick Sang was in a dispute with the IRS over thousands of dollars and had quit work. A deeply religious man, he erupted in church on a weekday and ran out of the church when the pastor attempted to calm him. Sang ran down the street and took hostage of a Dade County school bus carrying elementary students with learning disabilities. During a low speed pursuit, he threatened that he had a bomb. Metro-Dade Police snipers killed Sang and dragged him off the bus. One child was slightly injured by flying glass. It could have ended in a more tragic manner.

Security has increased on busses. Communications with drivers and video monitoring has been installed to monitor activities inside the bus. GPS locators can provide real-time tracking of each bus.

In August 2012, an expelled student named, Jared Cano targeted Freedom High School in Tampa, Florida. Cano, who shared a two-bedroom apartment with his mother, had planned to target his former high school on the first day of class. His mother, who was a schoolteacher at a different school, was unaware of her son's bomb-making efforts in his bedroom or his marijuana farm. The subject's Facebook page gave a clear indication of his addiction to marijuana. Cano's mother, when asked by Tampa Police, provided consent to search the apartment.

The interesting part about his plot was that he shared his thoughts in some homemade videos. The videos demonstrated his intent to eclipse the death count of the Norwegian killer, who killed seventy-seven students. Cano diagrammed the school and plotted where he planned to plant explosive devices. He pointed out where he intended to stash his weapons in the woods and how after the explosions, he planned to retrieve his weapons, return to school, and conduct an assault on the administrative offices. He specifically named two members of the faculty he planned to kill, while naming another member of the faculty who he admired and intended to keep safe during his attack.

Cano was undeterred by the fact that an armed school resource officer (SRO) would also be in the administrative office, as he pointed out the general location of the SRO. His plot was detected after an individual in whom he confided his plot contacted authorities. The suspect was taken into custody and was subsequently found guilty. His attorney advocated that the subject did not intend to do any harm. If Cano had been collecting stamps instead of constructing explosive ordnance and drawing plans for an assault on the school, I might listen to those assertions. The subject has never displayed any remorse for his actions. Ironically, a number of years earlier, I conducted school shooter training for the Tampa Police school resource officers at Freedom High School.

Chapter 35
Waiting for the Police

According to George Mason University, the average duration of active shooter incidents in institutions of higher education (IHE) is 12.5 minutes. In contrast, the response time of campus and local law enforcement to these incidents is 18 minutes. On average, every year 35 students are murdered and another quarter of a million are seriously injured in acts of school violence. Not all of these deaths and injuries are restricted to school shooters but would also include schoolyard violence and edged weapon attacks.

The tactical response prior to Columbine used the 5 Cs concept. This theory, taught to first responders, is *contain* and *control* the threat, *call* SWAT, *communicate* with the shooter, and *create* an action plan. This theory worked until Columbine, when the shooters had no interest in complying with being contained, controlled or establishing communications. They terrorized the students and teachers for forty-five minutes.

Since Columbine, the likelihood of a slow and deliberate police response has been greatly reduced. Once the initial attack occurs, and law enforcement is notified and resources dispatched, the active shooter will have substantial time to concentrate their shooting in a confined area with little or no chance of armed opposition. Keep in mind that 50% of all active shooter scenarios are concluded prior to the arrival of law enforcement. In an urban environment, police response to an active shooter could be 3 to 5 minutes. In a rural environment where police resources cover much greater distances, the response could be considerably longer. Remember, John Hinkley fired six rounds in 1.8 seconds with a revolver, striking four individuals. Seconds and minutes count.

After the shooting in Columbine, Greg Crane, a former SWAT officer and his wife a former school principal, developed a program called ALICE. This acronym stands for *Alert, Lockdown, Inform, Counter, and Evacuate.* Although the program was developed in the mid-2000s, ALICE has gained considerable traction after the Sandy Hook massacre.

In an ABC news interview, Greg Crane shared his observations of the Columbine students in the library: "They were all sitting down. Why were they there for five minutes when they had five minutes to do something else?" He was referring to the students who hid under the desks in the library, of which eighteen were shot. Despite critics of the program, I believe the overall philosophy of the program has merits.

Once an attack commences, it is essential for school personnel to sound the alarm and *alert* all school campus population, as well as summon law enforcement and first responders. The quicker the alert is made, the quicker potential victims can take evasive action. The *inform* part of the program calls for pushing out information as quickly as possible to allow responders and possible victims to evaluate and make an appropriate response.

The other three aspects of the program are dependent upon the individual evaluation of those impacted by the attack. If the attacker is walking down the hallway, the best option may be to shelter in place, or *lockdown,* and seek the best means of cover and concealment, which may be getting under desks or inside cabinets and closets. It would also be essential to secure the entry by either locking or barricading the door. This may be accomplished by pushing a desk or heavy object in front of the door provided the door open in toward the class. If the door opens outward and it cannot be locked from inside, it will be dependent upon teachers and/or students to restrain the door from being opened. This would expose those individuals to being shot through doors that are not ballistic. Most school doors are made of wood and provide minimal protection from bullets.

If it is determined that the shooter is not in close proximity to the exit of the classroom, the best option would be to *evacuate* the students and make a mad dash for freedom. Unlike fire drills, where students routinely assemble in the parking lot or the basketball court, distance is your friend in an active shooter scenario. It is important to get as far away as possible, and not return until summoned by law enforcement personnel when the scene is safe. If students are trapped in the classroom, they may have the option of climbing out through windows. This is dependent upon the exit area and type of window as well as whether the classroom is located on the first floor or second floor. Anything above the second floor would almost ensure significant injury to students jumping to the ground below.

The last and least desirable of the options is to *counter*. This means when all else fails and you have no other options, the best alternative may be to fight back. On numerous occasions, active shooters have been subdued by unarmed individuals who took it upon themselves to stop the rampage at great risk to their personal safety. Individuals who assess that they have no alternative but to die or fight back must be resourceful in choosing potential weapons. These weapons could include a fire extinguisher, staplers, whole punchers, weighted backpacks and purses, marbles or any other projectiles that have the potential to inflict injury or distract the shooter while you counter his attack.

The *counter* option has been the most criticized aspect of this program. It certainly can place individuals in harm's way who may have avoided injury by concealing themselves or fleeing. The counter response should be evaluated as an age appropriate response. A shooting can be quite traumatic for second grade school children, and they may lack the maturity to understand the gravity of the situation. High school and college students are more able to understand and evaluate this concept on an individual basis.

Chapter 36
Campus Security

Dorm inspections and locker inspections or lack thereof are often pointed to as a weakness in security on school and college campuses. Although routine locker inspections may uncover drug paraphernalia, narcotics, and an occasional weapon, most shooters conceal weapons on their person and do not take the chance of storing guns in their lockers. For schools that employ magnetometers to check students for weapons, this can be a costly expense in equipment and the resources necessary to operate the equipment. In schools that utilize magnetometers, these screening devices are limited in their use during the school day. Therefore, a student coming in after school hours to attend afterschool activities with nefarious intent can easily conceal a weapon in either a locker, unattended classroom, or behind a fire extinguisher. The San Diego State University shooter concealed his weapon in a first aid kit.

Dormitory inspections present a greater challenge. Although most college housing contracts stipulate routine inspections these are cursory searches at best. The resident advisors who are conducting the inspections, are ensuring compliance with safety protocols, maintenance issues and open display of prohibited contraband. They are not conducting an extensive search like the one a police officer would perform while executing a search warrant. Without cause, this type of search would be unreasonable and too time-consuming. The resident advisors are not lifting mattresses, checking the underwear drawer, the bottom of the trashcan or any other location where weapons could be easily concealed. Dormitory inspections have no impact on potential shooters who reside off-campus or store weapons in their vehicles.

The smaller the school campus, the more easily lockdowns can be achieved. In an elementary, middle or high school setting, classroom doors can be secured and perimeter fencing can secure the property. Fences will rarely prevent a determined individual from scaling the fence to obtain access.

Aaron Alexis was able to defeat security at the Navy Yard with legitimate access to the base. He was issued credentials for approved access. In July 2013, a homeless person placed a trashcan against a wall taken from an adjacent park and used it as a ladder to scale the fence at MacDill Air Force Base in Tampa. This was the fourth time this homeless person defeated the perimeter security for a military installation. MacDill houses the headquarters for Special Operations Command and Central Command. If the military cannot adequately prevent a homeless person from gaining unauthorized access to one of the most critical bases to our fight against terrorism, how is a school to ensure one hundred percent security?

To lock down most college campuses would be virtually impossible. Depending upon the number of access points for motor vehicle traffic, the campus police force may be able to close these access points. At the University of South Florida, they have seventeen entrances to the campus property, which is also home to a number of hospitals and associated medical facilities. Most college campuses would be unable to attend to all the pedestrian access points. Larger universities have a student population of between 25,000 and 50,000 students. It is just not feasible to conduct an entire lockdown.

Many college campus buildings are opened in the morning and are not secured until the end of the day. The student body and anyone else is free to access the buildings at anytime.

Key access to campus buildings can also be vulnerable. Students easily lose track or misplace their key cards that provide access to dormitory buildings. There is a frequent occurrence of students tailgating other students to gain access to dormitory buildings. At Lehigh University, Jeanne Clery was murdered after students propped the doors to the dormitory building open with pizza boxes allowing access for the killer. The armed intruder at McNair School in Decatur, Georgia, gained access by tailgating a visitor that was granted authorized access. Sometimes, tailgating is often due to a students laziness. These lost access cards many times will be accompanied with the students personalized pin number adhered to the back of the card by the student. A lost card with corresponding access code can provide entrance to un-invited visitors. Universities must be diligent in removing lost or, expired cards, or the names of persons who have had their access restricted.

Cross training and drills with other agencies is essential and has been demonstrated in both Virginia Tech and Columbine. When a crisis occurs in a school setting, speed and efficiency is paramount to reducing fatalities. Local departments that may not routinely patrol the campus setting would benefit from the exposure and training opportunity. This greatly leverages an efficient response protocol and breeds familiarity between various agencies.

When developing a threat management team, the size of the team can vary, but at a minimum, it should include campus police, counseling centers, student conduct, student affairs, and others with a vested interest. This is similar to the private sector, where corporations conduct threat assessments of employees exhibiting behavior of concern.

Communication is essential in the school environment. In this day and time, the school must assume that there could be multiple shooters, and it is always best to err on the side of caution. It is essential to not only keep students, faculty, and staff apprised of developments but also worried parents of students. In this day of social media, there is no excuse for not pushing out notifications via Facebook, Twitter, text messaging, emails and website portals. Bandwidth must be sufficient to withstand the enormous traffic during a crisis. Communication platforms are easily overwhelmed and crash during the ensuing increase in volume.

As I have learned through the aftermath of hurricanes, cell towers and telephone lines may be knocked out. In a crisis, these platforms could become so congested that telephones and cell phones became almost useless. However, text-messaging using a different SMS protocol may be more reliable.

Schools must also be cognizant of crisis management protocols after the event has concluded. This may include the temporary relocation of students who have been displaced from either classrooms or dormitories. It is essential to have counselors on call to respond in an emergency and provide needed counseling and therapy. For the displaced students, temporary shelter and immediate needs will also have to be addressed. This would include food, water, restroom, and shower facilities. In some instances, students who had to scramble with only their bedclothes or workout clothing may have to be provided blankets or disposable jumpsuits and footwear.

In a crisis in which explosives or other hazardous materials must be neutralized and removed, students may have extended delays in returning to the dormitories. If this is the case, it may be necessary to procure off-campus temporary housing at nearby hotels.

If there are injuries among the student body, a faculty liaison must be established and contact maintained with family members. Although Virginia Tech was heavily criticized for their threat assessment of Cho and their response to the initiation of violence, their post-crisis response was impressive. Family members of the victims, many of whom had to travel from out of state, were provided an empathetic response as well as local lodging, food, and counseling. A short time after the horrendous shooting, the school was able to organize a candlelight vigil and memorial service with tens of thousands in attendance.

No crisis management response plan is complete without considerations for the media. In the 24/7 news cycle, the media response will be quick. A staging area will have to be provided, large enough to accommodate satellite trucks. It may be necessary to identify the location on campus and an alternate location off-campus in close proximity depending upon the enormity of the catastrophe. Most school districts and colleges have a spokesperson, public affairs, or media relations department that is proficient in addressing the needs of the media. Limit the information flow in the beginning until the facts can be further substantiated and validated. Consolidate the data dump to alleviate the agonizing drip, drip, drip, of information that merely continues a frenzy and insures prolonged front page, above-the-fold coverage and leadoff stories on the evening news. Schedule joint press conferences with members of the school and law enforcement community. During a crisis, it is best for the school to maintain a one-voice policy, meaning the media has a single point of contact for news inquiries concerning updates.

A command post is necessary to consolidate and unify the command structure. This could include separate command posts for staff and law enforcement, which have different priorities in responding to the crisis. Intercommunication between different command posts is vital. This is best maintained by the physical presence of a high-ranking staff member stationed in the other's command post to provide a continuity of communications. Many larger universities have a physical emergency operations center staffed full-time by skilled and trained emergency management personnel.

According to the Centers for Disease Control and Prevention (CDC), from 1992 to 2006, less than 1% of all homicides involving children ages 5-18 occurred at school. This data does not account for the number of planned school shooting attacks that have been prevented. According to National School Safety and Security Services, there have been 120 prevented attacks between 2000 and 2010.

I believe the prevention of school-centered attacks is vastly underreported and could be considerably higher than the 120 cited. The intervention of the school shootings can be attributed to a number of factors. Students have become more willing to share concerns over inappropriate statements or threats with either their parents or school administration. Schools have become much better at identifying and mitigating concerning behavior among their student population. This has been achieved through training, awareness, and vigilance by our wonderful and dedicated teachers. Teachers, while reviewing writing assignments are less willing to dismiss violent passages. Inattentive parents are now forced to become engaged in their children's lives. More schools are employing a trained threat assessment teams to analyze disturbing behavior.

School resource officers have become a unique and specialized group. The SRO's are now staffed with enthusiastic officers who embrace the community-oriented policing concepts first used in high-risk neighborhoods. The officers assigned to schools are often selected volunteers who learn to integrate their activities to monitor the community. They develop a relationship of trust with students and are more likely to be sought out by students who are concerned by the conduct of another student or inappropriate communication they have overheard. The SRO's and teachers now have a joint hand in monitoring the pulse of the school community.

As much as I support active shooter training in schools and first responders, when the first shots are fired, we have already failed. We must make every attempt to identify troubled students whose behavior is a concern to others, and divert them to the help that they need to prevent violence.

Chapter 37
Public Killers

In Aurora, Colorado, in April 2012, James Holmes dressed in black ballistic clothing and blazing orange hair entered a movie theater and began shooting during a screening of the Batman movie, *The Dark Knight Rises*. After the smoke cleared, twelve were dead and fifty-eight victims lay wounded. You could speculate that James Holmes was obsessed with the diabolical Joker character from the movie, or the symbolism of the title. The Joker enjoyed causing mayhem and fear, all the time while laughing.

Prior to the shooting at the Aurora movie theater, James Holmes rigged his apartment in a Rube Goldberg type interactive puzzle that would result in a fiery inferno. At precisely midnight, an alarm triggered blaring music inside of Holmes' apartment, with the intent to draw law enforcement to investigate the loud music. Instead, one of the residents, awakened by the music, attempted to confront the noisy resident. She knocked on the door and turned the doorknob. She thought better of it, and returned to her apartment. After his arrest, Holmes confessed to the arresting officers that his apartment was rigged with explosives.

Holmes was a Ph.D. student in neuroscience at the University of Colorado. Initial media reports puzzled over why a brilliant

Ph.D. student would engage in the act of mass murder. It appeared unfathomable. Did he just snap? He must have; what other explanation could there be?

It appears that Holmes was not quite the brilliant student he was initially portrayed to be. He was denied admission to the University of Iowa. The individual on the admissions board wrote that Holmes was not to be admitted under any circumstances. Holmes had been an intern at the Salk Institute in San Diego. Larry Jacobsen supervised Holmes while he was an intern. Jacobson said in a post-shooting interview that Holmes should not have been admitted into the summer program, as his grades were mediocre. Jacobson said, "I've heard him described as brilliant. This is extremely inaccurate. My experience with him was quite bad. He never completed the project. What he gave me was a complete mess. I basically fired him." Jacobson described Holmes as a shy and socially inept person. Holmes named Jacobson as his mentor. Jacobson was offended by the assertion, and said this is not true, and is almost slanderous. "I was never his mentor," he told the New York Times.

Holmes apparently related to another student that he would kill when he thought his life was over. He must have felt his life was indeed over when he engaged in his murderous rampage. He was failing in his studies at the University of Colorado, and he was in the process of withdrawing or being expelled. He interacted with Jane Felton, a psychology professor. Dr Fenton was not only a psychiatrist who was perhaps tending to Holmes mental stability, she was also a professor at the university, as well as the founder of the behavioral assessment unit that was established to identify and manage troubled students.

At the writing of this book, there are conflicting stories as to the timeline. There were some assertions that she was directly threatened and brought this to the attention of the behavioral assessment unit. There were also claims that since he was withdrawing from the school, perhaps they took the view that he was no longer their problem. Another report indicates that she was alarmed enough by Holmes' homicidal thoughts that she reported his disturbing behavior to campus police. According to reports,

Fenton notified a campus police officer that she was making the notification under her legal obligation and duty to warn. This occurred thirty-eight days prior to the shooting. We know that the campus police department conducted a criminal history check of Holmes and that his key access card to the school was disabled.

At this point, I do not have clear knowledge as to what was done and not done by the university police. I will not speculate. I will share with you what I believe the proper course of conduct at that point in time should have been. The concerns shared by Felton bare considerable weight, considering the fact that she was not only his psychologist, and a faculty member, she was also the founder of the behavioral assessment unit.

After Fenton's notification to the campus police officer, supervisors should have been notified and an email distributed to campus security to be aware of the subject and his possible intentions. Contact should have also been made with the Aurora Police Department. At a minimum, the Aurora Police Department could have created an intelligence file on Holmes, so that if a police officer happened to notice the subject with his Batman garb driving round town at 11 P.M., a curious officer who ran the license plate number of Holmes's vehicle could be alerted that the subject posed a danger.

I am not aware of the peace officer jurisdiction and arrest powers of the campus police in Colorado. If possible, they could have accompanied the Aurora Police Department to James Holmes' apartment, attempted to conduct an interview with him, and obtained consent to search his apartment. He may have refused to open the door, or perhaps if he had opened the door they could have at least peeked over his shoulder to see anything in plain view in the apartment. The officers could have asked him to step out of the apartment, where they could have asked him to accompany them to the police department for further questioning, or at least conducted an interview in the hallway in a worst-case scenario.

Even if Holmes failed to come to the door or refused to speak with the officers, they could have checked the parking lot for his vehicle and looked through the windows. It is purely speculation that any of these strategies would have disrupted the thought process and the ultimate outcome. These notifications would have at least alerted the law enforcement community and satisfied the future inquisition that will occur. The University of Colorado essentially kicked the can down the road and off the campus, since he was no longer a problem to the campus. Holmes could have just as easily targeted the school that he perceived as turning its back on him.

After the Boston bombing, many people were alarmed that the Boston Police Department was not directly notified by the FBI or DHS of the suspicious behavior of the oldest brother, Tamerlan Tsarnaev. The Boston Police have publicly stated they were not aware of concerns raised by Russian authorities. Having worked on the Joint Terrorism Task Force (JTTF), communication among the various agency representatives can be challenging. Daily participation is fluid among the members, some of whom are not assigned full-time. Case updates comprised in a synopsis format, compiled in a bi-weekly update, and distributed to each member would help to alleviate noncritical updates. Time sensitive issues must be handled accordingly.

It is always the best policy to notify everyone possible who could be remotely affected by the conduct of an individual. When it came to threat cases, I always aired on the side of caution and notified anyone who could be affected. Those notifications were always documented. In this day of emails, you have a built-in documentation system and a secondary backup to a precursory telephone call. When I became aware of a stalker of a tennis star who lived at a tennis resort, I notified the head of security for the resort community. The security director in turn directly notified the tennis star and her family.

In the Holmes case, it will be interesting to see the disclosure of the contents of the package that he mailed to Dr. Felton prior to the shooting. According to news reports, the parcel contained at least some renderings of what appears to be Holmes shooting people.

A number of psychologists have offered their own assessments that Holmes was suffering from schizophrenia, paranoia or narcissism. It is unknown now what his exact diagnosis will be, except to say that he did suffer from some form of mental health illness.

When all the evidence comes out, I believe there will be some very clear indicators that were missed or ignored concerning James Holmes. We all have a duty to warn and notify affected parties. It is not acceptable to take the position that you do not have a responsibility to notify others once that person walks out the front door or off your property. Your due diligence is now mandated to notify others of the possible conduct that could lead to violence.

Despite Holmes' apparent mental health instability, he had a high enough level of functioning to conduct detailed planning for his attack. I am sure he had attended a number of movies in that movie theater. One could assume that at some point in time, while attending a movie in that theater, he exited the rear door to check if there was first, an audible alarm; second, if left ajar, the door would emit an audible alarm; and third, if staff from the theater would respond to the opened door. I do not believe he would have ignored this preoperational check with the level of planning that he displayed. It was only at the fortunate jamming of his rifle magazine that his killing spree was brought to an end.

From his perspective, his dreams were no doubt to become a successful Ph.D. in neuroscience. This is a difficult endeavor. For Holmes, failing out of the Ph.D. program meant he would have to return home, live under the roof of his parents, and face the humiliation not only with his family, but also with neighbors and friends. Exacerbated by his mental illness, this mass killing was his opportunity to give some significance to his meaningless life. It was also a way for him to deliver a revengeful message to the University of Colorado that chose to reject him and ruin his life.

In 2011, Jared Loughner walked up to a gathering for Congressperson Gabby Giffords in Tucson, Arizona. After he finished firing and was subdued by an aide to Giffords, six innocent people were dead and eleven wounded. Among the dead were a U.S. federal judge and a nine-year-old girl, Christina-Taylor Green. Among the wounded was Congresswoman Gabby Giffords.

Loughner was a complete loser in life. He could not hold a job, and he was a heavy substance abuser. There was not a drug that passed by him he didn't try, including psychedelic mushrooms, Salvia, LSD, marijuana and anything else he could get his hands on. He was besieged by paranoid beliefs of the government manipulating currency, various frauds involving the NSA, a government 9/11 conspiracy, and so on. One of his closest friends, Zach Osler claimed that Loughner was obsessed with an online movie, *Zeitgeist: The Movie*. The two-hour movie explores and promotes various conspiracy theories, including the possibility of a North American government unification that would lead to the government planting RFID tracking chips in humans. For someone suffering mental health issues, this was probably not the healthiest movie to become obsessed over.

He attended a public meeting where Gabby Giffords was present and asked her a bizarre question, "What is government when words have no meaning?" She apparently responded in typical political speak. Loughner was further insulted when he received a form letter from her thanking him for his appearance and input at the recent meeting. He wrote on that letter, "Die bitch."

His parents were viewed as being isolated from their neighbors. His former friend, Osler, said that he did not enjoy visiting Jared at his home. According to Osler, the mood was unwelcoming. Friends said that they noticed a behavior change two years earlier, in which Jared had become isolated and consumed with conspiracy theories.

Loughner attended Pima Community College and there were at least five instances in which the campus police documented concerning behavior. The final straw came when he posted a YouTube video alleging that his school was an illegal college and was involved in the Holocaust. One of his fellow students was fifty-two year old Lynda Sorenson, who attended an algebra class with Loughner. Sorenson painted a disturbing picture of the suspect and shared her own concerns in a Facebook posting: *"We have a mentally unstable person in the class that scares the living crap out of me. He is one of those whose picture you see on the news, after he has come into class with an automatic weapon. Everyone interviewed would say, Yeah, he was in my math class and he was really weird. I sit by the door with my purse handy. If you see it on the news one night, know that I got out fast..."* Sorenson's post was insightful and embraced the concept of exploring your options for safety.

The community college campus police went to Loughner's residence and served him with a letter of suspension from campus. The two officers at the residence were backed up by two additional officers, who waited down the street in case there was trouble. It is unknown if this information was shared with the Tucson law enforcement community. After this incident, his parents took away his guns and disabled his car at night, so he could not drive away. They obviously had deep concerns over his stability. There is no evidence that Loughner received mental health treatment.

On the night before the shooting, he posted a farewell on Facebook and apparently took a number of pictures of himself, including one posing in a G-string with his gun. In the morning, he drove to a nearby Wal-Mart and attempted to purchase ammunition for his handgun. The minimum wage clerk at Wal-Mart was alarmed enough at Loughner's behavior that he declined to sell ammunition to Loughner. This clerk made a conscious decision to listen to his inner voice and respond to the alarm bells. This one clerk had the opportunity to alter the tragic consequences of the day. He deserves a bonus and a promotion.

Not to be deterred, Loughner went to another Wal-Mart. Unfortunately, the clerk completed the transaction and sold the ammunition. As he was driving back home, Loughner was stopped by a Fish and Wildlife officer for a traffic violation. The officer was concerned about Loughner's mental health stability, as he asked a number of times if he was all right. He allowed Loughner to drive away with a warning. When Loughner entered his residence with a backpack, his father demanded to know the contents. Loughner fled the residence with his backpack and took a cab to the Safeway. Giffords was holding a public rally in the parking lot. No arrangements had been made to have local police stand by for crowd control or security. Loughner walked up behind the stage and began shooting.

The Sandy Hook shooting by Adam Lanza is very sad and tragic. A great deal is still not known and may never be known about what went on behind the façade of the Lanza home. It is obvious that he was deeply disturbed and had antisocial behavior. One person I spoke with said Lanza was known as being "weird." Perhaps through mental illness, he, like Seung-Hui Cho, felt more comfortable in a self-imposed isolation. Lanza's refuge was his bedroom or basement, where he found comfort in playing hours of violent video games and researching previous mass killings.

As reported in the New York Daily News, it appears that Lanza conducted extensive research on previous public shooters, and developed an obsession with the Norwegian shooter, Anders Brievik. According to this story, Lanza had generated a spreadsheet that was seven feet long and four feet wide, which included a detailed analysis of approximately 500 mass murders. The windows in his room were covered in black plastic to keep the outside world from leaking into his cloistered world. According to the Hartford Currant, which provided excellent coverage in print and for PBS, Lanza also provided editing to mass murder postings in Wikipedia. His edits were of small errors pertaining to firearms and ammunition.

Lanza's tactical precision in his rampage simulated the actions necessary for success in his first person shooter video games. Some offered the explanation that in the video game, if your opposition kills you, they take all the points you accumulated. Was suicide Lanza's last act to deprive the police the opportunity to terminate his slaughter? Somewhere in his wrecked hard drive, his computer may provide the answer to this speculation. As simulated in the video games, he repeatedly changed magazines in his gun, despite it not being empty.

According to those involved in the investigation, Adam suffered from Asperger's syndrome, which is a milder form of autism and makes communication challenging. There are various levels of severity, but those with autism have not been previously associated with premeditated acts of violence. In all probability, the deeply disturbed Adam may have been impaired with other mental health disorders.

His mother, like so many other parents of children affected by mental illness, cared deeply about her son and struggled with her own frustration. His mother stockpiled weapons, and she would take her son target shooting. Kip Kinkel's father was encouraged to embrace the joint exercise of shooting guns in an effort to deepen their relationship. Adam's mother's interest in weapons may have been to the extreme, but her love and advocacy for her child has never been disputed.

I have been asked why he chose the school. It could have been symbolic related to some event in his past. With certainty, we know his killing field was a familiar target, as he attended elementary school at Sandy Hook. He would have minimized the chance of resistance and virtually no chance of armed conflict. The enhanced security protocols at the entrance did not deter him, and I doubt the presence of a lone police officer would have stopped him either. A police officer on campus could have altered the dynamic, but a murderer set on the slaughter of innocent children, would have thought little of killing a police officer in an ambush.

It is well known within the community and in his school that Adam Lanza had mental health challenges. The exact nature of his demons is not known. Despite his mother's doting nature, he would have benefitted from professional treatment and intervention. Nancy Lanza's decision to remove Adam from public school was criticized. Robert Novia, the moderator of the A/V club, witnessed an improvement in Adam's socialization skills and felt continued improvement could have been achieved. He also thought that the decision to remove Adam from school and the support system for special needs students was detrimental to his stability.

The final catalyst that pushed Lanza over the precipice has been speculated. With his long term planning, it is also a strong possibility that there was no final catalyst. It is known that his extensive research was not conducted in a single night. This evil plan was contemplated and planned for an extended period. Was the killing of his mother to spare her the anticipated humiliation of being the mother of a monster, or to exact some revenge over on his hovering parent? Again, we may never know.

Could you imagine sitting in front of a slot machine, thumbing tokens into the slots, and pulling the arm, hoping to hit the jackpot, but instead shots are fired from the mezzanine level above? Just put yourself in the chair in front of the slot machine and imagine the hysteria that ensued as people scrambled for safety and self-preservation.

In July 2007, that scene played out at the New York New York Casino in Las Vegas. Stephen Zegrean, a 51-year-old Hungarian immigrant told investigators, "I was trying to create a conflict." Two days prior to the shooting, relatives concerned about his emotional stability appropriately called police and paramedics to report that he was suicidal. He was assessed at that time and apparently, he did not meet the threshold for an involuntary commitment.

Police report that over the next 24 to 36 hours, Zegrean was observed walking up and down the Las Vegas strip wearing a trench coat in the sweltering July heat. Police theorize that he was seeking to elicit a conflict with law enforcement. For reasons unknown, he entered the New York New York Casino where he was observed loitering for approximately twenty minutes. Police were not able to make any associations between the shooter and the casino that he targeted.

A cousin of the shooter described him as, an unemployed house painter, who may have been dealing with financial difficulties associated with gambling. The cousin went on to say the shooter got divorced five years earlier after his twenty-year marriage deteriorated and he lost custody of the children. The cousin also stated that the shooter's temper had increased, and he had been threatening family members.

Zegrean wounded four gamblers before running out of ammunition. He dropped the empty magazine to his pistol, and before he could reload, he was tackled by two members of the military and two agents from the Florida Department of Law Enforcement. All these courageous souls were off-duty. Zegrean died in prison in 2010, of natural causes.

On a daily basis throughout the United States, police and paramedics are continuously faced with assessing the mental stability of individuals who have allegedly made statements that they intend to kill themselves or others. Having stood in the shoes of the police officer, I know that many of these individuals will deny the alleged claims. The police have limited discretion on the commitment of an individual who is in his own home and does not cross the threshold of being a danger to himself or to others.

The shooters family, being concerned about his emotional stability, took the responsible course of action and summoned law enforcement officers to assess his behavior. The officers are typically on the clock to resolve their call as quickly and efficiently as possible, so that they can become available for additional calls waiting in the queue or to provide backup to other officers. In a city like Las Vegas, individuals acting bizarre on the strip are a frequent occurrence. Had an officer become suspicious of his behavior, in all likelihood the interaction would have lead to an armed conflict on the heavily populated street. The casino surveillance cameras could have analyzed the subject's behavior, but again, individuals loitering in the casino are common. Not being a gambler myself, I have stood in casinos, people-watching, and taking in the sights and sounds.

Chapter 38
Political Assassins

Despite the fact that there have been few political assassinations in the United States, they are still considered high-value targets for would-be assassins. Although most will not result in mass killings, they have the same mindset and often, there are additional casualties. Many readers of this book may be associated with providing dignitary protection throughout the world.

High-level security and planning have made it very difficult for assassins to be successful in carrying out political assassinations. Every year the U.S. Secret Service investigates thousands of individuals whose behavior caused concern. Meanwhile, there are many individuals who have come to the concern of security details for Supreme Court Justices, members of congress, governors, and mayors. A successful attack on a political dignitary will forever raise the profile of an assassin.

In 1963, President John F. Kennedy was assassinated by Lee Harvey Oswald. To this day, there is a considerable community that embraces that a conspiracy existed by the government, the Mafia, the Russians or Fidel Castro, who orchestrated the assassination. I had a brief conversation with retired Secret Service Agent Clint Hill, who was assigned to provide protection to

Jackie Kennedy on that horrible day in Dallas. Clint Hill was the agent viewed sprinting and leaping onto the back of the presidential limousine. Mr. Hill said that it was his opinion that Lee Harvey Oswald had the same characteristics as many of the other individuals we investigated for raising our concerns about their behavior and safety of the President. Oswald was a loser who failed in the Marines, failed out of Russia, failed in his marriage, and failed at all of his jobs.

In March 1981, John Hinkley attempted and nearly assassinated President Ronald Reagan, while wounding three others in addition to the President. Hinkley was the son of an oil executive in Evergreen, Colorado. He was an indifferent student who just appeared to be wandering through life. He filled his days by writing poems and songs and ventured to Los Angeles in an attempt to find a purchaser of his songs. He drifted along in Los Angeles and lived off the substance and financial support of his parents until they finally reached the point of cutting him off.

Hinkley divested stock, and sold most of his gun collection and his guitar for financial support. He enjoyed reading *Catcher in the Rye* and identified with the protagonist, Holden Caulfield, who railed against the phonies of the world. John David Chapman, who would kill John Lennon, was also enamored with *Catcher in the Rye*.

Other books that were of interest to Hinkley included books on John Lennon, the serial killer Ted Bundy and *Romeo and Juliet*, which he viewed as a historical couple that exemplified his perceived relationship with Jodie Foster. In his hotel room, other books were found: *The Fox Is Crazy, Too: The True Story of Garrett Trapnell, Adventurer, Skyjacker, Bank Robber, Con Man; Lover,* by Eliot Asinof, which was a true story of a conman who faked mental illness to manipulate the criminal justice system; *The Skyjacker,* by David Hubbard was an examination of the suicidal tendency of those that hijacked airplanes; *The Fan*, by Bob Randall is the story of an overzealous fan's obsession with an actress; and *Taxi Driver,* by Richard Elman on which the movie was based.

We have discussed earlier that Hinkley was motivated and obsessed by the movie *Taxi Driver* in which the main character Travis Bickle was played by Robert DeNiro. The character of Travis Bickle was very loosely based on Arthur Bremer, the shooter of George Wallace. Bickel became enamored with an aide to a political candidate and when she rebuffed the taxi driver, he targeted the political candidate for assassination. Hinkley reportedly had seen *Taxi Driver* in excess of fifteen times, and he became obsessed with the character of the 15-year-old prostitute portrayed by Jodie Foster. The movie poster for *Taxi Driver* read, "On every street in every city, there's a nobody who dreams of being a somebody." Besides being voted one of the best movie taglines of all time, it also embraces the deranged thoughts and spirit of many of the mass killers. During his trial, Hinkley watched with rapt attention as the movie was played in its entirety during the trial.

Hinkley learned of Jodie Foster's enrollment at Yale University in New Haven, Connecticut, through media accounts. He told his family that he was going to Yale to attend a writing class and they provided funds to finance his studies. He never enrolled in any classes. Upon his arrival at Yale, Hinkley penned love letters and left them in Foster's mailbox. He was able to acquire her dormitory phone number, and he called Foster and spoke with her. She was polite to Hinkley, but was firm that she did not intend to carry on a conversation with a complete stranger. He was not deterred, and made another phone call. In the subsequent phone call she was dismissive of him, mispronounced his last name, and apparently there was laughter in the background of some fellow students. When Hinkley inquired as to whether they were laughing at him, she admitted that in fact that was the case. He felt rebuked, humiliated and was convinced now that he had to kill himself to become noticed.

He continued stalking Foster from afar and sent additional letters. Hinkley was crushed, disappointed and devastated by Jodie Foster's rejection. His feeling of rejection was despite the fact that there was never any reality-based connection. He had never personally met Foster, and she never provided any encouragement that a romantic relationship was possible.

Rebuffed in his attempts to explore his romantic fantasy with Foster, he returned home to Colorado. He began therapy with a psychiatrist. He confided in the psychiatrist that all he really cared about in life was writing and Jodie Foster. However, this obsession was never explored by the therapist.

His final love letter to Foster detailed his intentions to kill President Ronald Reagan to grab her attention. Before he focused on President Reagan, he initially stalked President Jimmy Carter six months earlier. He stayed three blocks from the White House and travelled to Dayton, Ohio during a campaign stop of President Carter. He was able to get within arm's reach of the rope line; however he did not have his gun with him. He then traveled to Nashville, where he was arrested at the airport for carrying a concealed firearm. In his possession was his journal, which detailed his entire plot, but this was not discovered by the police. His firearms were confiscated, and he paid a fine. Upon his release, he quickly replaced his confiscated firearms with the purchase of two additional weapons, and he destroyed the journal that could have exposed his intentions.

Hinkley's interest in targeting the president shifted to the president elect, Ronald Reagan. While Reagan was staying at the Blair House across the street from the White House, Hinckley was photographed standing in front of the fence at the White House and in front of Ford's Theater. An ironic setting, considering Lincoln was assassinated at the theater. Hinkley stalked Reagan while he stayed at the Blair House.

On December 8, 1980, John Lennon was assassinated by Mark David Chapman. This event could have been a possible catalyst for pushing Hinkley further down the path to violence. He was in despair over the death of his hero, who he admired, and he attended the vigil for John Lennon in New York City. At one point, he contemplated committing suicide in front of the Dakota apartment building where John Lennon lived and died. Hinkley had a history of failed suicide attempts and suffered from depression.

Hinkley's parents viewed their son as a youth without direction and discipline. They were concerned about his future and were unaware he was suffering from mental illness. Being supportive and loving parents, they became concerned that they were enabling his lifestyle. In an effort to practice tough love, they provided some pocket spending money and sent him on his way.

Hinkley made his way to Los Angeles for a brief stop, then he decided to make one final trip to New Haven, Connecticut to Yale University, where he planned to take his own life to demonstrate his undying love for Jodie Foster. The cross-country bus had a stopover in Washington D.C., and he spent the night at the Park Central Motel.

When he awakened that morning, he looked at the newspaper and noticed that the president's schedule indicated that he was planning on attending an event at the Hilton Hotel. While in the shower, apparently while he was mixing in his cream conditioner, the thought crossed his mind that instead of killing himself, he could demonstrate his love for Jodie Foster by killing President Ronald Reagan. After exiting the shower, he concluded that assassination of the President would be his best course of action.

After the assassination attempt, he was quickly apprehended, taken into custody, and transported to the Metropolitan Police Department. According to witnesses, Hinkley appeared calm during his detention and even offered to assist the arresting officer with the spelling of "assassinate." He did provide some information that the motive could be found at his motel.

FBI agents began interviewing Hinkley, but they noticed a stilted and uncooperative yes/no response to the questions. The interviewing FBI agent had detected that Hinckley appeared to be disappointed that he was not being questioned by the Secret Service. In an effort to alleviate some of the tension, the FBI agent requested the presence of the Secret Service liaison agent. The Secret Service agent began inquiring about Hinkley's background such as where Hinkley was from, his family upbringing, his education, and interests, which opened a degree of rapport and eased the tension within the interview room.

The Secret Service agent, Steve Colo, analyzed the contents of Hinkley's wallet, which contained a number of magazine photos of Foster and a phone number scribbled on paper with a Connecticut area code. Colo asked Hinkley about the telephone number. At that point, Hinkley said, "If you know about her, then you know about everything." He sighed heavily, displaying the first leakage of emotion. He admitted that the telephone number was linked to their one-sided relationship. He also added that he had taped their telephone conversations and the tapes were in his motel room. His statement was later suppressed, as he apparently asked the Metropolitan Police for a lawyer and the FBI had again read him his rights and began questioning before his appointed attorney had arrived.

The Hollywood version of good cop and bad cop interview tactics does not work well with those suffering from mental health issues. The tactic of asking background information allows the interviewer the opportunity to develop rapport and diminish the tension of the interview. The idea is to talk about everything but the act that resulted in the police intervention. I want to hear, from the suspect's view, what the contributing factors were that can provide clarity and explain the actions, thus determining the dangerousness of the individual.

Chapter 39
Celebrity Killers

As in the case of political assassinations, the celebrity is a lone target. They are often accompanied by security or associates, who could easily fall victim to the killer. The celebrity killers, are close cousins to mass killers in their mindset and actions.

In December 1980, John Lennon, one of the most popular Beatles, was slain by Mark David Chapman outside of his residence in New York. Chapman was the son of a violent father, and he became a substance abuser in high school. He later found refuge in Christianity and became a born-again Christian. Chapman, following his new passion, became a camp counselor at Christian camp and achieved high marks from those who worked around him.

Chapman became obsessed with the book *Catcher in the Rye*. He found a refuge and affirmation in Holden Caulfield's observations of the hypocrisy of the world. Chapman was an underperformer in life and had a number of failed suicide attempts. He was a wanderer through his early years and settled in Hawaii, working as a security guard.

He initially focused on several targets for possible murder, including Johnny Carson, Jackie Onassis Kennedy, Elizabeth Taylor and George C. Scott, but ultimately focused on John Lennon as he felt that Lennon was easiest to locate and gain access to as opposed to the other celebrities. Chapman was enraged at John Lennon's hypocrisy of wealth, while advocating for the poor. Lennon was heavily criticized when he made the claim that he was more popular than Jesus. Chapman felt Lennon's life was in conflict with the humble teachings of Jesus.

Travelling to New York, Chapman began stalking Lennon, but initially he was unable to carry through with his plans. He returned to Hawaii, where he confided to his wife what his plans were and that he changed his mind. His wife made no effort to call the authorities.

He eventually developed enough strength to return to New York, where he began stalking Lennon outside of the Dakota apartments. As Lennon departed his residence, Chapman had enough gumption to ask Lennon to sign his record album and shook hands with the singer. Chapman lingered around the outside of the Dakota apartments, waiting for the return of the musician. When Lennon returned with his wife Yoko Ono, Chapman pulled out his gun and shot John Lennon four times. While Chapman was waiting for the police to arrive, he calmly reached into his back pocket and removed his copy of *Catcher in the Rye,* which he began reading. He had signed the book, "This is my statement."

This deeply troubled man had shared his thoughts with his wife, which apparently caused no alarm. The Dakota apartment building was used to having John Lennon fans camping outside with the paparazzi. A lone fan camped outside provided a limited profile that he would engage in such a villainous act.

Chapman told the parole board in 2010, that his initial target list was selected because "they are famous; that was it," and he thought that by killing them he would achieve "instant notoriety, fame." "It wasn't about them, necessarily," Chapman said. "It was just about me; it was all about me at that time." This reiterates the mindset of many mass killers, whose motive is one of achieving fame.

Actress Rebecca Schaeffer appeared in the television series *My Sister Sam*. In 1989, she was stalked and killed by Robert Bardo, an obsessed fan. Bardo, like many others, was infatuated with her beauty and sent a fan letter to her. He received a stock studio photo, which he perceived to be an affirmation of his love. A simple gesture like this photo is enough for some of these subjects to misunderstand the reality of the situation. Bardo traveled to Hollywood on at least three occasions and visited the studio, where he was rebuffed by security. At one point, he returned to the studio with a stuffed bear and knife, hoping to get close to her.

Daunted by his inability to get close to Schaeffer, he began to focus his attention on other female celebrities including Tiffany, and Madonna. He had previously focused his attention on Samantha Smith, who had garnered worldwide celebrity status after her letter writing campaign with Russian Premier Mikhail Gorbachev. She was killed in a plane crash in 1985. *My Sister Sam* filled the void as it was on air from 1986 until it was cancelled in 1988.

Robert Bardo was one of seven children from what was described as a dysfunctional upbringing. He struggled with mental illness and was seen by a psychiatrist, but was no longer receiving treatment. His neighbors viewed him as emotionally unstable, as he often would become enraged, and he was described by one neighbor as a "psycho." Bardo threatened to get his .357 magnum and shoot another neighbor. He had a few minor arrests for disorderly conduct and domestic violence. Bardo worked as a janitor at Jack in the Box.

From all accounts, Bardo worshipped the innocence of Schaeffer. In one letter he sent to Schaeffer, he told her that he identified with her character's yearning to be famous. His path to fame would be following a different road to infamy.

He became upset and jealous of Rebecca Schaeffer's changing lifestyle and more risqué roles in Hollywood after *My Sister Sam* was cancelled. Bardo asked his brother to purchase a .357 revolver for him. In one letter to the actress, he included lyrics from a John Lennon song and a self-authored song. Bardo wrote to his sister, "I have an obsession with the unattainable and I have to eliminate (something) that I cannot attain." He was not specific about his intentions to his sister.

After reading that another stalker hired a private investigator, Bardo used the same tactic to determine Schaeffer's home address. He told the investigator he was searching for an old friend and presented himself with established roots in Tucson. As disturbing as this conduct is, in today's society, it is much easier to locate addresses through public database searches or for those willing to pay for online services.

Bardo went to Schaeffer's apartment. He rang her doorbell. Her intercom was not working, and she answered her door in her bathrobe. She was polite to him, but told him to leave. He complied and went down the street, where he called his sister and confided to her that he was about to complete his mission.

He returned to her apartment and again rang the doorbell. Schaeffer answered, now out of patience, and told him to leave. Bardo upset at her treatment of a fan, pulled out his gun and shot Schaeffer in the abdomen, fatally wounding her. I have seen videos of the interview of Robert Bardo and his description of the murder. When he provides details of the shooting, I sensed an excitement from him, as he revels in the details and explains how she screamed and blood spurted out from her abdomen.

Bardo claimed that he was inspired to shoot Schaeffer by the song *Exit*, from the rock group U-2. Bardo believed that some of the lyrics were references to Schaeffer and himself. Reviewing the lyrics of the song provided some insight to his mindset. "He wanted to believe in the hands of love." The song describes the mixed emotions of love from black to white and "fingering the steel" of a pistol in his pocket. What other influences may have held sway with Bardo? When he was fleeing the scene of the shooting, he tossed away a copy of *Catcher in the Rye*. He had previously written letters to Chapman after the assassination of John Lennon. He fled the scene and was subsequently arrested the next day while running through traffic in Tucson, Arizona. His sister, upon hearing of the murder of

Rebecca Schaeffer, called Tennessee authorities and reported her brother may have been the suspect.

Bardo was influenced to utilize the services of a private investigator by media reports of the stalker of the well-known actress Teresa Saldana. In 1982, Arthur Richard Jackson stalked Teresa Saldana. He utilized a private investigator to obtain Teresa's mother's telephone number. He called her mother and posed as an assistant to director Martin Scorsese to obtain the address of Teresa, so that they could send her a script for her review. Most mothers looking to be helpful to their daughter's career would have complied.

After obtaining her address, Jackson made contact with Teresa Saldana outside her home and stabbed her 10 times. The attack was so vicious that he actually bent the knife in his assault. She survived the assault and Jackson was returned to Scotland to serve time. He died in an asylum in 2004. Robert Bardo read an article in People Magazine on Jackson's assault, and he learned from the article that Jackson used a private investigator.

Chapter 40
Interviewing

When you are interviewing suspects related to these investigations the road can be filled with potholes. Many of these individuals are challenged with mental illness and as a result, you have to exercise a great deal of patience and provide a great deal of latitude. You must view the world from their flip-flops. The world is viewed from their own fractured or altered sense of reality. Many of these individuals have a high degree of functioning and are extremely intelligent. You will have to be crafty in determining their motivations, plans, intentions, and agenda. As we saw with John Hinckley, it is best to use the strategy of "once upon a time." Start from the beginning. You will have a much better understanding of their psychological makeup if you can determine their background; most times, they are willing to discuss their biographical life.

I always try to avoid discussing the initial conduct or allegations that have brought the suspect and me together. On occasion, they may ask what my concerns are, but I try to minimize that approach and focus on their background. This usually helps to establish a degree of rapport with these individuals. I prefer to utilize a casual approach and avoid the hardball tactics seen in the movies and the television world of Hollywood. I will admit that it does become challenging as some of these individuals will not only run off the road, but continue running through the weeds for extended periods of time. I allow this for a time, so I can ascertain their psychological makeup, but when I realize that they are straying too far off the path, I will then give a gentle tug to guide them back to the road. Once I focus their attention on a new subject, they will often once again stray off the path. This repetitive process allows me to explore their personality and their reality.

The interviewer should understand that many of these individuals are not approaching life from a rational standpoint. Reality is based on their viewpoint of life. I one time spoke with an individual, who at the end of the conversation, I bid good luck. My intention was that he would stay out of trouble and enjoy stability in his mental health. He took that farewell salute as a positive affirmation for his journey of discovery and bizarre behavior. Perception is reality.

The areas that should be explored during the interview where they are from, their family upbringing, their relationship with their parents and siblings, how they would characterize their family life, and what their current relationship with their parents and siblings is. Ask them where they have travelled and for what purpose. This provides an insight into possible stalking behavior and how organized or capable they are of completing the logistics of travel.

Determine where they have been employed, what they enjoy or dislike about their jobs, and what their passions are in life. You want to determine the stability, longevity and organizational abilities of their employment. Ask if they had any disciplinary problems, and how they interacted with co-workers and supervisors.

Also, gauge their grasp of reality by asking them where they obtain their news and if there are any current events that they find alarming or concerning. Try to ascertain if they know the date, the month of the year, where they are living and their address. One police department made the unfortunate mistake of asking one of these individuals if he knew who the president was. This had the effect of throwing chum in the water for the sharks. It unfortunately baited him into making some disparaging remarks toward the president. During my subsequent interview of the individual, I determined that he had little interest in the affairs of the president, but I was also able to determine that he was deeply disturbed and could potentially pose a significant threat to the public at large. The last I heard, that individual had moved out of state and returned home, where I hope his family is providing the social support that he needs.

Ask questions concerning their social support system. Who are his friends and how often does he see them? For many families, the level of frustration has reached the point that they can no longer tolerate the disruptive and aggressive behavior. When interviewing a former NFL player, he said that he had no contact with former teammates. His bizarre behavior had alienated him from the locker-room friends. This trend is understandable. Those who are residing in assisted living facilities (ALF's) often reported isolation due to their aggressive tendencies.

This former player eventually moved back to his hometown to be closer to his family. When you are exploring the family dynamics, you want to determine the depth of the relationship. How close are they and how often do they have contact? One individual, who had retreated to a closet and armed himself with a knife, was convinced to drop the knife after an armed confrontation. His mother and grandmother drove up as we loaded him in the police car. Despite their best intentions to provide loving support, this individual was facing a long-term commitment because of the depth of his mental illness.

Eventually I will ask if they have ever sought mental health treatment. This will be an area to investigate in depth. This is where I will determine where they have sought treatment and who their past and current psychiatrists are. I ask them if they recall what their diagnosis is and what kind of treatment or medication they are currently taking. It is useful to find out the last time they were seen by a clinician. Many of these subjects will deny having a problem. I discussed earlier the pharmacology cycle. Are they currently compliant with their prescribed medication therapy?

The one element I want to stress concerning the exploration of their mental health is to determine their level of functioning. Find out how well they are able to focus and whether they would be capable of developing a plan, maintaining discipline long enough to follow that plan, and execute it through completion. I have seen individuals that were stoic and refused to communicate, and on the opposite spectrum, those who had ideological racing thoughts in a manic state and found it difficult to control their emotions.

It is always important to explore whether or not they are experiencing any sort of hallucinations both visual and/or auditory. Many will not admit to visual hallucinations. Auditory hallucinations were quite common in the individuals I interviewed. Auditory hallucinations mean that they are hearing voices. I always want to determine what these hallucinations are telling them to do in order to gauge the strength that the voices hold on them and whether or not the voices are dictating their decision-making and behavior.

I have interviewed a number of individuals who believed very firmly that they were receiving commands from the president through the television. It is important to determine, again, the extent that these individuals are complying, obeying or considering action based on these commands. As is this case, it is important to explore whether or not they have homicidal or suicidal thoughts. I have found that most will volunteer previous incidents but will avoid admitting current ideations. It is for the same reason that mental health facilities become a revolving door, as these individuals know how to play and manipulate the system and realize that admitting any such thoughts could have dire consequences to their freedom.

On the other hand, I had others who willingly manipulated the system by stating their intent to commit homicide when in reality I felt comfortable that these individuals had no intent of acting upon their verbalizations. You must also determine whether or not they are suffering from obsessive delusions, delusions of grandiosity, or of feeling persecuted. I sat down with one individual who was convinced he was God. He provided an interesting conversation, as I explored his delusions of grandeur.

It should be easier to determine those suffering from bipolar disorder or schizophrenia and especially those suffering from paranoia. Some individuals may be suffering from more than one form of mental illness. I am not a trained clinician, and I am not interviewing these individuals to attach a diagnosis. My main goal is to determine how dangerous they are and how organized their thought pattern is in accomplishing their tasks.

I will repeat that depression is probably the most easily concealed mental health disorder. I have known numerous individuals who were able to conceal the depravity and darkness of the world they were experiencing. Their suicide was viewed as a complete shock and out of character by those closest to the victim. It is important to try to determine whether the individual is experiencing the factors that would be pulling them down the negative emotional vortex. This can only be achieved by an empathetic interviewer who can try and stand in the flip-flops of the individual and view the world from his or her eyes.

Ask them about their military history to determine if they were able to fulfill the obligations of their enlistment and what their view of their military history was. Their own personal recollection of their military service is quite often skewed from reality. It still can provide a certain level of insight into their functioning level during their late teen and early twenties when mental illness often begins to develop. It is also interesting to determine how they endured the structure of military life.

One fellow I interviewed pleaded with me to incarcerate him. He felt he could not function outside the structured environment of the military or prison. He told his public defender that he did not want her help. He only wanted to return to jail. Upon his release from prison three years later, he took a cab an hour and half to my office. He assured me that he was determined to keep his life in order. I was not as confident. I expected to hear from him within two months. Two weeks later, I was called by the local police after he made threats to kill someone if not arrested. He was provided a one-way ticket back to the penitentiary.

Many will brag that they were snipers or Navy SEALs. I have never found one of those claims substantiated. I am not as concerned about their specialty or the precise training. I feel that anyone who completed basic training in the military has now acquired the skills necessary to fire a pistol or rifle and has some degree of training in planning and engaging in combat.

According to a 2011 Gallup poll survey, 36% of the American public own at least one gun. I have a number of friends who I refer to as gun enthusiasts. They never passed a gun they did not find attractive and wanted to purchase. I also know that these individuals have never engaged in criminal activity or targeted violence. I caution you to use a common sense approach when assessing the danger of someone who owns firearms.

What is the gun owner's emotional stability? I investigated an individual who embraced a white supremacist ideology and was emotionally unstable. This individual frequently espoused the approval of violence. He developed a reputation by those closest to him as being "crazy." He lived in a neighborhood that was predominantly housing retirees, and his entire neighborhood felt tormented by his incessant bullying. He had former military training, and an undiagnosed mental health disorder. Without notice, he vacated his residence, loaded his car and headed north to visit his mother. At his mother's residence, he had a cache of weapons at his disposal. These were legally purchased firearms by the subject but were maintained by his mother. This individual's behavior was disturbing before he was able to obtain access to the firearms, and now the situation had become extremely volatile.

Gun ownership in the United States is a legal entitlement for all, with the exception of those convicted of felony offenses, and those who have been adjudicated as mentally ill. A voluntary or involuntary commitment to a mental health facility is not considered being adjudicated mentally ill. Typically, an individual is initially committed for a short time normally 48 to 72 hours. If a clinician determines that the individual is a danger to himself or to others after that prescribed examination period, the patient must be seen by a judicial official, who will determine whether that individual needs to remain a patient in the mental health system. It is only after that mandated treatment by a judicial official, that a person becomes adjudicated mentally ill and is no longer allowed access to weapons.

In Illinois, any individual who has been a patient of a mental health facility, either voluntarily or involuntarily, is prohibited from owning a firearm within five years of their release. This is one of the strictest laws in the country. Unfortunately, it did not impede the firearm acquisition of Stephen Kazmierczak, the Northern Illinois University shooter. He deliberately deprived himself of mental health treatment so that he could continue the clock ticking on that five-year time restriction.

USA Today reported in an article in October 2012, that one third of the states reported less than 1 in 100,000 of the population was adjudicated mentally ill to the FBI database. When you consider the fact that according to the National Association of Mental Illness, 1 in 17 Americans suffer some form of mental illness. The surprising statistic is that the states of Alaska, Hawaii, Massachusetts, Pennsylvania, and North Dakota reported only one person to the database. The State of Rhode Island, reported zero individuals to the database.

It should always be of concern when an individual who is enduring what most people perceive as unbearable stressors in life and displays signs of emotional instability has access to firearms. However, according to current laws, these factors in themselves do not prohibit weapon ownership. It should still give caution to an investigator. Investigators should also note any recent changes in weapon ownership. An individual whom has never expressed any interest in firearms who suddenly purchases several weapons and ammunition and begins attending gun ranges to hone his or her skills is concerning.

When it comes to the proficiency of utilizing weapons, it takes a limited skill set to aim a handgun and pull the trigger. That is not to say that practice will not improve proficiency, because it will. We have seen instances of individuals who have never fired a weapon before who were able to pull the trigger and hit their target. Again, I will point to the fact that video games can be a virtual simulator, providing real-life training scenarios and experience in a virtual setting. As an earlier example, I described Michael Carneal in Paducah, Kentucky, who was able to hit 100% of his targets despite never firing a weapon. He had vast experience with video simulators. Adam Lanza the Sandy Hook shooter, also spent hours playing video games, and accompanied his mother to live fire target practice with legally acquired weapons.

An inquiry about their history of substance abuse never hurts, and I have found that in most instances they will be providing a rough estimate of their current and previous usage. Many will distort their usage, but I have had a few who admitted to trying everything but the kitchen sink. The investigator needs to ascertain whether the subject's substance abuse is causing mental impairment or clouding his judgment. Many of these individuals will self-medicate with drugs or alcohol. This usage can exacerbate their agitation and mental illness.

Their view of their arrest history could be slightly altered or so extensive they will fail to recall all of the events. It is always important to conduct an in-depth criminal history check to confirm and verify the veracity of their statements. Many of the individuals I interviewed had the assortment of annoyance arrests, such as disorderly conduct, minor assaults and so forth. When I see on their rap sheet, carrying a concealed weapon, stalking, battery or murder, this grabs my attention. It demonstrates their proclivity to resort to violence.

One female that displayed an unusual level of interest in a politician, had shot her husband seven times on Christmas Day and claimed self-defense. She was ultimately acquitted by a jury. She had become overwhelmed with paranoid beliefs and obsessive-compulsive behavior. Before surveillance cameras became the rage, her entire perimeter was covered by video. She was hoarding enough survival supplies to endure the next five hurricanes. Her being a former professional boxer and having several weapons caused a great deal of concern. The local officers who accompanied me, convinced her to allow them to keep her weapons for safekeeping.

The arrest history and allows me to segue into whether or not they have had previous incidents of harassing behavior or stalking and a history of restraining orders. TRO's will indicate a difficulty in getting along with others either in the workplace, home or at school.

As I have discussed, a number of these individuals have displayed a keen interest or obsession with previous assassins, assassinations, or public killers. It is usually better to avoid a frontal assault and again use a velvet glove approach. Try to enter in through the back door to obtain your information.

It will always help if you can interview them inside their domicile. This will allow you to have a look see and ask for consent to search the premises. Their interests in music, movies and books are worth exploring. If they say they are currently reading *Catcher in the Rye,* I will quickly look for the nearest exit and run for safety.

When you are dealing with an individual who has had difficulty maintaining employment, it is best to ask why in his or her opinion, he or she was unable to maintain continuity of employment. You want to determine whether the individual holds any grudges against any former employers or employees. You want to explore if these individuals are harboring any hostility or are wound collectors, keeping score of everyone that has ever crossed them. It will be worth verifying their version of the job separation with the employer. The level of skill for their job provides some insight into their level of functioning.

Again, I want to stress the importance of determining the organizational ability of the subject. Many of these attacks do not have to be sophisticated and planning may be a minimum of effort. I have seen some individuals who acquired a Ph.D. who were more disorganized in their thoughts than individuals who had only achieved a high school education, but because of their mental illness were unable to complete secondary education. The underachievers were still highly intelligent and organized enough to cause a great deal of concern and danger.

As you are interviewing these individuals, keep in mind the four basic motivations that I described earlier. That is to achieve fame, bring attention to a cause, to achieve suicide by cop, or revenge. The bottom line is you need to determine whether this individual is considering committing an act of targeted violence in order to attach some significance to his or her meaningless life.

I want to caution you never to underestimate the determination of these individuals. This is clearly evidenced in a case that had a profound influence in my career. Fifteen-year-old Kip Kinkel went on a shooting rampage in Springfield, Oregon. I recall walking through the campus of Thurston High and looking into the small cafeteria where Kinkel had launched his senseless attack, and I imagined the students sitting there eating their lunches and exchanging gossip with one another only to have their lives shattered with the sound of gunfire.

Kinkel struggled in his studies and had a difficult relationship with his parents who were respected teachers. Despite their best efforts to provide a nurturing environment, they recognized his challenges and brought him to therapy. The psychotherapist recognized that Kinkel had a significant interest in guns and explosives. Kinkel's father reluctantly explored this hobby as a mutually beneficial interest for building rapport with his son. Kip had confided to the therapist that detonating explosives and shooting alleviated some of his anxiety. Unfortunately, his father's interest did not abate Kip's interest or obsession of firearms, and he was suspended from school after he was caught in possession of a stolen handgun. Realizing that his world was crashing down upon him, Kip began making plans to alter the outcome of his future discipline from his parents.

He executed his father in the kitchen. Kip waited until his mother arrived home and executed her. He contemplated suicide throughout the night. Driving his mother's car, he drove to Thurston High School, entered the cafeteria and began shooting. He killed two and wounded twenty-four students. When he stopped to reload, students, including one who had been wounded in the assault subdued him.

Kinkel was so committed in killing himself that he had the forethought of taping one bullet for each of his guns to his chest. This reflected the depth of his planning. He wanted to provide provisions in case he ran out of ammunition; he would have a reserved a bullet of each caliber weapon to use on himself. Due to the fact that he was subdued by others, he was unable to utilize his hidden bullets.

In the interview room, a detective who interviewed him just two weeks earlier over the firearm at school stood up and left the interview room for a brief moment. When the detective returned, Kinkel who was handcuffed, was able to bring his hands to his front, reach down to his leg and pulled a knife, which he had taped to his leg. This knife had been previously missed during a pat down after his arrest. He lunged at the detective and pleaded with the detective to kill him. The detective, with the assistance of others, was able to subdue Kinkel and disarm him.

In the interview, Kinkel provided a full confession. He displayed remorse for killing his parents. He blamed some of his action on voices in his head, said how fucked up he was, and that he had no choice. He was unable or unwilling to provide a motive for the school shooting. The purpose of the interview was to obtain a homicide confession and not explore motives or psychological background that may have impeded his prosecution. Kinkel was highly emotional during the interview, and the detective was challenged to obtain an in-depth exploration of the crime.

In October 2007, Luke Woodham also killed his mother before travelling to Pearl River High School where he shot and killed two individuals including his former girlfriend. He confided in a friend just before the shooting that he was tired of being ridiculed, beaten, and hated. He said his rampage was not a cry for help but, "a scream in sheer agony." He too said he felt that he had no choice.

Despite the volatility of many of these subjects, it is always best to deescalate the hostility by using genuine empathy. Hardball tactics will only increase tensions and shut down the individual's communication path. They are often guarded and defensive when they are first are exposed to authority figures. You do not want to come across as being patronizing. They will be more likely to share if they feel you are providing an empathetic ear.

Many of these individuals latched on to me because I was willing to listen to their far ranging conversations. You will have to exercise a great deal of patience and give them plenty of leeway to explore their behavioral thoughts. It is the only way to determine their mindset.

Chapter 41
Other Interview Sources

Witnesses

When interviewing witnesses you must assess the veracity of their statements. Most trained investigators understand that witnesses may have agendas; they might want to either conceal the conduct of an individual or erroneously report conduct of an individual. I have seen individuals who became so consumed with the ideology of their agenda that the clarity of their perception had become disrupted and this could result in the lack of reliability in their statements. Unfortunately, information that is provided by a witness who you deem to be perhaps unreliable must still be vetted to protect yourself from future scrutiny for not acting upon information that was provided.

This is clearly evidenced in the recent Boston bombing in which the FBI was notified prior to the bombings that the Tzarnaev brothers were embracing radical ideology as reported by the Russian FSB. Despite the unreliability of some of the information that was passed along, and being skeptical of the agenda of the Russians, the FBI still had to conduct a thorough background investigation of the subjects. The diligence of their investigation will now be closely scrutinized to confirm that their investigation was completed with the knowledge that was known at that time.

An individual called to notify me that a former friend of his was associated with a Russian terrorist group, and she was planning a bombing operation. I was initially skeptical of the motivation of this witness. I knew he had a previous intimate relationship with the alleged suspect, and I suspected that he wanted to exact revenge and destabilize her immigration status. He refused to take a polygraph exam, which further increased my suspicion of this supposed Good Samaritan. My personal interview of the witness became hostile, and he left angry.

Despite my reservations, I had no choice but to follow up on this serious accusation. I confirmed that their intimacy had ended poorly, and she had sought sanctuary with a battered women's shelter. I entered the intriguing journey through the underground protection system for abused women. I located the alleged suspect and conducted an interview with her and a number of other individuals, who undermined the credibility of the witness. The suspected Russian terrorist was the victim of a spiteful and abusive ex-lover. I asked the subject to call her abusive boyfriend in an effort to obtain an admission of his wrongdoing. Although he did not admit to criminal wrongdoing, the conversation provided a clear picture of his intent.

Neighbors

Our relationships with neighbors have changed over the last decades. We have become a much more transient culture. The neoclassical architecture of homes in which the front porch was a basis of external activity has now been replaced with homes that have external activity facing out into the privacy of the backyard. While conducting background investigations, the most common response I obtained from people was that they really did not know their neighbors. They passed each other on the road and just waved as they drove up and down the street. On my last transfer with the Secret Service, I spent seven months in an apartment complex waiting for my family to arrive for the completion of our home. In seven months, I had contact with two neighbors, who provided a brief hello, nice weather, and goodbye. Those neighbors knew nothing about me either.

I described the façade effect, in which we really do not know what goes on behind the front door of the home or apartment. This was clearly evidenced by the most recent example in Cleveland, Ohio. Three girls were held hostage inside a home on a residential street for years. The neighbors were clueless, despite having interactions with the owner of the home.

There will be times that problem children will be known to the neighbors. Neighbors may initially be reluctant to be forthcoming with information concerned that there could be retribution to the statements that they make. When a legal entity is looking into the behavior of one of their neighbors who could potentially pose a danger to them, they may have a vested interest in providing insight into the behavior of that individual.

I described earlier the individual who terrorized his elderly neighbors. This case was one of the few I experienced in which every neighbor spoke of a completely different and negative experience with the suspect. This ranged from conversations that provided insight into his embracing of the Nazi spirit, to anger management issues, to road rage incidents, harassment and stalking of the president of the homeowners association.

People in apartment buildings may have limited engagement with their fellow neighbors, but quite often neighbors will share a common wall with the subject. They may not know exactly what is going on in their neighbor's apartment, but they can provide information about the subject's behavior, daily schedule, and any arguing that may have been overheard. They may also be aware of complaints from other neighbors.

When I was a police detective, a robbery was profiled on our department's Crime Stopper show. A motel resident was watching the show on his television. He overheard the suspects in the next room laughing and critiquing the portrayal of the crime. The motel neighbor called the police and collected the reward. The robbers were apprehended and sent to jail.

The challenges I have found in interviewing neighbors is first trying to find them at home, and second, getting them to open their doors. Even when I identified myself as a law enforcement officer and displayed a badge with government-issued credentials,

I found neighbors reluctant or guarded in their responses. Many times, they were concerned about sharing information on an unstable neighbor who might seek retribution against them after my departure. There were times when I had to make multiple trips into a neighborhood to do an adequate canvas of neighbors. Sometimes I would have to find people early in the morning and return that evening. I often achieved the best success during the noon hour, when some people would return home for lunch. If time was limited, I would leave a business card in the unanswered door. The overall value of the interview was dependent upon his or her willingness to share and knowledge of the subject.

When interviewing neighbors, if the subject is a tenant or renter, make sure you check with the landlord or maintenance person. If the property owner lives on-site, their information will be more valuable than an absentee landlord, who may have limited contact with their tenant. The maintenance person may be able to provide information concerning their dealings with the renter and the condition of the apartment as well as anything of interest that they observed in the apartment such as guns, knives or hand grenades.

Teachers

For students in middle or high school, teachers can provide great insight into the behavior and interaction of their students. Teachers are in direct contact with the student on a daily basis five days a week. They have the opportunity to observe students not only a structured environment, but also their interaction with other students. English teachers in particular have the ability to provide a clear insight into the thought process of students during writing assignments. Teachers and administrators can also share the disciplinary conduct of the student.

On the college level, teacher insight becomes more limited. This is due primarily to the large volume of students in lecture halls, and frequent delegation of classroom activities and grading of papers to teaching assistants. In addition, a higher proportion of college classes are now administered in an online environment. There is limited personal interaction with students. You may have better success with college teachers who are instructing students in their core curriculum, where the classes are smaller and more intimate.

If you are checking on a current student, other students may be able to provide some input as to the behavior of the student. This can be a mixed bag, as some again do not want to be labeled as cooperating with the police, and thus are guarded or protective of providing damaging information. This would be particularly true if the subject student had any degree of popularity or was a close friend. If the student was ostracized or a loner, the information will probably be freer flowing. No trip to the school campus would be complete without conferring with the assigned school resource officer or campus security. They too may have records or recall of non-documented incidents involving the student.

Friends

When interviewing friends, the investigator must be aware of potential allegiances with the subject. Friends may not provide damaging evidence, but they will be in a position to provide information concerning the stability and behavior of the subject. It is always best to ask general questions concerning the overall behaviors and interactions that the subject had with others. Inquire if the friends had any concerns for their own personal safety or that of others. They may not have been concerned for their own safety, but they may have had concerns that the subject was targeting others.

The associates may have discounted these discussions as either reckless talk or jokes. Many a truth is told in jest. It can sometimes help if you approach the interview from an empathetic point of view, minimizing the information that was shared. As an example, you might suggest to the individual that he or she may have thought the subject was joking, but did the subject ever make any statements that you thought were troubling?

Intimate Friends/Spouses

Interviewing intimate partners and spouses can be a double-edged sword. Some, who ended their friendships with consternation, could provide information with an agenda. The motives could include revenge or using the investigation as leverage in future judicial proceedings, including child custody battles. At the same time, these individuals have shared hours of intimate time in conversations with the subject. They can share some significant insight into the mindset and difficulties that the subject may have been experiencing. Any information that I obtain from intimate friends and spouses I assess with a scrutinizing eye. I still believe that interviews with these individuals can provide significant value.

One individual I was investigating was uncooperative during the interview. I asked an associate to locate the subject's ex-wife out of state. She provided complimentary assessments of the subject and believed the behavior was out of character. She also provided a morsel of valuable information that the subject may have been seeing a therapist in another state because of stress and anxiety.

Family

Interviewing family members can be a challenge. There is a saying,"Blood is thicker than water." I have often witnessed family members circling the wagons to protect one of their own. After the Boston Bombing, the parents of the two brothers were in absolute denial of the overwhelming evidence against their children. They launched counter accusations and advocated a conspiracy targeting their children. The school bus hijacker's family was critical of the police sniper who killed their loved one, despite the fact that the hijacker's actions placed innocent children at risk. Family will often be in denial and are defenders of the honor of their family.

As any police officer who has encountered a family disturbance understands, the dangerousness and volatility of the situation increases when the two battling domestic partners unite forces and attack the meddling police officer. The same holds true in these investigations involving targeted violence. At times, particularly when the family has become extremely fatigued and frustrated with a loved one who has endured the pharmacology cycle and revolving doors of mental health system, they can provide some honest input into the history and disposition of the subject.

I recall one individual who shared an honest evaluation of his brother, in which he professed his concerns that his brother would in fact kill someone someday. Timothy Hill, the brother of the armed intruder at the McNair School, shared his family's frustration over his brother's mental illness and inability of the system to address his brother's behavior.

I always approached family members with genuine empathy and sympathy in my heart. I understood that they were torn between being honest and possibly implicating their loved one, and recognized that they had an internal desire to obtain help and support for their family member. I rarely experienced hostility from the loved ones; at times, they were guarded or defensive, but most times, I found them to be cooperative.

Family members can provide tremendous historical knowledge into the thought process and path that the subject followed. They can usually point to the time in the subject's life when he or she pursued the wrong fork and deviated from the path of acceptable behavior to one of aberrant behavior. They can also share societal influences that could have played a part in altering the subject's state of mind, such as head trauma or addiction. They can inform you about the subject's experiences in the criminal justice system, mental health systems previous friends, education, and employment. They may also have knowledge of weapon ownership. The family may be also aware of a genetic predisposition to mental illness stemming from a family history.

It is best to chart a course of interviewing family members with the genuine belief that you want to obtain the help and necessary social services to assist their loved one. I have lost track of the number of family members who have become frustrated with their attempts to obtain help for the family member. The family that is engaged can also become victims through direct action by the killer or the onslaught of the media frenzy after the attack.

Mental Health Professionals

Mental health professionals will not discuss their past or current clients without the permission of the patient. They have a legal obligation to protect the privacy and confidentiality of their patients and clients. If you are able to obtain a release from the patient, the mental health professional can be of great value in assessing the stability of the individual. I would always ask the professionals whether the patient or client or poses a potential danger to others or if he or she was capable of violence. The mental health professional will probably say, "At the time of the patient's release, they were not a danger." The most important element is to determine the patient's thought process, how organized he or she was, and how capable he or she was in formulating a plan that the subject could follow.

Mental Health Records

Mental health records are protected under the confidentiality and privacy laws afforded by HIPPA. Unless the individual has verbalized threatening behavior, it is unlikely that the information will be willingly shared with law enforcement or other investigators. I have also noted on a number of occasions that threatening behavior by the patient was recorded by mental health staff but was never reported to authorities. Either you will have to obtain a release from the patient, a court subpoena, or court order in order for mental health records to be released to you. The records will provide significant input into the functioning, stability, and biographical data of the subject.

This assignment was much easier in the days of paper records. It afforded me the opportunity to flip through charts and identify records of value. In this day, with the digitalization of medical records, you will be forced to sit in front of a computer terminal and become accustomed to reviewing medical records on a monitor. Individual reports can be printed, but keep in mind that due to budgetary restrictions, more facilities are charging for copies of records. It is best to be judicious in your requests.

The two documents that provide the greatest value are: the initial intake summary, which records the initial interview with the subject and the conditions in which they were hospitalized; and the discharge summary, which summarizes the psychiatrist's summation of the patient's progress and stability. It will also include the diagnosis as well. I will also typically peruse the nurse's notes and any notes from group therapy to gauge the patient's behavior and conduct during their admission.

There will also be documentation as of physical examinations, which had lesser value unless there is a head injury or terminal illness. There will also be a recording of prescribed medications. I have less concern over their drug treatment as quite often these individuals are noncompliant for extended periods. Drug treatments often have to be adjusted as the patient's body metabolizes drugs and goes through its own adjustment period. If you are unsure of what ailment the drug is used to treat, you can look these up on the Internet to find out their intended purpose and side effects.

In 2002, a fifteen-year-old stole a plane and flew into the Bank of America building in Tampa, resulting in his death. His mother subsequently filed a $70 million lawsuit against Roche Laboratories. She blamed the drug Accutane on her son's depression and death. The lawsuit was eventually dropped. Most drugs have side effects. When in doubt, your local pharmacist is a plethora of reliable information.

Co-workers

If you are interviewing coworkers, you should gauge the proximity and level of contact they had with the subject, as well as the role in which they interacted with the subject. Were they true coworkers, or were they supervisors? Some supervisors ascribe to the caveman mentality of supervision. That is that they enjoy the safe confines of their cave and have limited interaction with or knowledge of their employees. Other supervisors are much more engaged and have a greater understanding of their employees.

Think of yourself in your own place of employment. Who is it that you interact with the most and who really understands and knows you the best? It is probably your fellow resident in cubicle city, in the adjoining office or standing next to you on the assembly line where you work eight hours a day, 40 to 50 hours a week. Some of these same employees may socialize with the subject outside the work place in a more casual environment, where they might feel more freedom to share their frustrations and thoughts. As an investigator, you want to make sure you determine whether other employees assessed the subject as being a concern to others.

Also helpful is to find out whether the individual was the subject of disciplinary action and how often the employee was disciplined. Was the individual abusing sick leave or filing disability claims or discrimination claims? Many of these allegations can be legitimate and substantiated, but if there is a pattern of claims that are deemed frivolous or fraudulent, those must be taken into context of your overall evaluation of the subject. This conduct is consistent with "wound collectors," who always feel slighted and hold a grudge.

If the subject is a member of the union or trade association, it can also be beneficial to check with the representative or shop steward to obtain their assessments of the subject's conduct and disciplinary record. Unions are looking to protect their members and are not typically willing to share much information. The NFLPA has filed an appeal on behalf of Aaron Hernandez, who was waived by the Patriots after being accused of murder. The faculties at a number of schools have supported members who were accused of egregious acts, including terrorism.

Arrest records

Arrest records will indicate previous arrests and display the original violation of that led to the arrest. Some departments fail to complete the record-keeping, and may not have provided conviction or acquittal updates. Keep in mind, that most of these individuals have had limited criminal history and most of their previous criminal history was relegated to minor or misdemeanor arrests. Items that should raise concern are crimes of violence involving assaults that demonstrate their willingness to use violence, such as the Navy Yard killer who displayed a history of firing a weapon because of anger. Other arrests that should lead an investigator to search deeper are those arrests involving weapons, harassment, threatening behavior, and stalking. These arrests provide a clear indication that the subject is willing to engage or has a history and pattern of showing or displaying this type of conduct.

Police Incidents

I encourage younger investigators not to limit their assessments solely to the arrest record. I felt that there was a significant opportunity to provide additional information by searching the local police departments for any incidents involving the subject. This could include field interview reports, intelligence reports, or reports involving family disturbances that may not have elevated themselves to the level of arrest. The same goes for stalking-related or trespassing cases, in which the individual was provided a warning but was not arrested. You may be able to identify additional witnesses and victims through this process. In addition, it may be helpful to contact the officer who generated the report and obtain his or her evaluation and assessment, which may not have been included in the written portion of his or her report.

Although there may not be a national database of gun ownership, you can obtain some useful insight into gun ownership through family, friends, and police reporting. For law enforcement agencies, you can also check with the Bureau of Alcohol Tobacco and Firearms (ATF) for possible assistance. An individual who has acquired weapons over an extended period or has access to weapons maintained by other family members will not raise any flags.

School Records

School records have limited value. These records will be able to provide information about what type of classes the student was taking and his or her grade achievements. If you are looking into someone who is perhaps considering assembling an explosive device, it may be helpful to see that he or she is an engineering student or has taken chemistry classes. Most of this knowledge can be obtained through the Internet. You will be able to identify teachers assigned to the classes so that you may interview them individually. Most schools will also have a record of disciplinary actions of the student.

Military Records

Military records are accessible through a court subpoena or court order. Military records can be obtained through the National Personnel Records Center in St. Louis, Missouri. The records will provide a truthful accounting of the individual's training, specialties, rank achievement, awards, disciplinary record, and discharge status. It has been my experience that military personnel files quite often are missing performance evaluations as individuals are commonly transferred every two years after their initial training phase. The DD 214 form will summarize their military service in one page.

Military medical records are maintained through the Veterans Administration Hospital. The same rules apply for accessibility; you must obtain either permission from the patient, a court subpoena, or court order. These records can provide insight as to any physical injuries or disabilities that the individual service member sustained while in the military. Of primary interest to me is whether the individual service member sustained a head injury, blunt force trauma, or is suffering emotional instability from PTSD.

If they obtained mental health services while in the military or outpatient post discharge, I will refer you back to the section on mental health records and interviewing mental health professionals. The same rules and objectives apply.

Chapter 42
Holistic Mindset

Having worked with various law enforcement agencies while conducting behavioral threat assessments, I can share with you that many agencies had different approaches. Some agencies are more measured and methodical in their approach to investigating subjects who are considering or threatening to engage in violence. In some instances, they were looking to build a criminal case for which they attempted to acquire witness statements and assemble evidence that could be used in a criminal prosecution of the individual.

The Secret Service approach was one in which they attempt to essentially throw a wet blanket on a smoldering fire in an effort to eradicate the threat. They were more concerned with identifying and disrupting the threat, and assessing the organizational skills and capability of the alleged perpetrator.

In my experience, local police agencies are very forthcoming with information when it comes to reporting threat activity. I was fortunate enough to have enjoyed a tremendous relationship and rapport with my local counterparts. I often referred to them as my safety net, and they were always quick to call me about an individual of concern.

On the federal level, due to the overwhelming size and bureaucracy of the individual agencies, I witnessed more delays in notification between federal agencies. This was again demonstrated by the 1993 World Trade Center bombing, the Fort Hood shooter, and the Boston Marathon bombing. I believe that federal agencies tend to have a myopic viewpoint when it comes to sharing information. All federal agencies are guilty of this conduct. It also comes down to bureaucratic oversight. Quite often, approval must be obtained to disseminate information outside of the agency's jurisdiction. This applies to criminal cases as well, where there are jurisdictional turf wars.

I have witnessed delays in notification that exceeded a month to two months after the conduct or statements became known. You must keep in mind that this is an extensive amount of time for an individual to travel further down the path to violence without being monitored. This will continue to be an ongoing issue until the institutional mindset is altered, and federal agencies recognize that they have a duty to warn. No one should want to be left holding the bag.

In the Navy Yard shooting, the Newport Police made the necessary notification to the Navy in Newport, Rhode Island. Their report indicated the name of the individual they alerted to the bizarre conduct and emotional instability of a contractor with access to their facility. It appears that information was never passed along or acted upon to mitigate possible danger. I would not want to be the person who failed to warn and have the knowledge that I could have prevented the deaths of twelve innocent people.

In the investigation stage of conducting behavioral threat assessments, your goal is to assemble a holistic overall assessment of the behavior of the individual being investigated. I never locked on one trait as being an immediate indictment into the conduct of the individual. You must avoid this trap.

When you consider that a third of the population owns firearms, gun ownership should not be an immediate alarm as to the dangerousness of the individual. Likewise, when you consider that 1 out of 17 Americans suffer from mental health illness of some form, that does not indicate they are considering violence.

Remember in the book, *The Insanity Offense,* only 1% of the mental health patients are considered a danger to society.

I cannot stress enough how important it is to approach the investigative process with a holistic standpoint in order to accumulate as much background and facts about the current behavior and state of mind of the individual as possible. Look at this investigative process as you would in assembling a jigsaw puzzle. You may never have all of the pieces to complete the overall picture, but you may acquire enough of the pieces that you get a general overall assessment of the viewpoint of the picture.

Chapter 43
Prosecution

When it comes to prosecution of the subject, it can be a challenge to identify a criminal act or violation. As we saw in the Boston bombing the oldest Tsarnaev brother, despite being on the radar of foreign intelligence services violated no laws that would have led to his arrest. It also must be kept in mind that most crimes are predicated by intent. Despite the fact that someone may have threatened to kill the president, the predication is based upon whether a reasonable person would have been reasonably alarmed by the statement. In my experience of various judicial proceedings, this was always the most challenging obstacle to overcome. Proving the intention of the individual can be formidable.

The question that I commonly faced from attorneys, judges and juries was not only the intent, but also the level of impairment from mental illness, drugs or alcohol. This is where a complete threat assessment investigation is crucial. You will need to demonstrate the subject's mindset and behavior. Exploring the subject's ability to focus and plan is helpful in proving that he possessed the ability to execute an attack. Did he have access to weapons and had he initiated the planning stage?

I can say that in light of the increase of targeted violence and mass killings throughout the U.S., prosecutors will now give pause and a closer examination of cases presented to them for deliberation. A paradigm shift occurred in the mindset of prosecutors after the Virginia Tech shootings and especially after the Tucson shooting of Gabby Giffords.

I feel much more comfortable and sleep better at night with the knowledge that someone who completed law school and passed the bar exam is the person to make a determination regarding any violation of laws or internal employee policy infractions that would warrant termination. Judicial oversight of your case is mandatory. If you are a business, it is always best to consult with your legal counsel to obtain guidance.

The Jefferson County Sheriff's Office in Littleton, Colorado could have easily processed the already prepared affidavit requesting a search warrant for the residence of Eric Harris and submitted the affidavit for review to the Jefferson County District Attorney's Office. If the district attorney had declined that there was sufficient evidence or probable cause, the sheriff's office would have been able to deflect their exposure with a clear conscience after the shooting. You must embrace this mindset. When the music stops, you do not want to be the last person standing, fully exposed.

Chapter 44
Management

The primary purpose of conducting behavioral threat assessments is to identify those individuals who pose a potential threat going forward. None of us has a crystal ball to be a clear predictor of future violence. However, as we have discussed in this book, there are clear indications that can be predictors of future violent tendencies and the goal is to identify and properly assess a person's conduct so that if appropriate, you can interdict and prevent a tragedy from occurring.

Interdiction stems from either conducting a personal interview that can disrupt the momentum of the individual's behavior, removal of the individual from the environment, or incarceration through the judicial process or mental health process. If it is an employee or a student, that person must be excised from the environment to ensure the safety and stability of those who could be impacted by that person's behavior. If the conduct rises to the level of legal scrutiny, it is incumbent to contact law enforcement authorities for consultation. The goal is to prevent and mitigate violence.

Documentation is essential. In the world of medical charting, if it is not written, it did not happen. The job is not complete until the paperwork is completed. In the Columbine shooting, we saw a lack of documentation, as well as misplaced or destroyed files. In the Boston bombing, there is indication that an employee of the Customs and Border Protection Department of Homeland Security was notified that Tamerlan Tsarnaev, the oldest brother, had returned to the United States after a six-month trip to Russia. There was no documentation that this employee shared that notification. That employee may have shared that information verbally, but in incidents like this, memories often become selective and faulty. Report writing takes a considerable amount of time, but it is essential in providing support for your protection. All notifications must be clearly documented with specificity as to date, time, and the individual who was notified.

In any human relations environment, you may be able to interdict and mitigate potential damage by providing individual counseling to the employee. This would again be utilizing the Grote Harvey discipline model. All employees would benefit from genuine feedback, both positive and negative. It is essential to monitor the manner in which you administer this council. An empathetic approach goes a long way to soothing an individual's emotional state. Options should be explored that will promote a restoration of harmony.

If the hostility cannot be abated through individual counseling, efforts should be made to refer the employee or employees to the firm's employee assistance program. The EAP can be a neutral based effort to moderate unacceptable or disturbing behavior. Some firms also utilize an ombudsman program to assist in mediating resolution of conflicts. The limits of both the ombudsman and the EAP are that in most instances, neither one have any teeth in which to require definitive action. They are there merely to assist in conflict resolution. It can be beneficial for the identified individual to have a sympathetic ear and the feeling that someone cares and is listening to his or hers frustration. This can provide an opportunity for the person to alleviate or diminish their pressure and perhaps learn to incorporate behavior modification that will have a positive outcome.

It remains vitally important to document all human relations interactions with a troubled employee, and you have a mandatory duty to warn individuals who may be impacted by this individual's potential violence. Failure to properly warn those who could be affected could have dire consequences, not only to their safety but for future litigious action for failing to practice due diligence. Although the Penn State incident did not involve workplace violence, the failure of the athletic department and administration's failure to act and notify the authorities of sexual abuse will cost the school approximately sixty million dollars. Hewlett-Packard (HP) and their subcontractor, "The Experts" have civil liability exposure concerning their hiring and retention of Aaron Alexis, the Navy Yard killer. The Experts contract was cancelled by HP, thus resulting in a huge financial loss that will also impact 250 employees.

It is helpful to maintain a liaison with essential contacts throughout this process of mitigating a potentially violent employee. I have observed individuals and threat management personnel fail to follow up and maintain liaison contacts. I suggest that you recruit allies during this process. These allies could be coworkers, neighbors, or family members who can provide status updates on the behavior and conduct of the subject of your inquiry. Mental health professionals will be restricted in providing follow-up information unless they have the patient or client's permission. Even if the employer is paying for the services, they will only be restricted to accessing the billing records, not the content of the visits.

Maintaining contact with the suspect can also be utilized as a tool to monitor his improvement and stability. There were a number of individuals who I maintained contact with for extended periods because I was willing to provide a listening ear. In some instances, I could filter my conversations with them through the voicemail. This had a similar effect as a counseling session, in which the individual could share his or her thoughts and feelings in a five-minute dissertation. Some of these folks would call back multiple times, frustrated with the time limit, but the outcome was positive for both of us, as they were able to unload their thoughts to a person they perceived to be listening, and I was able to monitor their emotional state.

One time, I called an individual the day before a protectee appeared in town. I made no mention of the protectee visit; I merely wanted to assess the subject's state of mind, and what she had on her agenda. A couple of days after the departure of the protectee, I received a call from the subject. She confronted me with her realization that I was, in all probability, monitoring her intended activity. Despite the fact that she was impaired by mental health illness, she was able to assess my conduct, which again is an assertion that these individuals are not to be underestimated.

I would like to comment briefly on computer modeling systems that are utilized for threat assessment. My concern is similar to that of those who rely upon eliminating crime by living within the confines of the gated community. The gated community does not eliminate crime, but the gates provide an element or extra layer of security that can have some influence on reducing crime, though it never eradicates the threat. Using computer modeling for threat assessments causes me concern. I am afraid individuals who rely on the analytical appraisal of the computer hard drive to analyze human behavior may defer decision-making to the computer.

In addition to the erroneous predictions of Hurricane Charlie's path in 2004 that I previously mentioned, many colleges claim to use a holistic admission process, but the process is heavily weighed by the SAT and ACT test scores. That one test determines the approval process. As you can see, I am not a big fan of computer threat assessment modeling. They may be useful in thinning a pool of suspects, but I would not stake my life or that of your family on the results.

Chapter 45
Run, Hide, Fight

The Houston Police Department in cooperation with the Department of Homeland Security has produced an excellent video entitled *Are You Ready? Run Hide Fight.* I would strongly encourage you to find this video on the Internet. It explores the mindset and options available to those in a workplace or school shooting environment. Our brain processes stimuli in rapid succession and threats to our human existence are quickly assessed in fractions of seconds. Some of the responses of the body include increasing the heart rate, redirecting blood from the capillaries back toward the major organs, increasing field of visual acuity and increasing the production of the stress hormone cortisol.

This is the body's primitive way of preserving itself. The body instantly assesses this incoming information to determine the best course of action: run, fight or freeze. Freezing is not an option in a violent encounter. It leaves you exposed for an imminent departure from the face of the earth. Fleeing an attack allows you to become a moving target while increasing distance between the assailant and you. Distance is your friend in a shooting situation. Your ability to survive an attack is much greater when you are able to use distance and movement as your ally.

There will be times when fleeing is not an option, as your escape route may be blocked due to the assailant's position or other obstacles. It is important that employees and teachers identify possible hiding locations to conceal their location from an assailant. This may be as simple as crawling under your desk and pulling the chair as far in as possible. It provides limited protection from gunshots, but it can afford you an opportunity to survive the attack.

The better option is to identify a number of hard-rooms, in which entry can be denied to the assailant. If there is not a locking mechanism on the door, perhaps the door or entryway can be barricaded with furniture. It is important to determine what direction the doors open. You must also assess whether or not bullets can penetrate the walls and if so, identify furniture that may protect you from bullets.

In a shooting in a dormitory at the University of Central Florida in 2013, gunman James Seevakumaran initially encountered one of his suitemates and pointed the rifle at him. The suitemate dove back into his individual bedroom, closed the door, locked it, and then hid behind the chest of drawers to provide additional protection from his assailant. He then dialed 911 to alert responding authorities. The assailant retreated to his own bedroom, where he took his own life.

A third alternative, once you have determined that there is no opportunity to flee or to hide, is to launch an attack on the assailant and fight back. This was demonstrated on 9/11 when the passengers of United Flight #93 rose up against the hijackers and forced the plane to crash into the field in Shanksville, Pennsylvania. In the shooting by Kip Kinkel in Springfield, Oregon, he was subdued by the bravery of a student who was already wounded. Other students, inspired by this display of bravery, came to the aid of the student and assisted in restraining the shooter.

In the Fort Hood shooting, autopsies provided evidence that a number of victims were killed while taking cover and lying with their backs exposed. Others, despite not being armed charged the terrorist and were shot or killed. One, a civilian, armed himself with a chair and was killed while attacking Hassan. No doubt these acts of bravery allowed others to escape. Decisions will have to be made regarding the best option for surviving. You must have a visualized plan with available options.

In a study conducted by Texas State University of 84 active shooter cases, 41 of those cases were resolved prior to the arrival of law enforcement. Nearly 50% of the active shooter incidents were resolved before the police arrived on scene. In 50% of those cases, the assailant committed suicide. It is noteworthy that in 31% of the cases that were resolved prior to the arrival of law enforcement, the assailant was subdued by others.

This is an important aspect to understand: sometimes the only opportunity for survival is to fight and attack the assailant. Quite often, if one individual makes this courageous decision, others may join the fray in what becomes a coordinated attack against the attacker. It may be necessary to utilize primitive weapons and restraining devices. Potential weapons would include fire extinguishers, chairs, bats, statues, lamps and so forth. Possible restraining devices could be belts, rope, electrical cords and so on. In 10% of the incidents that were resolved prior to law enforcement arrival, the assailant was shot by others.

According to Texas State University study, 51% of cases resolved after the police arrived on scene, 30% of the assailants ended the active shooter scenario by taking his or her own life. This leaves 60% of the active shooters who were still engaged when the police arrived and were shot, subdued, or surrendered. Keep in mind that there will always be significant hysteria and pandemonium as a consequence to an active shooter.

As I dug through the rubble at Ground Zero, I often contemplated what went through the minds of those individuals who did not survive the attack that day. I wondered what they were thinking as they brushed their teeth, grabbed a cup of coffee to go, failing to savor the aroma, and closed the doors of their residences, not knowing that they would never see their home again.

People do not prepare for combat on a daily basis. Even law enforcement and military are not anticipating violent encounters each and every day, although they understand the possibility does exist. For citizens making their way to school or to work, a violent outcome or altercation is not anticipated. They have received little training to prepare themselves for a sudden act of violence. However, in light of previous shootings and the probability of future shootings, we must change our mindset and be prepared for an emergency response.

Keep an eye out for exits, where you sit and listen to your inner voice. If you perceive danger, quite often there is a reason for the concern. Gavin DeBecker wrote that humans are the only animals that will override instinct. The fellow student in class with Jared Loughner sat near the door with her purse in her lap. She listened to her inner voice and had a plan.

Chapter 46
News Media

The news media has a job, as well as a duty to inform the public with fair and accurate reporting of events. As the news industry is under intense pressure in the digital age to remain competitive, the nightly news has become overshadowed by the 24/7 news organizations and now bloggers, Twitter and Facebook. The consumers of news demand immediate updates and access to information. This creates a highly competitive market as all these platforms make an effort to be the first to report or have an exclusive interview.

After any mass shooting, there will be a thirst for information by news media outlets. In today's technologically advanced society, everyone who is armed with a cell phone or camera is a potential citizen journalist and capable of capturing graphic, real-time images as well as monitoring the response of first responders. In the 24/7 news cycle, as news alerts are pushed out, viewers are beckoned to plug-in to the source of their news.

The media has become compelled to provide input from subject matter experts (SME) on the crisis. Many of these SMEs are commonly referred to as talking heads. I have often witnessed news outlets relying on individuals who have either weak resumes or are discussing topics outside their defined area of expertise. As a result, quite often the initial assessments are highly inaccurate and factually wrong. Some of these assessments are based upon the fog of the crisis, and initial reports are not accurate.

Some of these experts are in fact very knowledgeable in their subject areas and can provide considerable insight and analysis. They will also be in a position to critique the investigation before during and after the incident. During every one of these major public shootings, whether it was Tucson, Aurora, Sandy Hook, Boston, or others, agencies must be prepared for the media onslaught, the subsequent examination, and critique of their actions.

After every one of these major incidents, I brace myself for the news of a copycat killer. Copycats may have already been deliberating the use of violence as an acceptable means of attaching significance to their meaningless lives. The success of the assault emboldens the individual, and this will provide them with the confidence to proceed forward and execute their contemplated act of violence. Many of these copycats will also be strengthened by the fact that they know that their message platform will be leveraged by the media circus, and that they will be able to place an exclamation mark next to their name so that everyone will remember them and understand the motivation behind their act.

As we have seen becoming more commonplace, many of these attackers are now going to the lengths of either writing or recording video manifestoes, which becomes essentially virtual suicide notes notifying those they hold responsible and asserting retribution for their collection of wounds. Quite often, the news media will unintentionally glorify these individuals and at times will even make them appear somewhat sympathetic. This is evidenced by the younger brother of the Boston bombing suspect, Dzhokhar Tsarnaev, who despite deliberately placing a backpack bomb next to an eight-year-old child, has developed a cult following on Facebook by shallow, idiotic followers. Rolling Stone Magazine has glorified his persona by placing a provocative photo of the killer on their cover. The magazines sales doubled with the killer's photo on the cover.

The news media has an obligation to inform and produce material for their viewership. The media is a big business and always on the hunt for ratings and advertising dollars. If it bleeds, it leads. Most organizations strive to maintain a sense of accuracy, but this is a difficult measure to achieve in the early fog of the mass hysteria, when the media is trying to determine and ascertain the accurate flow of information while attempting to be the first news outlet to break the news.

Unfortunately, the news media has been used as a leveraging platform for many of these mass killers. After the University of Texas shooting, Charles Whitman appeared on the front cover of all the major magazines of the day. Today, shooters are prominently featured on every cable news outlet and Internet blog. The shooter in death is now memorialized forever by those willing to research the archived accounts of their murders and the killers' own dedicated Wikipedia pages. Dr. Katherine Ramsland calls this thought process, "the rehearsal fantasy" as the potential killers dream of the coverage of his or her carnage.

One area that I would like to address is that in the post-catastrophe interviewing of witnesses, their recollection of events can be significantly impaired. Our biological brains' processing of a crisis stimulates the release of the stress hormone cortisol, which can impair memory formulation in the hippocampus area of the brain. As a result, in these catastrophic events, eyewitness testimony can vary significantly, even among those who witnessed the same event.

The Innocence Project identified that in 75% of all false convictions were directly attributed to inaccurate eyewitness identifications of the suspects. These convictions were overturned due to contradictory DNA evidence. In almost every case, eyewitness or victim testimony was considered the most compelling evidence in the case against those individuals wrongly convicted.

In an experiment conducted by Gary Wells and Amy Bradfield of Iowa State University, they displayed a grainy surveillance video of an individual man to test participants, who were told that the subject in the video later shot a security guard. The test participants were then asked to view five mug shots and identify the perpetrator. The five mug shots did not include a photo of the individual in the surveillance footage. Despite the difficult task of identifying a mug shot from a grainy surveillance video, every one of the 352 test subjects wrongly identified one of the mug shots. Thankfully, these test subjects were not testifying in a court of law and their misidentification would not lead to the unnecessary incarceration of an individual.

I believe the experiment still holds value in demonstrating that we must be careful in assessing the accuracy of eyewitness testimony, especially after a catastrophic event that has been a shock to the conscience. First reports are often wrong.

Chapter 47
Protective Orders

It may be necessary to obtain a restraining order or protective order to be served on the individual. These orders are not a silver bullet. They will only be effective against offenders who fear the ramifications of possible arrest. For those who have little concern of being arrested and little regard for their own lives, and who have embraced suicide as a viable option, these restraining orders will have limited impact.

Professors T.K. Logan and Robert Walker of the Department of Behavioral Science at the University of Kentucky have conducted extensive research on the effectiveness of civil protective orders. In a study of 213 females, which was split between 107 in urban environments and 106 in rural settings, they determined that half of the victims of partner violence indicated the protective order was not violated. In 86% of the rural and 87% of the urban participants, the women believed the protective order was effective. The research did indicate that enforcement of the protective orders by law enforcement could be at times problematic.

Gavin deBecker, author of *The Gift of Fear*, proposes the theory of engage and enrage. The principle of the theory is that violence can increase once law enforcement becomes involved. This includes the obtaining of protective orders. Those who have a chronic stalker are often faced with the dilemma of whether to obtain a protective order or to ignore the behavior in hopes that the stalker will turn his or her attention elsewhere or that the conduct will eventually abate. When the stalker's behavior increases in intensity or frequency, this pattern should not be ignored.

Alissa Blanton, a former Hooters waitress was stalked by an older customer for years. She sought a protection order against her stalker. The judge failed to issue the restraining order, but this would have had little impact on an attacker who was not only committed toward homicide, but also suicide. Laura Black was in the process of obtaining a restraining order against Richard Farley at ESL. He intended to commit suicide and conducted a murderous rampage. The judge who approved the order after the shooting said that paper will not prevent bullets.

Regardless of the effectiveness of restraining orders, it is a necessary tool to be utilized in the legal documentation and legal enforcement and to assist in providing safety to you and your community. Although restraining orders are often ineffective, you cannot take the approach that the process will not work and therefore why waste the time and money. Rest assured, if violence breaks out, you will be on the witness stand addressing the reason why you chose not to obtain a temporary restraining order against the individual.

Restraining orders or protective orders are typically enforced to ensure that the person of concern remains at a certain distance from their target and restricts contact. Restraining orders are quite frequently enforced for a specific and limited duration. Depending on the jurisdiction, they are sometimes not enforceable by local or municipal law enforcement agencies but must be enforced by the county sheriff. The order is issued by a judge after reviewing the facts of the case.

The approach of these individuals who ignore the restraining order is that if he/she cannot have you, no one will. For a school or a business, you do not have the luxury of anticipating the future conduct of the individual who has posed behavioral concerns to your organization. You must document your attempts to obtain a protective or restraining order against the individual if they have posed a threat.

Chapter 48
Removal of the Individual

When it is deemed necessary to terminate the individual or to remove that individual from the environment, it is essential that all employees in the security department be notified of the pending termination. This will allow security to heighten their alert status and be prepared if the individual makes a spontaneous act of aggression, sabotage, or returns with the intent of engaging in targeted violence. If concerns are heightened enough concerning the behavior of the individual, it may be necessary to incorporate the hiring of additional armed and trained security personnel. Not all security companies are comprised of armed and well-trained individuals. Many professional security companies can provide security officers who fit that model. Off-duty police officers may also be a viable option.

It may also be in your best interest to hire either a private investigator or off-duty law enforcement officers to conduct surveillance and monitor the individual for the next few days to assess his behavior. If the surveillance team observes the individual conducting his own surveillance of the organization's members or the physical location of the organization and appears to be engaging in stalking behavior, this should become an immediate concern. Evidence of this behavior should be documented and photographed, if possible. If the subject strolls into a firearm dealer, this would be considered a clue as well.

You cannot conduct surveillance on the individual for an indefinite period. This process is not applicable toward the individual who, upon learning of his or her termination, appears to accept the separation without harboring any violent intentions toward the organization or its members. For those whose conduct clearly indicates there is a threat, it may be advantageous in the short-term to conduct this surveillance. This can become an expensive proposition, and may not be feasible for a small business. For a larger corporation, it becomes more important to take this extra step to ensure the security of your organization.

If the individual at some time in the future engages in a violent path of targeted violence, the organization will be questioned as to why they did not continue surveillance for a longer period. This will always be a judgment call, but the fallback response should be that in an effort to provide adequate safety for the members of your organization, you conducted a short-term surveillance on the individual to ensure that he was not preparing to engage in an immediate act of aggression toward the organization or its members. Your surveillance team was unable to observe any pattern of disturbing behavior that would've brought concern to anyone within the organization, and the determination was made to cease the operation, as you did not want to be construed as violating the rights and privacy of the terminated employee.

When it comes to the safety and security of the organization, surveillance and alarm systems become a force multiplier. These systems incorporate utilization of an integrated camera surveillance system, perimeter alarm system, panic alarms, adequate door locking and access control devices. Those organizations that are lacking in these devices are exposing themselves to a huge liability.

I would encourage you to obtain the services of a security consultant. This should be someone who does not have a vested interest in an individual security company or products from which he or she will potentially profit. Security should be approached from the point of view of what is reasonable and expected to ensure basic level of safety and security, while still providing accessibility to customers, clients or students.

With security consultants, you must scrutinize their qualifications. Certifications can be good and a series of initials after their name looks impressive, but what do the letters mean and how does one acquire these designations? Look for those that are familiar with crime prevention through environmental design (CPTED). The six main concepts of CPTED are defining territory, surveillance of defined areas, access control to property and buildings, maintenance of infrastructure, promoting activity to decrease crime opportunities and target hardening.

Many police departments have crime prevention practitioners who can conduct security surveys of your organization and provide valuable input. While the service may be offered as a service to the community, you may have to be placed on a waiting list to obtain your survey. It is always best to obtain a survey before you need one as opposed to responding as a crisis is developing and not being able to obtain a survey.

One of my clients wanted to enhance her security and integrate a surveillance camera system. I provided suggestions and input. Based upon those recommendations, she obtained an estimate from a vendor. I was asked to assess the proposal and was astonished at the price. I encouraged the client to obtain an estimate from another company. The second installer submitted a proposal that was half the price. Being the security advocate in this situation allowed me to save a considerable amount of money for the client. My fee, as it turned out, was a small percentage of the total savings.

In addition to the notification of the security department upon termination of an individual, your IT department should also be notified. You should coordinate with the IT department that at a predetermined time after termination, the individual's access to all computer and access platforms in the building be removed. This will eliminate the possibility of sabotage and reduce the possibility that the individual will walk out to the parking lot, retrieve a weapon, and return through one of the access points.

It is always essential that after the employee has been terminated, all other employees are notified that the subject is no longer a member of the community, and his or her access to the property has been removed. The employees should be instructed that any future observation of the individual on the grounds should be immediately reported to the security department. It is best not to include the cause of the separation but only to indicate that the person is no longer a member of the business or school community.

Chapter 49
Threat Management Unit

The purpose of the threat management unit is to identify individuals who are displaying concerning behaviors and assessing what risk that those individuals pose to the organization and attempt to manage a successful outcome. The organization could be a school, community, or business enterprise. I will use the term "threat management unit" (TMU) but I have heard various terms used, including threat assessment team, threat analysis unit, crisis intervention team, behavioral intervention team and others. One university informed me that their legal counsel advised them to avoid using the words "threat" and "assessment" to avoid potential legal liability down the road.

Regardless of what you call your threat management unit, the purpose and mission must be the same, and that is to keep your assets safe. Assets include students, visitors, employees, infrastructure, equipment, and intellectual and physical property. The number one asset is always the human asset. You can always rebuild the infrastructure or replace equipment, but you can never replace the existence of human life, and the impact on those around that person.

The threat assessment process involves several steps, beginning with the intake of an initial report indicating observable behavior that is of concern. Some advocate assigning a preliminary risk level of low to high. I do not like this approach. I believe the person either presents a danger or does not. Someone who is initially assessed as being a low threat may experience a crisis in his or her life. This crisis could serve as a catalyst to propel the person from a low threat to a high threat in a very small time frame. Labeling someone as a low threat can provide a false sense of security. I believe that any time somebody rings the alarm bell, it should give cause for a threat assessment to be conducted of that troublesome individual.

The roster of the threat management unit must be published and accessible to all individuals within the organization. This avoids the confusion of a single point of contact, who might be on vacation or unavailable to field the call. Every member of the unit should have the responsibility and ability to contact the hierarchy within the organization to make a notification of a rapidly changing safety environment that should be addressed immediately. In the absence of an immediate threat, the individual who is initially notified of the problematic behavior should have the ability to assemble the threat management unit.

Upon the initial intake of the complaint, the broadest view of the behavioral picture must be assembled. That includes any and all biographical data of the individual, longevity with the organization, previous conduct within the organization, what steps have been utilized to address the behavior, observations of direct contact and interactions with the individual suspect, and detailed descriptions of the concerning pattern of behavior or behavioral incidents. Concerning the individual incidents, dates, times, and witnesses should be obtained. These are all critical keys to documenting a problematic individual.

As in the medical world, if it is not written in the chart it did not happen. People often take a lazy approach and claim they did not have time. They might say that that the behavior was confined to a single event, or they thought the employee would change his or her behavior. You can document the verbalization;

however, if this incident enters into the legal arena, the absence of previous documentation will significantly weaken the case. Again, I cannot stress enough how important documentation is to provide legal support for any disciplinary or mitigation efforts in the future.

Despite the lack of documentation, you still have a responsibility to provide a safe environment for your human assets. You must approach the management of the threat from the point of view that it is better to be sued by one individual and substantiate your actions than to believe the barn door is already open, and it is too late. As a result, an unrestrained individual engages in a mass shooting directed toward other members of the organization.

To manage an assessed threat, there are a number of actions that may be incorporated in the management process, including: supervisory counseling, mediation through the use of an ombudsman-type approach, referral to the EAP, referral to anger management counseling, behavior modification through disciplinary measures which could include from a minimum to maximum actions. Disciplinary procedures could be gradually increased through the following steps: oral reprimand, written reprimand, probation, suspension in varying degrees, reassignment and separation.

I cannot stress enough the absolute importance in threat managements unit's duty to warn. If at a later date it becomes known that you were aware of a threat toward another individual and you failed to notify the intended target, you may as well just open up your checkbook and put a lot of zeros at the end of it.

When I was with the Secret Service, many of the individuals I interviewed displayed unusual interest toward others, including politicians, celebrities or others that the person viewed in a revengeful manner. It was always incumbent upon me to notify those individuals either directly or indirectly through their security apparatus and those notifications were always documented as to whom I spoke to, the date and time.

Any threat should be immediately reported to the local law enforcement agency. Many larger departments have individuals within their ranks who have received some degree of training in conducting threat assessments. Those in the law enforcement community who have experience and training in threat assessments can be a great comfort and an excellent resource. Many agencies lack those resources; however, most police officers through their basic law enforcement training and experience with dangerous individuals, provides better insight and experience to draw upon in conducting threat assessments, despite the lack of formal education in the particular field of threat assessments.

Chapter 50
Composition of the Team

Some organizations have utilized the approach of hiring outside threat assessment professionals to conduct behavioral threat assessments. This is always beneficial to see if you have the liberty to obtain a second opinion however, this can be a costly process. It is best to have an organization that is based internally, is familiar with the culture of the organization and has the ability to blend essential entities from within the organization that can either provide essential insight or have a vested interest in the threat assessment process.

Another aspect is that familiarity breeds responsiveness. When I was assigned to the Joint Terrorism Task Force (JTTF), there were a number of occasions when a representative from another agency would see me and bring to my attention a matter that they may not have considered important. Another advantage to an in-house threat assessment unit is proximity and timeliness of response. They have the ability to immediately respond to a threat that has been reported. They can quickly assemble within minutes or hours in a conference room to discuss the matter at hand.

If you are utilizing an outside vendor to function as your threat management unit, you perhaps have some liability protection in that you can take the pose of the Heisman Trophy by claiming you delegated this to an outside professional organization and their failures are not your failure, because you relied upon their expertise and training. An in-house unit essentially has no expense outside of the cost of the initial training and man-hours devoted to their mission.

Obviously, if you are a small company with less than a couple hundred employees, a threat management unit may not be feasible. In a smaller company, where the owner or manager personally knows all of the employees, there is less need to have an overall team assessment approach. In a school environment, a team approach will usually be necessary. When in doubt, it is best to obtain an outside expert opinion.

When determining who the members of the threat management unit should be, it is essential to include all of those who can provide insight into developing a holistic behavioral threat assessment approach. The larger the group, the less agile it becomes. It has always been my experience that larger groups have a greater challenge in reaching a consensus opinion and being responsive to the needs of the organization. Alternatively, you should have more than two or three members so that you can draw upon the knowledge and wisdom of various aspects of the organization.

In all organizations, whether it is academic or business related, representation from human resources is essential. In an employment situation, HR will be able to provide a detailed assessment of the individual's publicly known private life, previous employment history, and performance evaluations as well as any previous disciplinary record. Even in an academic setting, HR analysts bring to the table a skill set for which they are routinely called upon to assess and make judgments concerning the character of applicants and employees. These are useful skills to have on the threat management unit.

Security should and must be an integral member of the assessment process. They may become aware of issues concerning their employees that administration may not be aware of concerning his or her behavior. Unfortunately, many organizations view security as a necessary evil and relegate them to a night watchman status. While on vacation, I watched as the loss prevention personnel at the resort pushed luggage carts laden with the tourist's belongings to their resort villas. This was an irresponsible utilization of security personnel. This view is common in the corporate world.

I have seen too often, administrators who feel they are omniscient and have a better sense of the activities in their organization than the security officers who were viewed as pariahs. Security can either be the Achilles' heel of an organization or a strength. Regardless of their positioning within the hierarchy of the organization, the security department can be the eyes and ears and are commonly the first line of defense during a crisis. I was told by a security professional that the president of his organization had been threatened in a graphic manner by a member of the community. The community member was banished. Security only became aware of the threat after the suspect was detained by local police, who reported the subject was on the path to violence against the president.

Security will be the immediate first responders to a crisis and provide stabilization efforts until municipal first responders arrive on scene. Besides being the eyes and ears, they quite often will have physical interaction with the individual on various levels and perhaps can provide input in the decision-making process.

If you are in a unionized environment, it is perhaps best to include the union as part of the process as opposed to an adversarial role in the threat management unit. This decision will have to be made on a case-by-case basis. Depending upon the union representation, they may take the position of placing the interests of the individual employee above that of all other employees. If the union representative is reasonable, he or she could be an ally while acting as an ambassador to the remaining workers to provide confidence in the fairness of the assessment process. Their inclusion in the unit should not be an impediment to providing an adequate, fair screening and assessment of individuals posing a risk.

Along the same lines as a union representative, we should also address members of student council or student campus associations. My viewpoint is that most of these individuals will lack the maturity and overall world experience to provide much insight into the process. It is also essential to maintain confidentiality while conducting a threat assessment, and this is another reason the scope of membership should be limited.

In-house legal counsel is a reliable participant in the assessment process. Legal counsel can provide advice and guidance, as well as providing a legal safety net. They can also present a devil's advocate viewpoint as to the ramifications of action versus non-action. There can be times when an attorney can become an impediment; however, the legal insight is beneficial for consideration. If you do not have in-house counsel, it may be best to consult with outside legal advice prior to termination or expulsion of the problem individual. Your legal advice should be obtained from an individual who has expertise in that particular field of law, such as in labor relations.

A member from the EAP should be included. EAP individuals can provide insight into referral-based programs that may be available in an attempt to manage and mitigate the concerning behavior. This particularly applies to substance abuse programs or social programs, for which referrals can assist in housing needs, food banks, Salvation Army, and so forth. I have always looked at the devoted individuals in the EAP as having the ability to provide a group hug to individuals who need a life preserver tossed to them. EAP members are extremely useful in providing support to troubled employees early in the process. EAP has limited ability when it comes commanding change or to address workplace efficiency in production.

In the workplace, it is essential to have the employee's immediate supervisor and perhaps mid-level manager involved in the assessment process. This member will be evolving on a case-by-case basis depending on who the problematic employee is. The immediate supervisor will be able to provide the greatest input as to the day-to-day behavioral conduct of the subject employee. This supervisor, if properly engaged, should be familiar with any personal turmoil the employees is experiencing, as well as ongoing hostility with fellow employees.

In a campus environment, the assessment group should also include housing, on-campus counseling services and academic affairs. Housing administration will be able to determine whether there were complaints by roommates or resident advisors. If room inspections were being conducted, the housing administrators will be able to provide results of any housing inspections. They will also be able to consult with the resident advisor for the particular dormitory building to obtain an objective analysis. A great deal of responsibility is placed on resident advisors, as they are asked to be an enforcer of rules and regulations, as well as on psychologists, social workers, and oh yes, students.

On-campus counseling centers will be able to provide advice concerning programs available to assist the problem student. They should also have knowledge as to whether the student is seeking treatment and abiding by the conditions of the treatment. They will only be able to share this information if the student becomes a threat to the health and safety of him or herself, or to others.

When it comes to the inclusion of academic affairs, they will be able to reach out to the instructors of the individual students to obtain feedback on their behavior within the classroom setting as well as observed interactions with other students. At Virginia Tech, the English department was loudly sounding the alarm for concern and properly notified academic affairs. Unfortunately, there was limited coordination between the various entities within the university environment. This lack of coordination is estimated to have cost the university and the State of Virginia approximately $48 million.

If there is a judicial affairs office on campus, they too should be included in the process. Judicial affairs are the primary administrator of the student rules and regulations for the individual university. Judicial affairs are routinely charged with the responsibility of the enforcement of college regulations.

In all threat management units, it is essential to have a quarterback who is coordinating and leading the activities and facilitating the assessment flow process. In other words, someone needs to be in charge. That person should have direct access to the CEO, president, owner, dean, or whoever has the ability to arbitrate a final decision.

It is also beneficial to consult a mental health professional trained in forensic psychology. Forensic psychology is the unique study of psychology with a focus on the assessment, diagnosis and treatment of individuals who have interacted with the criminal justice system. As in medicine, there are unique areas of specialty. You would not go to an orthopedic surgeon for a cold.

The mission and focus of the threat management unit is based upon enhancing the security of the organization and its members. All members of the threat management unit must consistently adhere to that focus. This is no place for those who have an agenda or are looking to pad their resumes. Their interest in being a member must be genuine and their selection is based upon their integral usefulness to the unit and organization as a whole.

Chapter 51
Conducting the Threat Assessment

Once the threat management unit sits down at the conference table to discuss a problematic individual, there must be a process and order to their examination. They must examine the initial complaint to ensure that there are no hidden agendas by the complaining party. They must look at the previous conduct of the employee to see whether this is out of character or perhaps an escalation of previously inappropriate behavior. In addition to the initial complaint, the unit must make every attempt to corroborate the disturbing behavior. This will be accomplished through direct interviews of those that who are listed as witnesses or are routinely in close proximity to the individual.

Corroboration is necessary as it is in criminal cases. In a criminal case, if someone claims that another individual struck him or her, you would not arrest the alleged suspect without first corroborating the initial statement. This is achieved by compiling evidence through statements of witness accounts, physical evidence in the case of an injury, or perhaps surveillance film.

The same holds true in corroborating statements during a threat assessment process. Despite the integrity of the reporting party, it is always best to obtain corroborating evidence from other sources. This could be obtained from determining entry and exit log times through access control devices, as well as computer examinations of emails, social media postings, cell phone evidence, or surveillance video footage.

When conducting the assessment process the largest concerns are whether this was a one-time incident, and if the individual is accepting responsibility for the transgression or there is evidence of an escalation of behavior that is concerning to those around the individual. You have to assess what the individual's coping skills are and whether they are incurring anger management issues, emotional instability, or mental health instability. If the individual is experiencing a great deal of personal turmoil, you must view the world from their flip-flops and determine whether that individual may be viewing the world from the position of being sucked into the negative emotional vortex with no way out.

Many of these individuals have narcissistic tendencies; perhaps they are consumed with paranoia and may be wound collectors. It may be difficult to determine whether this individual is already working on plans, but the reality is that many of these incidents are not very complex. It does not take a highly skilled assassin to purchase a handgun, walk into a crowd, a classroom, or an office building, and begin shooting. Most people who have some degree of functioning within society have the capacity to execute the attack of targeted violence.

To obtain the means, such as a firearm, most people live close enough to a pawnshop, gun dealer, or sporting goods store. In some instances, the individual stole legally owned weapons used in the attack. As has been demonstrated in previous attacks, it was not difficult to obtain the means to execute the attack.

In November 2012, a suspect entered a classroom at Casper Community College in Casper, Wyoming. The suspect was armed with a crossbow. The teacher was killed at the hands of his own son, who then took his own life. In December 2012, in Chenpeng, China, a 36-year-old armed with a machete stabbed 23 children and an elderly woman. Fortunately, all of the victims survived. In April 2013, Dylan Quick, a student at Lone Star College in Cyprus, Texas, used a razor edged weapon to wound 14 students.

Quick, who is hearing-impaired was described by neighbors as being a nice, quiet boy. He apparently also harbored visions of committing mass murder for many years.

In March 1996, Thomas Hamilton, armed with four handguns entered the Dublane Primary School in Dublane, Scotland, where he killed 17 students and wounded 14 before committing suicide. Hamilton had been accused of inappropriate touching of boys, and he blamed the accusations on his business failure. Despite the UK's strict gun ownership laws, Hamilton was able to engage in a murderous rampage. I am not arguing for or against stronger gun laws; the point is that those committed to violence and suicide will not be deterred by legalities.

Chapter 52
Getting Help & Training

Although someone who has a degree in psychology and is a member of the employee assistance program as a counselor may have a basic understanding of psychology and displays compassion to others, he or she are not necessarily well versed in the practices and concepts of threat assessments. This is why once the full-time members are selected, they must be properly trained in the process.

Training is not simply reading this book or others on the subject. Imagine yourself on the witness stand, and the defense attorney asks where you obtained your training and skill for the threat management unit. Your response is that you have read a number of books written by other individuals. This will provide limited value in terms of legal standing in a lawsuit.

The quarterback or designated leader of the group must ensure that the entire process of conducting the threat assessment is clearly documented. The initial complaint must be documented, all follow-up fact gathering investigations and attempts to mitigate or manage the behavioral conduct must be documented. You must assume that these documents will be analyzed by attorneys in judicial proceedings stemming from civil or criminal actions.

You may be fortunate in the case that there are no legal proceedings associated with the assessment, but you must approach your documentation from a legal standpoint.

There are many so-called experts in threat assessments. There are also a number of folks who claim to be criminal profilers. You must make a careful analysis of the person's knowledge and experience in this field. Whoever you select should be well-vetted. Always ask for curriculum vitae and scrutinize this document closely for accuracy and experience with the subject matter. Some folks are collectors of initials following their name. The initials can provide a degree of competency, but sometimes they merely mean they passed a paid examination. Just because someone claims to have been in charge of security for a major corporation, a police officer, FBI agent, or Secret Service agent, that does not make him or her proficient in conducting threat assessments. I cannot stress how important it is to scrutinize their resumes. I do these routinely on so-called experts and find often their backgrounds are embellished and overstated.

In the absence of the financial resources to contract a threat assessment-training program, you may be able to locate an individual who possesses those skills at your nearby FBI or Secret Service field office. If your local law enforcement or state law enforcement agencies have a threat assessment unit, you can tap into their resources as well.

Upon request, many government agencies upon request will provide training free of charge. This will be based on availability and budget resources. Normally, you will be required to assemble other similar threat management units in the area to consolidate the training effort. If you have a university or college in close proximity, they may also have someone within their faculty who may be proficient in providing this training. They may be able to provide a full semester class or a more intensive one-day class on an adjunct basis, which will again require funds.

Another aspect of the training should include practical, hands-on role-playing scenarios. Video scenarios are also helpful, but as my first field-training officer, Jack Matlock told me, "Michael, you learn by doing."

Too often, I've seen organizations with the best intentions that engage in initial training, but failed to procure follow-up training to reinforce not only the concepts learned earlier, but also to demonstrate the importance that the unit holds within the administration of the organization. Perhaps you can either start or join a local threat assessment association. The Association of Threat Assessment Professionals was founded in 1992 and is comprised of law enforcement, judicial, mental health, and corporate security professionals who are involved in the area of threat assessments. If you can identify other local threat management units, you can perhaps get together on a quarterly basis to exchange ideas and bring in guest speakers to strengthen the community.

Your threat management unit meetings should be conditional on the size of your organization. With a large organization, you may have to meet on a weekly or monthly basis. With a smaller organization, you may only meet on a quarterly basis or bi-monthly. The most important aspect of establishing your meetings is that you can quickly assemble to address concerns related to a problematic employee who is raising concerns of safety to other members of the organization.

In many organizations, the duties of the threat management unit will be ancillary to their full time responsibilities in their individual departments. The members' supervisors should be supportive of these duties. Each member should have at least one alternate in the event of a crisis and in case they are unavailable. This also provides an opportunity to prepare the ascent of future members and provide them with the necessary training and experience to move into the vacated roles. The unit must be viable and not just a paper tiger. The formation of the unit on paper will quickly dissipate upon the scrutiny by attorneys.

Chapter 53
The End of this Book

This wraps up our exploration of conducting behavioral threat assessments of mass killers. This field has grown exponentially over the last decade. According to Texas State University, there has been a significant increase in active shooter cases over the last few years. The reason for this increase has not been determined or researched at this point in time. I heard an interesting hypothesis, which I believe may hold some relevance. A seasoned homicide sergeant proposed the theory that the individuals who were perhaps most impacted by first-person shooter video games are now coming to the age of being able to carry out these horrendous acts. If you add in the current state of the economy, an increase in narcissism, and the heightened media exposure and fame garnered from such exposure, it can all add to the increase of mass killers. Going forward, I believe those focused on engaging in targeted violence will become more creative in their site selection in an effort to garner the largest attention by the news media.

In early 2013, there was a shooting at the Marine Corps base in Quantico, Virginia. The reports indicated that there were three dead, and it appeared to be a double homicide and suicide. I was surprised that most media outlets gave minimal coverage to this event. Ten years earlier, this would have been widely reported and perhaps even front-page news. As we have become more de-sensitized toward these acts of violence, the reporting becomes no more newsworthy than an IED explosion in Afghanistan. The acceptance of violence in the world is a sad reality. The shooting at the Marine Corps base turned out not to be workplace violence, but the result of a lover's quarrel.

While I hope that you will find this book useful in conducting behavioral threat assessments, it in no way will take the place of continued research and development of your knowledge and experience in this developing field. Do not make the mistake of reading this book and expecting to become an expert on conducting threat assessments. Not all of those engaged in targeted violence could easily be identified, and I make no assertion that all individuals can be identified. I merely hope to shed some light on some common factors and characteristics displayed by the killers, as well as techniques that I found helpful in conducting investigations of these individuals.

Bibliography

Achor, Shawn. 2010. The Happiness Advantage: The Seven Principles of Positive Psychology That Fuel Success and Performance at Work. New York: Crown Business.

Adamo, Felix. January 14, 2013, Suspect in Taft Union High shooting charged as adult., *The Bakersfield Californian*.

Allen, Stephanie & Matthew Pleasant. September 10, 2013. Lakeland Girl Commits Suicide After 1½ Years of Being Bullied. The Ledger.

American Psychiatric Associstion. 2000. Diagnostic and Statistical Manual of Mental Disorders DSM-IV. American Psychiatric Association.

Arkansas Business. September 30, 2002. 15 years later, murder-suicide fades from view.

Atlas, Randall. *21st Century Security and CPT-ED: Designing for Crotical Infrastructure Protection and Crime Prevention.* CRC Press, Boca Raton. 2008.

Avila, Jim and Reynolds Holding, Teri Whitcraft, Beth Tribolet. June 11, 2008. School Shooter: 'I Didn't Realize' They Would Die. *ABC News*.

Bachman, Richard. Rage. New York: Signet, 1977

Bacon, Doris. June 05, 1989. Vicious Crime, Double Jeopardy In 1982 Arthur Jackson Nearly Killed Actress Theresa Saldana; Now, on the Eve of His Parole, She Fears He's Not Through Trying. *People Magazine.*

Barnes, Patricia. 2012. *Surviving Bullies, Queen Bees & Psychopaths in the Workplace.* Amazon.

Barnes, Rebecca and Lindy Lowry, Church Leaders Lead Better Every day, 7 Startling Facts: An Up Close Look at Church Attendance in America. *Churchleaders.com.*

Barton, Laurence. 2008. *Crisis Leadership Now: A Real World Guide to Preparing for Threats, Disaster, Sabotage, and Scandal.* New York: McGraw Hill.

Bender, Michael and Mark Niquette. Mar 23, 2012 "Bales Had Troubled Broker Career Before Allegations." *Bloomberg.*

Bickford, Glen Pastor, July 18,2011. Bickford Mediations, Review: *The American Church in Crisis* by David Olson.

Biles, Patricia (Editor). 2011. *Halt The Violence: Readings in the Workplace Violence Educations and Prevention.* Lauderhill:The Alliance Against Workplace Violence.

Blair, J. Pete, Martaindale, M. Hunter. 2013. United States Active Shooter Events from 2000 to 2010: Training and Equipment Implications Advanced Law Enforcement Rapid Response Training (ALERRT) Texas State University, School of Criminal Justice.

Blankstein, Andrew, Robert J. Lopez and Ruben Vives, February 17, 2012. "Shootout between federal agents kills 1, wounds 1." *Los Angeles Times.*

Bradfield, Amy, Gary Wells, and Elizabeth Olson, Iowa State University. 2002. The Damaging Effect of Confirming Feedback on the Relation between Eyewitness Certainty and Identification Accuracy. Vol.87, No1, 112-120. *Journal of Applied Psychology.*

Braun, Stephen and Charisse Jones Victim. July 23, 1989. "Suspect From Different Worlds : Actress' Bright Success Collided With Obsession. *Los Angeles Times.*

Bremmer, Arthur, 1973. *An Assassin's Diary*, New York: Pocket Books.

Burke, Kerry and Larry Mcshane. August 24, 2012. Profile Of A White-Collar Murderer: Jeffrey Johnson Called A Sweet, Friendless Man Who 'Deserved A Nice Girlfriend.' *New York Daily News.*

Burke, Mary and Jennifer Schramm. 2005. Getting to Know the Candidate Conducting Reference Checks. Society for Human Resource Management Research.

Calhoun, Frederick and Steve Weston. *Threat Assessment and Management Strategies: Identifying the Howlers and Hunters.* CRC Press, Boca Raton.

Career Builder.Com. April 20, 2011. One-In-Four Workers Have Felt Bullied In The Workplace, Careerbuilder Study Finds.

CBS News, War On Words: NYC Dept. Of Education Wants 50 'Forbidden' Words Banned From Standardized Tests 'Dinosaur,'

'Birthday,' "Halloween,' 'Poverty,' 'Divorce' Among Those Suggested, March 26, 2012

CBS News. January 10, 2011. Jared Loughner Had 5 Run-ins with College Police.

Censer, Marjorie, September 25, 2013. Following Navy Yard shooting, HP terminates subcontractor The Experts. *Washington Post.*

Centers for Disease Control. 2013. School Violence: Data & Statistics.

Chabris Christopher and Daniel Simons, 2010. *Invisible Gorillas and Other Ways our Intuition Fail Us.* New York. Crown.

Chung, Connie. 2002. Connie Chung's interview with John List. ABC *20/20 Down Town.*

Clouston, Erlend and Sarah Boseley. March 14, 1996. Dunblane Massacre Gunman mows down class of children leaving 16 dead with their teacher. *Guardian.co.uk.*

CNN. June 12, 1998. Teen guilty in Mississippi school-shooting rampage.

CNN. February 27, 2002. Decorated WWII veteran detained, searched at airport.

CNN. 1998-10-05. Kentucky School Shooter - Guilty but Mentally Ill.

CNN. November 2, 1995. Police kill Miami school bus hijacker.

CNN. December 14, 2012. "Knife attack at Chinese school wounds 22 children."

CNN. August 12, 2008. Lennon's killer denied parole again.

Conger, Krista. 2008. Stanford University Study: Limiting TV Viewing Reduces Aggression In Children. Stanford Report

Corcoran, Michael and James Cawood. 2004. *Violence Assessment and Intervention: The Practitioner's Handbook*, CRC Press, Boca Raton.

Cracchiolo, Dan, Ilyse A. Reutlinger, J. Mills Goodloe, Jim Van Wyck, Joel Silver (Producers) Richard Donner (Director) 1997. *Conspiracy Theory*. Warner Home.

Cullen, Dave. 2009. Columbine. New York: Twelve-Hachette Books.

Cullen, Kevin. January 24, 2010. The Untouchable Mean Girls. The Boston Globe.

D'Urso, William and John Taylor. April 29, 2013. "Metro officer asked for forgiveness when he reported shooting wife, child." *Las Vegas Sun*.

Danielson, Richard. March 22, 2000. Programmed to Kill. St. Petersburg Times.

Dao, James. February 16, 2010. A Muslim Son, a Murder Trial and Many Questions. *New York Times*.

Dao, James. March 18, 2012. At Home, Asking How 'Our Bobby' Became War Crime Suspect. *New York Times*.

De Becker, Gavin. 1997. *The Gift of Fear*. New York: Dell Publishing.

Department of Justice. 2007. Intimate Partner Homicide

Dewan, Brian. November 8, 2009. Lawyer Cites Mental Illness in Shooting . *New York Times.*

Drysdale, Diana A., William Modzeleski, Andre B. Simons. April 2010. Campus Attacks: Targeted Violence Affecting Institutions of Higher Education United States Secret Service, United States Department Of Education, Federal Bureau of Investigation Washington, D.C.

E. C. Gogolak, June 17, 2013. "New York City Graduation Rate Remains Steady." *New York Times.*

Eagleman, David. Jun 7, 2011. "Ideas, The Brain on Trial." *The Atlantic.*

Emerson, Steven. 2001. *American Jihad: The Terrorists Living Among Us.* New York: Free Press.

Ergenbright, Charles E. And Sean K. Hubbard. June 2012. Defeating The Active Shooter: Applying Facility Upgrades In Order To Mitigate The Effects Of Active Shooters In High Occupancy Facilities. Naval Post Graduate School.

Fein, Robert A. and Bryan Vossekuil. 1998. Protective Intelligence and Threat Assessment Investigations: A Guide for State and Local Law Enforcement Officials. National Institutes of Justice, Washington D.C.

Fein, Robert A., Bryan Vossekuil Marisa Reddy, Randy Borum,William Modzeleski. May 2002. The Final Report and Findings of The Safe School Initiative: Implications For The Prevention Of

School Attacks In The United States. United States Secret Service & United States Department of Education. Washington,D.C.

Forliti, Amy. 04/23/13. Bulletproof Whiteboards Installed In Minnesota School District. Huffington Post.

Frontline. February 19, 2013. *Raising Adam Lanza*. PBS.

Frontline. January 8, 2000. *Killer at Thurston High*. PBS.

Garcia, Courtney. February 12, 2013. Friend: Christopher Dorner was 'sensitive' to race, but 'not militant.' *TheGrio.com*.

George, Justin. June 25, 2013. Maryland 'joker' threat charge against Neil Prescott dismissed Judge rules charges against Crofton man were too vague. *The Baltimore Sun*.

Gibson, Gregory. 2000. *Gone Boy: A Walkabout*. New York: Anchor Books.

Gillespie, Mark. April 6, 1999. U.S. Gun Ownership Continues Broad Decline. *Gallup*.

Goldman, Russell. Dec. 20, 2012. "Schools Face Threats Nationwide Following Sandy Hook Shooting." ABC News.

Goleman, Daniel. October 31, 1989. Dangerous Delusions: When Fans Are a Threat. *New York Times*.

Grabmeier, Jeff. 12/10/2012. Violent Video Games: More Playing Time Equals More Aggression. Ohio State University.

Graczyk, Michael and Nomaan Merchant. Aug. 14, 2013. Experts: Fort Hood Victims Shot While Lying Down. *Associated Press*.

Griffin, Alaine and Josh Kovner. June 30, 2013. Mass Murders Captivated Online User Believed To Be Adam Lanza."*The Hartford Courant*.

Grossman, Dave and Gloria DeGaetano. 1999. *Stop Teaching Our Kids To Kill: A Call to Action Against TV, Movie and Video Game Violence*. New York: Crown Publishers.

Gruver,Mead. 12/01/12. Casper College Attack: Man Kills 2, Self in Murder-Suicide." *Huffington Post*.

Hadaway C. Kirk and Penny Long Marler. August 25, 2005. *Journal for Scientific Study of Religion*, Vol 44, Issue 3.

Hare, Robert. 1993. *Without Conscience: The Disturbing World of Psychopaths Among Us*. New York: Guilford Press.

Harms,A.G. Jr. May 31, 2013. Final Report. UCF After-Action Review Tower #1 Shooting Incident March 18, 2013. University of Central Florida.

Heim, Joe. August 07, 2012. Wade Michael Page was steeped in neo-Nazi 'hate music' movement. *Washington Post*.

Henry, David April 10, 2013. "Read confession in Center City doctor murder." Philadelphia, 6ABC.

Hochwarter, W., Summers, J., Thompson, K., Perrewe, P., & Ferris, G. 2010. "Strain reactions to perceived entitlement behavior by others as a contextual stressor: Moderating role of political skill in three samples." *Journal of Occupational Health Psychology, 15,* 388-398.

Hoover, John 2003. *How To Work For The Idiot Boss*: Survive & Thrive- Without Killing Your Boss. Pompton Plains: Career Press.

Howard, Ron and Brian Grazer (Producers). A Beautiful Mind DVD. 2002.

Hseih, Tony 2010. *Delivering Happiness: A Path to Profits, Passion, and Purpose.* New York: Hachette Books.

Hudson, Jeremy. 2007. Dozens sue over Lockheed shootings, clarionledger.com.

Huffington Post. 02/06/2013.Floyd Lee Corkins Pleads Guilty In Family Research Council Shooting.

Ingold, John. 04/04/2013. Aurora theater shooting documents: Doctor reported James Holmes was threat to public. *Denver Post*

Innocence Project: http://www.innocenceproject.org/Content/DNA_Exonerations_Nationwide.php

Jeane Clery Act 20 U.S.C. § 1092(f) Disclosure of campus security policy and campus crime statistics.

Jones, Jeffrey. 08/29/13. "Parents' School Safety Fears Haven't Receded Since Newtown." Princeton, NJ. *Gallup*.

Kass, Jeff. 2009.*Columbine: A True Crime Story*. Golden: Conundrum Press.

Keefe, Patrick Radden. February 11, 2013. A Loaded Gun: A Mass Shooter's Tragic Past. *The New Yorker*.

Kelly, Jon. February 16 2013. Christopher Dorner: What made a police officer kill?" *BBC News, Los Angeles*.

Kemp, Joe, Jennifer H. Cunningham And Barry Paddock. August 26, 2012. Maniac gave back keys to apt. before Empire State Building slaying Jeffrey Johnson told super, I'm not going to be back after Friday anyway. *New York Daily News*.

King, Stephen. 2013. Guns. Bangor: Philtrum Press.

Kotz, Pete. February 11, 2010. Alissa Blanton, Ex-Hooters Waitress, Killed by Stalker Roger Troy. True Crime Report.

Kusey, Mitchell and Elizabeth Holloway. 2009. Toxic *Workplace!: Managing Toxic Personalities and Their System of Power*. Hoboken: Jossey-Bass.

Las Vegas Review Journal July 7, 2007.Tourists take down shooter.

Leyton, Elliot. *Hunting Humans: The Rise of the Multiple Murderer*. New York: Carroll & Graf Publishers, 2001.

Lim, Sandy; Cortina, Lilia M. 2005.Interpersonal Mistreatment in the Workplace: The Interface and Impact of General Incivility and Sexual

Harassment. Journal of Applied Psychology 90 (3): 483–96.

Logan,TK and Robert Walker. 2011. Civil Protective Orders Effective in Stopping or Reducing Partner Violence. Carsey Institute.

Lotz, CJ. February 14, 2013. My Friend, Chris Dorner: Dorner's "best friend" in the Navy recalls a "happy, bubbly, smiley" officer. A "man's man" with few traces of the anger that drove a murderous spree. *BuzzFeed*.

Low, Rob. November 29, 2012. Surveillance Video Shows Woman Shot in Head by Ex-Boyfriend. Kansas City: Fox4News.

Lozano,Juan A. 04/11/13. Dylan Quick, Lone Star Community College Stabbing Suspect, Due In Court. *Huffington Post*.

Lupica, Mike. March 25, 2013. Morbid Find Suggests Murder-Obsessed Gunman Adam Lanza Plotted Newtown, Conn.'S Sandy Hook Massacre For Years . *New York Daily News*.

Lupkin, Sydney. Nov. 10. 2012. "School Shooting Protocol Shifts From Lockdown-Only." *ABC News*.

Lysiak, Matthew and Bill Hutchinson. April 8, 2013. Emails Show History of Illness In Adam Lanza's Family, Mother Had Worries About Gruesome Images. *New York Daily News*.

Maag, Christopher. November 28, 2007. A Hoax Turned Fatal Draws Anger But No Charges. New York Times.

Maezav, A.R., Ilya Feoktistov (co-director). 2012. *Losing our Son's*. Americans for Peace and Tolerance.

Malnic, Eric and Kim Murphy December 10, 1987. PSA Gunman's Note Told Boss He Was About to Die : Message Written on Paper Bag. Los Angeles Times.

Mantell, Michael and Steve Albrecht. 1994. *Ticking Bombs: Defusing Violence in the Workplace*. Illinois: Irwin Professional Publishing.

Marimow, Ann E., February 6, 2013. Family Research Council shooter pleads guilty to three felonies. Washington Post.

McCarthy, Terry. Mar. 11, 2001. Warning: Andy Williams here. Unhappy kid. Tired of being picked." Time Magazine.

Meloy, J. Reid. 1998. *The Psychology of Stalking: Clinical and Forensic Perspectives*. San Diego: Academic Press.

Mitchell, Kirk Evan 03/28/2013. Ebel threatened to make prison guard beg for her life. *Denver Post*.

Morain, Dan and Mark A. Stein. February 18, 1988.Unwanted Suitor's Fixation on Woman Led to Carnage." Los Angeles Times.

Morgan, Piers. August 22, 2013. The brother of Michael Brandon Hill speaks exclusively to Piers Morgan. *CNN*.

Murderpedia - Huberty: http://murderpedia.org/male.H/h/huberty-james.htm.

Murderpedia - Weston: http://murderpedia.org/
male.W/w/weston-russell-eugene.htm.

Murderpedia - Whitman: http://murderpedia.org/
male.W/w/whitman-charles.htm.

Murderpedia - Williams: http://murderpedia.org/
male.W/w/williams-doug.htm.

Murphy, Bridget and Jay Lindsay. August 6, 2013.
Marathon bombing suspects met conspiracy theorist. The Associated Press.

NAMI - National Association of Mental Illness:
What is Mental Illness: Mental Illness Facts.

Nash, John. 2002. PBS Interview: Medication.
PBS.org.

Navarro, Joe. 2004. Hunting Terrorists: A Look
at the Psychopathology of Terror. New York:
Charles C. Thomas Publishers.

Navarro, Joe. April 7, 2013.Wound Collectors:
Who are they and how they impact on all of us.
Psychology Today.

New Employment Law Alliance Poll. March 21,
2007. Nearly 45% of U.S. Workers Say They've
Worked for an Abusive Boss.

Newcomb, Alyssa, June 2013. School Cites Allegedly Abusive Ex-Husband in Teacher's Dismissal. ABC News.

Newport, Frank. June 25, 2010. Americans'
Church Attendance Inches Up in 2010. *Gallup*.

O'Connor V. Donaldson, 422 U.S. 563 (1975).

OSHA: General Duty Clause, Section 5(a)(1) of the Occupational Safety and Health Act (OSHA) of 1970.

Path to Violence. 2012. PBS.

Pefley, Al. 2013. New details have been released in a murder-suicide at an office building in Boca Raton. Boca Raton CBS12 News.

Perry, Tony. May 28, 1997. Ex-San Diego State Student Pleads Guilty to Murdering 3 Professors." *Los Angeles Times*.

Pew Research Center, October 9, 2012. Religion and the Unaffiliated, Washington, D.C.

Pinsky, Drew and Mark Young.. 2009. *The Mirror Effect How Celebrity Narcissim is Seducing America*. New York: Harper Collins.

Pocono Record. August 31, 2013. Accused Ross Township shooter says he was 'an innocent victim, In a jailhouse interview, Rockne Newell says he's 'sorry innocent people got hurt.

Pollock, William. 1999. Real Boys : Rescuing Our Sons from the Myths of Boyhood. New York: Owl Books.

Puterski, Steve. February, 7 2013. La Shooting Suspect Has Ties To Nas Fallon." *Tahoe Daily Tribune*.

Ramsland, Katherine. 2005. *Inside the Minds of Mass Murderes: Why They Kill*. Westport: Praeger Publishers.

Ramsland, Katherine. John List: Straight to Hell. *Crime Library*.

ReadyHoustonTX.Gov. 2012. *Run, Hide, Fight*.

Redeker,Bill and Dean Schabner . March 9, 2001. Pa. Shooting Called A Cry For Help. *ABC NEWS. com*.

Reiss Steven. 2008. *The Normal Personality: A New Way of Thinking about People*. UK:Cambridge University Press.

Reitman, Janet. July 17, 2013. Jahar's World: He was a charming kid with a bright future. But no one saw the pain he was hiding or the monster he would become. Rolling Stone.

Reyes, Ray. May 14, 201.3 Woman testifies salesman raped her. *Tampa Tribune*.

Rivera, Geraldo. January 6,1972. Exposé of Willowbrook State School. WABC-TV.

Rivera, Jeannette and Henry Pierson Curtis, Jason Garcia, Hal Boedeker, Heather McPherson, Mary Shanklin,. November 6, 2009.'They left me to rot,' Orlando shooting suspect says. *Orlando Sentinel*.

Roche, Mike. 2012. *Face 2 Face:, Observation, Interviewing, and Rapport Building Skills: an Ex-Secret Service Agent's Guide*. Amazon.

Rosenhan, D. L. January 19, 1973. On Being Sane in Insane Places. Vol. 179 no. 4070 pp. 250-258. *Science*.

Rubin, Joel. February 21, 2013. Dorner's mentor cracked the case: The LAPD sergeant who played a central role in the rookie's firing told Irvine police about ex-cop's link to victim. *Los Angeles Times*.

Rubinkam, Michael. August 7, 2013. Pa. shooting suspect's dad saw warning signs. The Associated Press.

Ruderman, Wendy. August 27, 2012. After Empire State Building Shooting, a Gunman's Mother Asks Why. *New York Times*.

Rugala, Eugene and Arnold Isaa. Workplace Violence Issues In Response. Federal Bureau of Investigation.

Sageman, Marc. 2004.*Understanding Terror Networks*. Philadelphia: University of Pennsylvania Press.

Sageman, Marc. 2011.*Leaderless Jihad*. Philadelphia: University of Pennsylvania Press.

Salinger, J.D. 1951. *Catcher in the Rye*. New York: Little Brown.

Sauter, Steven. December 3, 2007. Workplace Stress. Centers for Disease Control (CDC).

Schulte, Brigid, Ariana Eunjung Cha and Carol D. Leonnig, September 21, 2013. Chances to intervene in Navy Yard shooter's problems missed for years by various groups. *Washington Post*.

Silber, Mitchell D. and Arvin Bhatt. 2007. Radicalization in the West: The Homegrown Threat. NYPD Intelligence Division.

Smith, Kendall (Editor). March 2013. CIP Report Center for Infrastructure Protection And Homeland Security. Volume 11 Number 9. George Mason University.

Smith, Mary Lynn and Abby Simons, September 28, 2012. Shooter, Business Owner, UPS Driver Among Those Killed. *Star Tribune.*

Smithsonian Channel. 2013. *Catching Killers: Criminal Profiling.*

Stout, Martha. 2006. *The Sociopath Next Door.* New York: Harmony.

St. James, James. 08/02/2013. Millikin University Prof Revealed To Have Killed His Family 46 Years Ago, Keeping Job *Huffington Post.*

Suicide.org: http://www.suicide.org/suicide-statistics.html.

Switzer, Michael (Director). 2005. Stalking Laura (DVD). Jef Films/Mvd.

Terry, Don. October 18, 1991. Portrait of Texas Killer: Impatient and Troubled. *New York Times.*

Torrey, E. Fuller. 2006. *Surviving Schizophrenia: A Manual for Families, Patients, and Providers.* New York: Harper.

Torrey, E. Fuller. 2008. *The Insanity Offense: How America's Failure to Treat the Seriously Mentally Ill Endangers Its Citizens.* New York: W.W. Norton & Company.

Tripp, Thomas and Robert Bies. 2009. *Getting Even: The Truth About Workplace Revenge - and How to Stop It*. Hoboken: Jossey-Bass.

Tucker, Eric . 07/28/12. Neil Prescott Makes 'joker' Reference, Threatens Boss In Maryland Shooting Plot . *Huffington Post*.

Turner, James and Michael Gelles. 2003. *Threat Assessment: A Risk Management Approach*. New York: Routledge.

*Twenge, Jean M. and Keith Campb*ell. 2009. The *Narcissism Epidemic*. New York: Free Press.

Twenge, Jean. *2007.Generation ME: Why Today's Young Americans Are More Confident, Assertive, Entitled--and More Miserable Than Ever Before*. New York: Free Press.

U.S. Bureau of Labor Statistics. August 2009Occupational Suicides Census of Fatal Occupational Injuries Fact Sheet.

U.S. Department of Education, Family Educational Rights and Privacy Act (FERPA).

U.S. Department of Health and Human Services, Health Insurance Portability and Accountability Act. (HIPAA).

USA Today. January 2, 2013. Editorial: Gun control database going to waste: Many states fail to do a simple task that would help keep guns from the mentally ill.

Vander Velde, Jessica. 12/02/12. What made Jared Cano plot destruction at Freedom High? Tampa Bay Times.

Vann, David. 2011. *Last Day on Earth: A Portrait of the NIU School Shooter*. Athens:University of Georgia Press.

Virginia Tech Review Panel. August 2007. Mass Shooting at Virginia Tech April 16, 2007.

Wikipedia Postal Murders: http://en.wikipedia.org/wiki/Going_postal.

Wilber, Del Quentin. 2011. Rawhide Down: The Near Assassination of Ronald Reagan. New York: Henry Holt and Company.

Wilgoren, Jodi. March 10, 2005. Evidence Links Man Who Killed Himself to Chicago Murders. *New York Times*.

Acknowledgments

This book would not be possible without the help from the folks at 52Novels, who formatted the book, Lynne Hansen, the cover artist, and Winslow Elliot and Fiona Quinn, who corrected and edited my many mistakes.

I would be remiss in not mentioning the researchers who have spent considerable time researching and studying mass killers and targeted violence. I relied upon their research to keep me safe and incorporated their lessons in my toolbox of essential tools while conducting threat assessment investigations. Many of the scholars are listed in the bibliography and I am humbled to call them friends. I have to thank all of those first responders who shared their stories and insights with me.

15650707R00186